THE WILD WORLD OF BARNEY BUBBLES

GRAPHIC DESIGN AND THE ART OF MUSIC

PAUL GORMAN

With contributions by Peter Saville, Clarita Hinojosa, Billy Bragg and Art Chantry

580 Illustrations

Thanks must go first to Aten Skinner of the Barney Bubbles Estate and also to Jenny Ross, who published the first two editions of this monograph. I am particularly indebted to Jake Riviera who has been a valuable adviser, supporter and friend over the years, particularly in regard to his pal Barney.

I am also indebted to Billy Bragg, Art Chantry, Clarita Hinojosa and Peter Saville for their contributions.

For their help down the years I'm also grateful to Belinda Syme, Brian Griffin, the late Brian and Jill Jewiss and Lorry Sartorio, Giana Skinner, Doug Smith and also to my agent Maggie Hanbury and the team at Thames & Hudson: Ben Hayes for pointing me in the right direction and Lucas Dietrich, Evie Tarr, Rosie Coleman-Collier and Darren Wall.

Salutations go out to the following, some of whom made available copies of artworks for inclusion: Alan Aboud, Nick Abrahams, David Allen, Andy Arthurs, Julian Balme, Peter Barnes, Reuben Billingham, Will Birch, Stacia Blake, Justin de Blank (RIP), Derek Boshier, Pippa Brooks, D.B. Burkeman, Marius Cain, Ted Carroll, Jon Carver, Jonathan Choat, Stafford Cliff, John Coleman, Glen Colson, Sebastian Conran, Paul Conroy, Jim Cook, Elvis Costello, John Coulthart, Alan Cowderoy, John Cowell, Michael Daks, John Davey, Sophie Demay, Jeff Dexter, John & Molly Dove, Baxter Dury, Jemima Dury, Andrew Easton, Richard Evans, Carol Fawcett, Diana Fawcett, Dominique Fenn, Pete Frame, Fiona Mathers and John Tate at Fred Perry, Chris Gabrin, Micky Gallagher, Pete Gardiner, Malcolm Garrett, Mychael Gerstenberger, Eric Goulden, Peter Gravelle, Jonathan Green, Bob Hall, Lee Harris, Ronnie Harris, Rian Hughes, Jonh Ingham, Tony James, Mushi Jenner, Peter Jenner, Val Jennings, John (KosmicKourier), Tony Judge, Wendy Kasabian, Ben Kelly, Pauline Kennedy, Paul Kindersley, Andrew Lauder, Cynthia Lole, Nick Lowe and Peta Waddington, Steve Maidment, Daniel Mason, John May, Lisa McErlain, Ian McLagan (RIP), Michael Moorcock, Pat Morgan, Aries Moross, Julia Muggenberg, John Muggeridge, Paul Murphy, Andy Murray, Muz Murray, Richard Neville (RIP), Frances Newman, Paul Olsen, Chris Overend, Kiki & Loulou Picasso, John Pidgeon (RIP), Tom Pogson, Tim Renwick, Dave Robinson, Samuel Rooker-Roberts, Jodi Routh, Antoinette Sales, Rat Scabies, Tom Sheehan, Phil Smee, Donald Smith, Sir Paul Smith, Neil Spencer, Suzanne Spiro, Martin Stone (RIP), Jason Stoll, Virginia Storey, Gavin Sutherland, Genevieve Terry, Uwe Tessnow, Nik Turner, Jan Vollaard, Brian Webb, Mark Williams, David Wills, Jah Wobble and Beau Wollens and the team at NOAH NYC.

This book is dedicated with love to Caz Facey, without whom...

On the cover (front and back): Artwork by Barney Bubbles for 'I Love The Sound Of Breaking Glass', Nick Lowe, Radar. 7in single. 1978.

Underneath the cover flaps: Detail from Barney Bubbles' artwork for Elvis Costello's *Armed Forces* album. 1979.

Page 1: Self-portrait. 1981.

First published in 2010 by Adelita Ltd under the title *Reasons to be Cheerful: the Life and Work of Barney Bubbles*

This revised and updated edition published in the United Kingdom in 2022 by Thames & Hudson Ltd, 181A High Holborn, London WC1V 7QX

This revised and updated edition in the United States of America in 2022 by Thames & Hudson Inc., 500 Fifth Avenue, New York, New York 10110

Original book design by Caz Facey

British Library Cataloguing-in-Publication Data
A catalogue record for this book is available from the British Library

Library of Congress Control Number 2021949905

ISBN 978-0-500-29645-5

Printed in China, by Artron Art (Group) Co., Ltd.

Author's note

'All it is is rock and roll and it's no big shakes. But at the same time I think commercial design is the highest art form.'
Barney Bubbles, *The Face*, 1981

In the 12 years since the publication of the second edition of this monograph, the work of Barney Bubbles has achieved wider recognition for its depth and breadth as well as for the unerring audacity, invention and wit the designer applied to his practice.

The person who was born Colin Maximilian Fulcher is now acknowledged among the greats of graphic design, and *The Wild World Of Barney Bubbles*, which is augmented by a selection of previously unpublished works and a foreword by American designer Clarita Hinojosa, seeks to further round out the portrait of this enigmatic character.

Proof that decades after his death Bubbles continues to touch the lives of fresh design generations was provided to me a few years ago by the creation of a film installation triptych from a diverse range of his existing artworks by the illustrator and designer Aries Moross.

This developed from a collaboration at the Glastonbury Festival 2011 where they VJed a digital light show while I DJed music for which Bubbles had designed. We found that this resulted in interesting and unusual collisions of sound and vision, and Moross' subsequent triptych, which I have included in exhibitions about Bubbles, juxtaposed his signs, motifs and patterns into a collaged and utterly contemporary proposition.

Today's wider understanding of Bubbles' work is a far cry from the bout of record-playing in 2006 when I showed my partner Caz Facey a selection of his designs for sleeves, posters and books, pointing to the detail, the accomplished art direction and the use of colour and typography.

She said: 'This is incredible. Has no one written a book about this guy?'

And that's how it all started.

This book – which owes its grid and overall look to Caz's brilliant design of the first edition – investigates the puzzle of the man's life, and in particular how he drew on his considerable educational and practical experience to problem-solve on behalf of unusual and often sympathetic clients, delighting in the process by interlacing his work with interventions, strategies and powerful symbols to engage and bewitch.

THIS PAGE: Colin Fulcher. 1965.

In his critique *Art Of The Sixties* (and Bubbles was very much a product of that schismatic decade), Hugh Adams expressed the view that the ideal artist 'usually opted for blankness and anonymity. For the most part he avoided confining himself to any single genre or medium and genuinely operated at the interstices of media.'

Substitute 'designer' for 'artist' and Adams may as well have called his unidentified exemplar Barney Bubbles, who, when asked to supply a photograph of himself to *The Face* magazine, delivered a manic self-portrait constructed from splashes, splotches and pieces of card.

These days we have a better understanding of not only the forces which propelled Bubbles, but also those with which he wrestled, though it remains difficult to unpick the effects on his mental health of substantial LSD ingestion in relation to what wasn't acknowledged at the time, his bipolarity. As I understand it, it is not unusual for those experiencing this to be attracted to complex stimuli, though there is much sadness attached to Bubbles' unfortunate and premature death at his own hand at the age of 41. This year, which would have been his 80th, we ponder what might have been and appreciate the achievements he left behind.

Barney Bubbles was a truly alternative designer, a radical thinker unable to conform to the norms of signature and recognition and unwilling to be pinned down to method, style or medium.

Yet – as American graphic artist Art Chantry points out – Bubbles' work is often recognisable. Maybe this is because his designs were rarely, if ever, static and reflective; they exude a kinetic force.

'That's Barney,' Britain's Malcolm Garrett explained to me. 'Looking at his designs is like being around Barney. He emitted nervous energy, you could feel it crackling off him, and that's what makes his work so intriguing. He was capable of injecting himself into it.'

Paul Gorman
London 2022

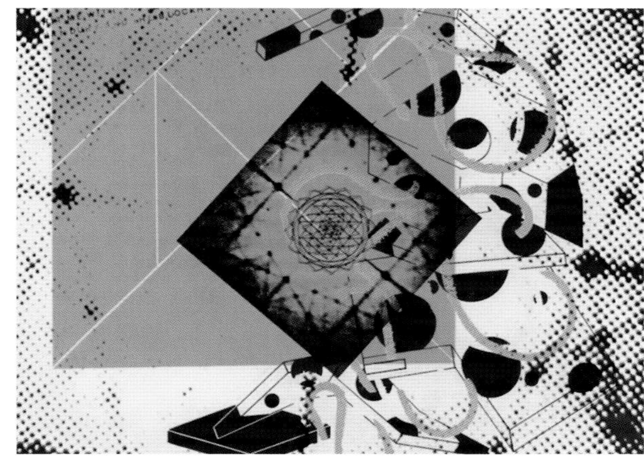

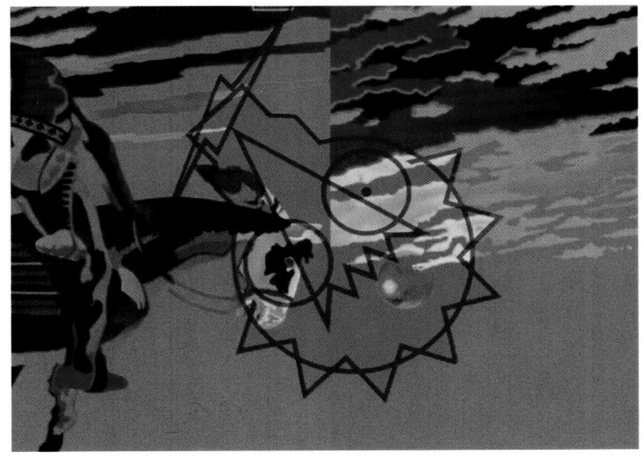

Four stills from Aries Moross' Barney Bubbles Triptych. 2011.

Towards the canonisation of Barney Bubbles

Peter Saville

The work of Barney Bubbles expresses post-modern principles: that there is the past, the present and the possible; that culture and the history of culture are a fluid palette of semiotic expression; and everything is available to articulate a point of view.

Even though we didn't know him personally, Barney Bubbles was a guiding inspiration to me and my friend Malcolm Garrett when we were at school and art college together in the early to mid-70s in Manchester.

Barney's presence in our lives was a combination of showing a way and/or reassuring us about our own inclination to a way. Just as, later, I was encouraged to investigate the imagery of Fantin-Latour – for the cover of New Order's Power, Corruption & Lies – by the opulence and juxtapositions of Scott Crolla and Georgina Godley's clothes shop in Dover Street; and just as Philip Johnson's proposals for the AT&T building in New York had reassured me that the later work of Jan Tschichold was of contemporary relevance, so Barney's work served as an exemplar.

In the summer of 1977, in Virgin Records' basement shop in Piccadilly in Manchester, I came across the cover he did for the single Your Generation by Generation X, which features the deconstructed numerals 45 in the style of Russian designer El Lissitzky. (I think Malcolm Garrett and I found the sleeve together, but he may remember it differently.)

We saw the Generation X cover and received a very clear signal: Mr Barney Bubbles – whose work we already knew from Hawkwind and Stiff – was saying, 'Constructivism has my blessing.' Our response was, yes, this is the way.

Barney's work was replete with anarchic intelligence and was often, in the context of commercial practice, entirely subversive. It was funny as well, though not in an exclusive, 'witty' way. Any kid could understand his concepts but simultaneously he was capable of highly intellectual interventions into the mechanisms of business.

To set the work of Barney Bubbles in context, it is important to clarify the cultural patchwork of the UK in the period of post-war socio-cultural democratisation.

We can see clearly now that, in the second half of the 20th century, that which had been almost entirely the exclusive domain of the privileged was disseminated through the medium of pop culture. This pretty much occurred initially through formative pop and then the attempts at broader engagement by institutions in response to the new society in the early 70s: the Royal Academy's Tutankhamun exhibition and the BBC's screening of Kenneth Clark's *Civilisation* spring to mind.

It's very easy to understand rock'n'roll and pop music as the first platform for the new element of society: the teenagers who gave birth to the notion of youth culture. Of course Jon Savage's book *Teenage* reveals that there was youth culture before rock'n'roll, but as a mass issue it didn't really kick in until the post-war period with the creation of a tangible audience *to be sold to*.

This dissemination of culture, and the political possibilities which were part of the gift, came about initially through rock'n'roll and pop. Music joined people together across the US and Europe to create a platform for civil rights, sexuality, gender, independence. In this way, popular music from Elvis to The Beatles provided the first political voice for the new society.

Then fashion entered the realm of possibilities, providing individuals with the ability to identify themselves. Pre-war, people had clothes. In the 60s, and in particular the 70s, there was fashion, which disseminated ideas, codes and opportunities.

It also empowered those like me inspired by such artists as Roxy Music and David Bowie.

The reason I mention all of this is that it's very difficult for young people to understand – and for some older people to remember – the cultural landscape into which the work of Barney Bubbles emerged.

Even as late as 1974 – when Malcolm Garrett and I entered art college – modernism and even the Bauhaus weren't discussed, let alone to be found on the curriculum. In the industrial cities of the north-west of England, we found ourselves growing up in a culture-free zone. Imagine a place where George Best's boutique is the pinnacle.

Add to that the fact that there was nothing modern in either the way we lived or our methods of communication. Every so often there might be something sexy in the *Sunday Times* colour magazine to do with fashion or pop art. With the remarkable exception of Peter York's essays in *Harpers & Queen*, that was it.

Our only access to an international – and in particular visual – cultural awareness was provided by the record cover. The regional element to this experience cannot be underestimated. And nor can Barney's role in this process.

Those were the days of division in pop: there was rock music and there was dance music, and there was no understanding between them. If you were into dance music you were beaten up by rockers and if you liked rock music you were beaten up by skinheads. It was as simple as that.

When Malcolm and I were at St Ambrose College, an independent Catholic grammar school in Altrincham, he was inclined towards rock while I preferred 'fashion music' – Bolan, Bowie and Roxy, and then definitely Kraftwerk. Malcolm was a massive Hawkwind fan, which is why I knew about Barney Bubbles. I loved his work but the music was not to my taste.

Then, when we left school, something occurred which was as important to our development as Barney, and which would in turn feed our appreciation of him as an avatar.

Malcolm was labouring under the illusion that it was better to go to a university than a polytechnic. So off he went to Reading, then the only university in the country with a graphics course. I, on the other hand, did a foundation year at Manchester Polytechnic.

Reading proved dry and academically oriented. When we got together at Christmas we compared notes. I told him the crazy things we got up to – mad, deliberately disorientating exercises, making buildings out of paper and painting them in the dark, that kind of thing. He sighed and said: 'Well, we looked at redesigning a Do Not Break label…'

We immediately conspired to get him off that course and on to first-year graphics at Manchester. And it came to pass that he joined me there.

Malcolm brought with him something we didn't have – the graphics books from Reading's prescribed list. During the foundation year they'd maybe recommended we read something, but we hadn't taken much notice. Now, here was a stack of volumes which, on investigation, led us directly to the moment in the early 20th century when modernism had informed what was to become graphic design. As the books beat a path to the Russian Revolution, the early period of German modernism and De Stijl in Holland, formative contemporary practices and principles were revealed.

While we were still absorbing this, in the summer of 1976, full-blown punk arrived, though Malcolm was initially antagonistic. Musically, he'd progressed to Frank Zappa and co; I think, to Malcolm, punk represented an anarchic rock sensibility which he'd already found expressed in a more mature way by other people.

By the time he'd come back to college for the second year, there had been a transformation. Malcolm embraced the new punk movement and was very soon working with Linder Sterling, who was a year ahead of us doing illustration.

He also became friendly with the Buzzcocks frontman Howard Devoto and was quickly full-on with the band, having single-handedly invented a kind of pop constructivism which drew parallels between Dada and the new punk sensibility. Malcolm was distilling the knowledge he garnered from the Reading University reading list and combining it with the new youth culture's day-glo aesthetic. He went on to work with the Buzzcocks and, eventually, alongside Barney Bubbles himself at Radar Records.

I, meanwhile, made my own way at Factory Records. It is interesting to note now, in the context of Barney Bubbles, how my Factory work is on a charmed pathway into the canon. It's been routed into fine art, served well by the fact that it was done outside commercial motivation. There existed at Factory an idealism and altruism which place it in a special capsule between business and art. This is a central distinction between my work and Barney's, and why I believe it has taken so long for him to achieve wider recognition.

At Factory, there was never the notion of trying to sell something: New Order recorded Blue Monday, a seven-minute single, which then had to be on 12in, and was put in a cover by me with nothing written on it, and the cost far outweighed the income. I think it is true to say that no one at Factory cared about profitability until 1990–1, when Tony Wilson borrowed £800,000 to refurbish a building. And that was the beginning of the end at Factory, but that's another story.

Certainly, in the late 70s and early 80s, I shared, alongside Malcolm, Neville Brody and Al McDowell at Rockin' Russian, Barney's palette of codes and directions.

For example, I was astonished by the cross-cultural transposition of his sleeve for Elvis Costello's Armed Forces in 1979. It is genius. The notion of appropriating (wildlife artist) David Shepherd for the cover came, as I understand it, from Stiff co-founder Jake Riviera, but Barney's realisation – he hired an artist and then art-directed the painting along with the sleeve's disparate elements – is a practice we would more likely associate with the late 90s period and one of the YBAs.

I sense from this and much else in Barney's work that, academically at least, he had not been taught up to the top of his head. From his experiments in modernism, constructivism and various other crossover points between design and art in the 20th century, it seems to me that he was both curious and intuitive.

This is another reason why Barney is exceptional and significant; he evidently had a natural artistic talent. My guess – since I didn't know him – is that he could draw, for example. And that is important because it takes the work to another level of sophistication. Because Barney wasn't handicapped by what he could photocopy or copy-camera, his work is more alive; he could just do it.

I always imagine Barney as somebody who didn't fear making a mark on the page, since he possessed genuine artistic skill. Of course, that is a great advantage, though strangely it can be a handicap: it is not unknown for such people to literally paint themselves into a corner.

In terms of his methodology, I can see what lay behind his use of scale when either condensing a larger image or blowing up a smaller one until the elements degraded. That kind of approach is only understood by praxis – you learn by actually doing it.

It is also a means of obtaining a better perspective on what you have created. Designers and artists find it very difficult to look at work until it is done, because you lose the ability to see clearly. I used to look at my stuff in the mirror in order to see it differently.

By contrast, I always worked at the size something was; if it was for a single, my frame was 7sq in. I think that is because, compared to Barney, I am maybe more insecure in my work. There is a tentativeness, which I don't detect in his.

Let me explain. Recently, I was reading a book about the culture of museums, and it came to me that there is a certain stillness to my work which comes from that insecurity. Barney's work, on the other hand, is active and very loaded. There is a pent-up energy, which is relevant to his compression of scale.

By reducing the graphic, Barney was containing it, and this is why his images appear as if they want to break out of the frame. This is a condition which pertains to graphic work, an impulse found in the work of graphic artists as opposed to graphic designers – to boldly go, to state, to push everything else to one side and say, 'Here I am.'

Yet, within the overloaded thoroughfare of commercial aesthetics, this can become another noisy element in an already noisy environment, which is possibly where my concerns stem from.

The negative aspect of the stillness in a Peter Saville cover is: he is a bit uncertain about what he is trying to do here. The positive side is that it creates space around itself – a gallery wall or white cube. That tends to happen with my covers – they impose themselves in a different way; you know, it is time to think now.

Everyone goes through a psychological reconditioning when they enter a gallery space, and I am fully aware there is a characteristic of my work which imposes that same mindset on the viewer. My feeling is that if you took Barney's work and put it in a white space, it would command the respect it deserves.

I wasn't in the least surprised to find out that one of Barney's personal traits was that he would sporadically go missing, disappear from contact. That was obviously his coping mechanism. Let's face it, the music business isn't even a formal business, so the demands and pressures on those who take pride in their work are often intolerable. And the only way to retain pride is never to say 'that'll do'. The evidence of Barney's work is that he never said 'that'll do'. His heart, soul, commitment, pride and sense of self are apparent.

The primacy of the record cover as a pre-culturalised pop medium was of vital importance to the work of Barney Bubbles. But in contradiction to that primacy is the continuing lack of importance the record cover has in professional graphic practice. Not that record covers are really significant any more. Music iconography is now familiar from childhood through to what we might call the establishment generation. There is a common awareness – the old guys know about younger culture (through their kids or even worse by trying to keep up). You're as likely to have a 60-year-old into Coldplay as a 21-year-old.

When record covers did mean something – from the 60s through to the 80s – the incumbent establishment of the graphics profession was predominantly male and already middle-aged.

They had been the first pop generation, so acknowledged the importance of their own culture in the 50s and early 60s. There was this notion that they were the ones who changed the world and anything which came afterwards received short shrift.

That's why the graphic work achieved on the margins of pop culture during the critically important period of the 70s and 80s registered nowhere on the establishment radar.

The more serious practitioners of problem-solving communication design have never thought much of the record cover. It is not seen as design – up until 1980, it wasn't granted a category in the D&AD Awards. Milk packaging and train timetables were and still are deemed to be more important, because they embody 'proper' communications design. And in a way they're right; as a communications medium, the record cover is not significant.

Its only function is keeping the primary artist happy. If you're doing a Madonna cover, there's only one thing that matters: is Madonna happy?

It is only in the last decade that I have even encountered the notion of selling an album through the medium of the cover. The proverbial brown paper bag story is true. The thinking is that this is a product that, if the market wants it, will be bought regardless of what packages it.

It is also a fact that, during Barney's lifetime, the graphics establishment did not have the language to decode his or other artists' work, because they were not part of youth culture, the finishing school in fashion, art and design.

But the record cover was the quintessential vehicle of an aesthetic language which spoke to millions, across continents.

It is also important to consider that visual material of Barney's level of creativity comes to the consumer in the context of cult-ish pop music, a medium of obsessive interest to young people.

The images on the Factory covers entered the consciousness of the audience because they were wrapped around the music of Joy Division, New Order and so on (the same visual material put on a postcard and posted through their letterboxes would have made little impact). The impression was made at an incredibly receptive time in the lives of the audience – usually boys between the ages of 15 and 20. Thus, Barney's work must have been of enormous importance to a generation of people who were just learning about the visual environment and considering art, fashion, photography and design as avenues of exploration.

The impact of, for example, Armed Forces on the 'fine art generation' would have been considerable. At that time, Elvis Costello was a mainstream figure in pop; he'd had hit records. So the cultural disorientation and aesthetic questioning were significant and the result is that we now have figures leading contemporary culture who were influenced by work such as Barney's in the late 70s and early 80s.

The era Barney was working in was influenced by fashion, if we understand that to mean the communication of a sensibility through a look. What happened in fashion and music was reflected in what happened at a more sophisticated level in graphics.

So, work such as Armed Forces can be seen as a blueprint for 'the now'; the fluency between disciplines, the silent form of ideas – these and other factors were part of a revolution in communications.

Personally, I am now not keen on the now. With a broader sense of appreciation have come the marketing people. And they use all of what has been achieved by artists and designers like Barney to seduce, corrupt and entice.

The appropriation into business of visual work of Barney's standard is depressing. I think I speak for him as well as myself when I say: 'We just wanted things to be better.' By which I mean we wanted to share our enthusiasm for what was possible with our contemporaries. Having that requisitioned by marketing to make a product look cool is saddening.

Nevertheless, Barney's achievements will survive. People say that design gives you answers, art asks questions. Barney's work fits into the category of asking questions.

Therein lies the disconnection between Barney's work and what we would call 'professional' design, which only understands the notion of answering questions.

When I was with Pentagram in 1990, it was suggested by one of my senior partners that my cover for New Order's Republic was 'not graphic design'. He could not see how it functioned even then, so imagine how Barney's work was judged, if at all. They categorically did not understand what we were doing.

The next edition of *Meggs' History Of Graphic Design* is being published soon, and they have finally acknowledged that, since the first edition came out in 1983, I have been overlooked. Barney died that year, so what chance does he have?

At the time he was working, contemporary art did not really figure in this country. If he had been in New York, he'd have been what he really was, an artist, not a record sleeve designer.

During the 80s, art was 'in-waiting' to become a popular issue in Britain as the cohorts gathered at Goldsmiths willing it into existence. And it finally arrived, in the early 90s, when Jay Jopling and Damien Hirst built the bridge between contemporary art and British society. The arrival of the YBAs marked the moment when it became viable again to practise fine art in the UK, for the first time since the 60s.

All of which makes it important that we now recognise Barney's contribution. I see it as a duty.

The publication of this monograph is, in my view, missionary work; Barney Bubbles should be canonised.

What would Barney Bubbles do?

Clarita Hinojosa

In December 2018 I dedicated an episode of my podcast Design Freaks to the work of Barney Bubbles.

My researches quickly revealed that this was no ordinary record sleeve designer. His combination of display and packaging instruction at Twickenham art school, lifelong fondness for codes and symbols, penchant for control and precision, subversive tendencies and transcendent style opened a universe of intuitive artistry and professional perfection that seemed to me to be beamed straight from the cosmos.

Even Bubbles' psychedelic work flies in the face of convention in that unconventional field, in particular in the ways he favoured typesetting and geometric intention over amorphous, hand-drawn lettering. See how the structural sensibilities of Art Deco, Futurism and sci-fi were applied to Hawkwind's space-rock universe, for example.

Yet it wasn't enough for my show to solely celebrate Barney's visual work and various professional accomplishment. And so I chose a guest, Seattle musician Bryan Standridge, to assist in introducing my listeners – the majority of whom would never have heard of Barney Bubbles – to this artist who, although he worked obsessively and experienced a degree of success, was also a vulnerable spirit.

Bryan and I talked on the podcast about the ways in which Barney and Hawkwind musician and performer Nik Turner were soulmates: 'A lot of people considered him their soulmate,' I said. 'A lot of people connected that deeply with him. He was just that kind of person… magical.'

During the show my first up-close encounter with Hawkwind's 1971 album X in Search of Space came to mind and so I described unfolding the glorious geometric wingspan and marvelling at the design.

Art director and graphic designer as an additional band member seems like an unthinkable extravagance, but it also makes perfect sense. Barney understood and actualised Hawkwind's vision and vice versa, his astonishing range of abilities embodying the intersection of music and design.

A section of our conversation ran like this:

Clarita: 'He wants to create a whole visual identity for Hawkwind, and this goes beyond record sleeves… He began to design everything from the logo, the letterhead… Hawkwind had letterhead?! I don't know if a band had been so well defined visually before.'

Bryan: 'A lot of bands do that now, but nobody was thinking like that back then. They would just think of maybe the LP cover and a special outfit for the stage… but not a full production like this.'

I also thought about the times I have studied the cover of New Boots And Panties!! and feeling that I understood Ian Dury through that record and sleeve. When considering designs for The Damned, Devo, Generation X, Nick Lowe,and Elvis Costello I have exclaimed, 'Wait, he designed that too?' These covers have stayed with me over the years because they share a distinct level of exceptional quality. Nowadays, whenever I'm working on a design job, I wonder, 'What would Barney Bubbles do?'

With much of Barney's work, I initially have a hard time deciphering his design process, particularly in regard to the analogue methods of the day vs our current digital design reality. 'How did he do that?' is a question which recurs.

It's as if a Faustian deal was struck with the unknowable to conjure the cryptograms that my subconscious seeks out. I think of Existence Is Unhappiness, the co-operatively designed multimedia poster for the May 1968 issue of *Oz*. This collage, one of a trio for the magazine and said to be influenced by the assemblages of Eduardo Paolozzi, is a fortune-telling dartboard that includes countless art references and religious iconography.

I'm equally fascinated the mischievously clever marketing concepts which took Barney's visual execution to another stratosphere. The manner in which he invited interaction with the audience, including instructional diagrams, packaging reveals and DIY options, created a tactile (and from a commercial point of view highly collectible) music experience.

The limited edition of 1977's Damned Damned Damned, with its exploding red paint sticker on the front wrapper and deliberately mistaken placement of a photo of Eddie And The Hot Rods rather than The Damned on the back, is an excellent example of Barney's punk sensibilities, valuing play and humour over earnestness/total authenticity. That's part of what resonates so strongly with Bubbles, since present-day design is less hand-touched and increasingly commodified.

Again from the Design Freaks podcast:

Bryan: 'I hope that he recognised that he did make beautiful art that a lot of people appreciated and loved.'

Clarita: 'And that he inspired so many designers to become designers.'

It's worth pointing out that absent Paul Gorman's monograph the podcast would have been very different. I used it as a road map to understanding this elusive artist, who was revealed as a wonderfully complex and sometimes contradictory human being. I also sought to alternately speak of his enduring work and the life in which it was created.

Colin Fulcher (AKA Jacuzzi Stallion, Heeps Willard and, officially, Barney Bubbles) was as enigmatic as his work was impactful. He proved time and again what visual communications could accomplish when a designer is given space to experiment, and he kept evolving, trailblazing new terrains and outsmarting public expectation. Every time I think I know him, Paul Gorman shares a design or some band ephemera I've never seen before on @_barney_bubbles_estate on Instagram. This perpetual discovery allows many of us the opportunity to experience his work for the first time again, and ensures that Barney's understated inspiration continues to live and grow.

Clarita Hinojosa is a Seattle-based graphic designer. Her Design Freaks podcast is at www.designfreaks.podcast.com

Making misfits magnificent

Billy Bragg

In an age of pretty boys, Barney Bubbles was a godsend. My first album had to stand out in a marketplace swamped with the high-gloss values of early 80s pop. Spandau Ballet set the tone, ABC camped it up, and the Human League, who outsold everyone, relied on the prominence of their lead singer's fringe. These were tough times for solo singer-songwriters. Think of the ridiculous lengths that Howard Jones had to go to in order to get into the charts. The hair! The clothes! The goofy dancing! The hair!

I had none of these advantages. In place of a 'look', I had an attitude, one that put me at odds with the image-obsessed artists of the day. Where they expressed themselves through style, I relied on content. With the charts full of records with glossy production values, my debut album was, in stark contrast, recorded straight to tape without any extra instrumentation or enhancement.

I was fortunate in finding Peter Jenner who, as manager of Ian Dury & The Blockheads, had worked with Barney during his Stiff days. He shared my disdain for 80s pop and was trying to set up a label that offered a more radical sound. These were austere times and Pete wanted to launch an austerity record label.

His suggestion that we should go to see Barney Bubbles for sleeve art was, for me, a dream come true. A massive fan of Elvis Costello, I'd admired the man as much for his album covers as for his songs. Frustratingly, there were never any design credits on Elvis' records. Yet there was a discernible signature to the work, visible in the detail on the sleeves: the way the slogan 'Surfing The New Wave' undulated on the back cover of My Aim Is True; the 'off-centre' image on This Year's Model; whatever that thing was that sat at the top right-hand corner of Get Happy!!.

And if, among the heightened illustrations that adorned Armed Forces, his typical flourishes were harder to discern, it was the functionality of the sleeve itself that gave the game away, the total redesigning of what is more or less a two-dimensional object into a multi-layered tour de force of artistry that was breathtaking in its audacity. This is pop art at its best – immediate, engaging, challenging on every level.

The brief for my debut album was somewhat different – how to reflect its back-to-basics approach in an eye-catching way. Jenner had the classic Penguin book covers in mind as a template, and Barney took that idea and ran with it. A light bulb – one of his favourite images – graced a front cover full of open spaces and clean lines. The back was similarly uncluttered, although it did contain a small signature Barney design in the shape of the 'Beware the Squander Bug' logo.

When Life's A Riot With Spy Vs Spy finally appeared in the summer of 1983, Barney's sleeve stood out from the other albums in the racks before anyone had even heard its contents. In a world filled with distractions, he had made me distinctive.

And that was Barney Bubbles' unique talent. I'm not talking about his amazing skill as an artist, the appreciation of which this book will surely enhance. I'm referring to his unerring ability to make unprepossessing blokes look cool. Elvis Costello, Ian Dury, Johnny Moped, me – we were misfits in the pantheon of pop and Barney made us look magnificent.

A chat with Art Chantry

US designer Art Chantry discovered the work of Barney Bubbles in 1977. In an e-interview with Paul Gorman, he discussed the impact on his own practices and his belief that Bubbles' ideas are now 'part of the shared language of graphic design'.

When did you first come across Barney Bubbles' work?
Living in the remote north-west corner of the United States, I was in college when punk started to emerge (in the Pacific Northwest, that was the mid-70s) and that's when I encountered him through the work for Stiff Records and Elvis Costello.

I was a budding young graphic design student, reared on hippie/disco culture, comic books/TV and fine art history. Encountering Barney Bubbles' work in a record store was like looking at messages from Mars; this was utterly alien to everything I had learned about design and art. Several things struck me. Of course, he had an intense colour sense. His personal palette comprised bright primaries and stark contrasts, unlike most of the work of the 1970s, when earth tones dominated in the designs produced by people like Gary Burden for the mainstream Southern California rock scene: Eagles, CSN&Y, Linda Ronstadt, Jackson Browne. To be suddenly smacked between the eyes by Barney Bubbles' colours was a sound jolt.

But the really contrasting aspect was his thinking. Whatever was going on, he did the opposite. It may not have seemed that way in his mind (for instance, his commercial work in your book beats a seamless path to the work on The Damned LP cover Music For Pleasure), but to the general pop culture trend around him, it came from an alternate position…

Compare his careful, studied, playful work to the other major design tastemaker of the period: Jamie Reid. Again, he is totally opposite. It was even startling from the punk perspective.

The other major factor that grabbed my attention was his sense of humour. He must have been a wonderful guy to hang out with. Every one of his covers is a carefully rendered inside joke. To me he is at his most marvellous when he references the very process of design itself – through intentional MISTAKES!

I found the off-register version of Elvis Costello's This Year's Model in the import bin and it blew me away. In America, they released the cover which eliminated the joke. Apparently, the captains of the music industry thought it was a real mistake, or something. You could only find the original design in the import section – along with most American punk, which had to be imported before it could be sold. Strange times.

This Year's Model completely flabbergasted me. It actually took me a long time to figure out it wasn't a misprint. And, when I realised it was a joke, I never looked at graphic design in the same way again.

I firmly believe that 'contrary thinking' was his biggest contribution to graphic design. His ability to step outside the accepted conventions and poke them with a stick endeared him to an entire generation of designers desperately trying to reinvent the language of design. And that's why punks loved him.

Do you detect a coherence given Bubbles multidisciplinary approach and unstylised use of form, method and materials?
Yes, definitely. I hate to use Picasso as a comparison in any context, but Barney Bubbles' use of medium precluded his method and style. It really didn't matter what his material or form, his work remained idiosyncratically his own and simultaneously reflective of the mood of the times.

Picasso worked in graphite, oils, assemblage, or metal or stone or ceramic etc, yet the end result was always 'a Picasso'. Barney Bubbles' masterful approach made his chosen method or style just a simple tool to convey his message.

The work was never anonymous. You could always spot him, no matter how dramatically his style shifted from project to project.

Tell us about your favourite Barney Bubbles design.
Aside from This Year's Model, that would be the imported-from-Europe, 'un-American' version of Get Happy!! by Elvis Costello And The Attractions. That carefully scraped 'wear ring' around the area where the record label would actually have rubbed through the printing as it was handled? That knocked me for a loop.

As I examined the cover further, I saw how he crudely overlapped colours to create new levels of imagery, just like the old-time album sleeve designers in the era he was referencing. It just nailed it for me. Get Happy!! is a brilliant tour de force of inside-graphic-design fetish-collector humour.

Do you detect his influence on other designers?
His influence works directly through people like me. Then there are the successive generations who not only see his work but mine and that of others like Paula Scher and Tibor Kalman, and follow the trail. His influence has become so diverse and foregone that it is used and referenced without awareness. His ideas have worked their way into the shared language of graphic design to such an extent that he is one of the most often imitated master thinkers, and it's all unnoticed. He has become a prime influence through his imitators.

Where do you think his work would be at today?
I think it would stem from his manipulation of processes. He would be one of those guys taking computer systems apart and exquisitely breaking them and rewiring them to do things they were never meant to do. I wish his voice were still active. We need more monkey-wrenchers.

Why is the interest in Bubbles occurring now?
The idea of 'graphic design' as a worthy discipline is still in its infancy and its history is still in the hands of academics and amateurs. They tend to gather around the imagined 'great men' of graphic design, ignoring the vast majority of design language that is created by direct interaction with popular culture.

Barney Bubbles' work is learned and intellectual, but decidedly outside academia, so he has been hidden from the mainstream of design culture thought.

Most of the truly great design dismissed as 'vernacular' by academia is unfairly judged to lack introspection, history and authorship. Nothing could be further from the truth and Barney Bubbles personifies my point. The historical and visceral power of his ideas is as plain as the nose on your face.

ABOVE: Front cover. US edition of Armed Forces, Elvis Costello And The Attractions, Columbia Records. 12in album. 1979.

A1 Good Guy 1942–1968

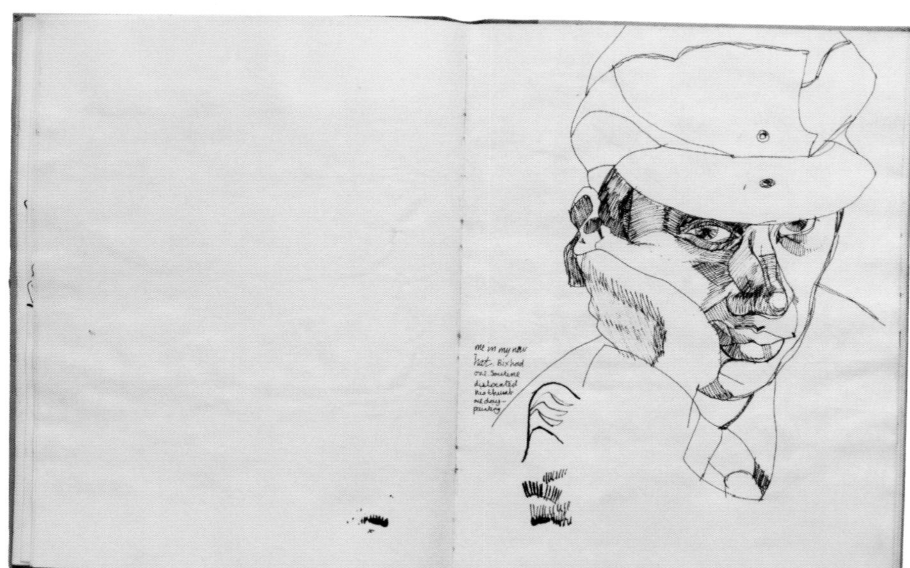

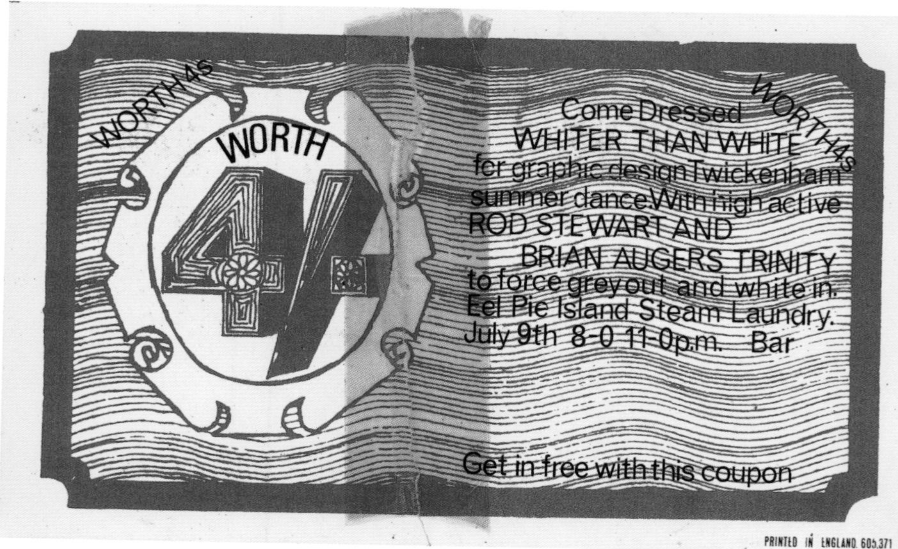

TOP: Self-portrait. Pen and ink. Sketchbook. 1963.

MIDDLE: Ticket. Eel Pie Island Club. 100mm x 155mm. 1965.

BOTTOM: Ticket. 'Eelpiland'. 55mm x 119mm. 1963.

The man who became Barney Bubbles was born Colin Fulcher on 30 July 1942 in Whitton, Middlesex.

The infant soon fell victim to a whooping cough epidemic, the lasting effect of which was to restrict his growth. 'First off he was a lovely fat little baby, but he fell ill and ever afterwards was thin and quite small,' his older sister Jill Jewiss told me in the sitting room of the house in the south-western suburb of London where she and Fulcher were born and brought up.

Their father Fred was a precision engineer, supplying dies and tools for manufacturers. At one time he operated his own factory providing parts for car-plant clients including Rolls-Royce and during the Second World War specialised in cameras (on his father's advice, the young Fulcher used a Minolta 35mm when he developed an interest in photography in his teens).

Fulcher's father met his mother Joyce (née Brooks) ballroom dancing, a fact which their son gleefully related in later life. Joyce Fulcher was gentle, forever bustling around the kitchen in a pinafore, doling out egg and chips for her family.

A bit of a stickler who maintained an interest in photography in retirement, Fred bestowed on his son a meticulous nature and the application to detail which characterised his commercial art throughout his professional life.

'He was a very clever boy, at school he was brilliant,' said Jewiss. 'Barney – or Colin as I sometimes still call him – was such a likeable fellow, really gentle and helpful, but with a wicked sense of humour. He was trusting and had a generous spirit, though he was shy and could be really secretive.'

Jewiss believed this aspect of her brother's personality is reflected in his refusal to take credit in later life. 'He didn't want recognition, because he felt it would interfere with the job at hand,' she said. 'He just wanted to get on with it.'

Colin Fulcher attended the local junior school Whitton Boys, where Jewiss remembers her brother even then emerging as a gifted child. Once, he startled the other family members by constructing a perfectly realised scale model of an ancient Egyptian temple – an early manifestation of a lifelong fascination with Egyptology, its codes and symbols.

'He was always active, drawing, painting, creating,' said Jewiss' husband Brian, who first met Fulcher in 1957. 'A few years ago we decorated what had been his bedroom and, when we stripped off the wallpaper, there was a painted self-portrait on the wall which he must have done when he was a student, using the mirror in his room.'

While Fulcher was indubitably an extremely talented and instinctive artist, it is clear that his practices were shaped by his formative educational experiences at Twickenham College of Technology in the late 50s and early 60s.

On leaving Isleworth Grammar School in 1958, Fulcher was steered by his father on to a display course for a National Diploma in Design (NDD), part of the further education structure which had been instituted in Britain after the war.

In his book *Art Into Pop*, music critic Simon Frith writes that the NDD is remembered as representing 'the halcyon days of art school life, when Bohemia was a viable career option… a time when shabby college buildings catered for fun and discovery, when artists were trained to be entertainers'.

Richard Guyatt, professor of graphic design at the Royal College of Art, might have been referring specifically to Fulcher when he wrote in 1958: 'The intelligent and lively art student has grown up in a beguiling, sparky, intellectual atmosphere of Outsiders, James Dean, Existentialism, the New Brutalism, Angry Young Men, Skiffle and Dribble.

'And they have twigged all this through the media of mass-communication – the telly, the flicks and the highbrow glossies, which bring them news about this exciting world, way outside their own actual experience. And materially they are the generation which has grown up in an atmosphere of war, violence, atom bombs, food rationing, restrictive boredoms, mass-produced foods, mass-produced entertainments. But through this hotch-potch of influences they have this intuitive desire to create, to become artists – a desire which I believe is inborn and not acquired.'

The establishment of colleges such as Twickenham was the result of increased support given to science and technology in the curriculum, mainly as a result of American technical assistance to western Europe, exemplified by the Marshall Plan – though educational policies were in fact dominated by British traditions, in Fulcher's case those rooted in arts and crafts.

In 1958 this was made manifest by Twickenham headmaster Osmund Caine's instigation of a broad-based vocational course which included illustration, exhibition and graphic design, typography and photography.

The autocratic Caine was described by David Buckman in his *Independent* obituary in 2004 as, 'one of the last of the old school, with an uncompromising skills-based approach. He believed that commercial artists should know how to draw, construct perspective, lay a wash or airbrush and understand photography, graphics and three-dimensional design.'

During this period the art departments of technical colleges in the London suburbs formed a ring around the capital, with the prominent art schools, particularly the Royal College of Art and the Slade School Of Fine Art, at its centre.

Technical college pupils were drawn from a widely cast net, with the entry requirements valuing promise and enthusiasm highly; Twickenham College was characterised by a boisterousness centred on the active local music scene engendered by the founding father of British blues Cyril Davies (whose revolving-door recruitment of young musicians in his group would lead to the formation of the Rolling Stones among others).

The display course was predicated on retail and advertising point-of-sale studies. 'In addition to painting, illustration and drawing, we studied the making of things: cardboard, book-binding and metal work, including silversmithing on Saturday mornings,' said Fulcher's schoolmate David Wills, with whom he later forged a working relationship and friendship.

'We were prepared for anything that came up. The display course was supposedly about "window display", something we considered corny but which was actually a good grounding in spatial awareness.'

Nurturing an interest in the Bauhaus and modern architecture, Fulcher talked excitedly of Frank Lloyd Wright's book on the modular, *The Natural House*. Also a devotee of Le Corbusier, he later constructed a scale model of a modernist pavilion.

This appreciation of the technical and, in particular, the geometrical aspects of the built environment was to endure: towards the end of his life Fulcher announced that his favourite book was *Delirious New York*, the so-called 'retroactive manifesto for Manhattan' by radical architect Rem Koolhaas.

'He was taught integrated design, a consistent house style,' said Wills. 'Everything was to be considered as a whole the furniture, the building, even the music in the elevators.'

During the school holidays the friends would hang out at the Fulchers' house, listening to rock'n'roll 45s on his cream-and-brown Dansette in the back bedroom. This overlooked a field which had been part of a local pig farm, used by Fulcher as the location for an 8mm 'cowboy movie' short made with other art students.

The tight-knit group of art students and friends were atypically rebellious, engaging in activities such as mailing each other increasingly wild missives made of collages, paint and ephemera, mainly as way of testing the Post Office delivery system.

Fulcher was an attentive and responsive student and, attaining his NDD after four years, opted to stay an extra year to gain his honours, absorbing such important texts as 1963's *Graphic Design: Visual Comparisons* by the decade's graphics exemplars Alan Fletcher, Colin Forbes and Bob Gill. Fulcher gave his copy of this, and the following year's *Illustration: Aspects And Directions* by Gill and John Lewis, to Lorry Sartorio, an elfin beat girl who started at Twickenham in his final year.

'I was 15, and had been there a couple of terms by the time I met Colin, but soon I was drawn into his gang,' said Sartorio, even in later life a slight, girlish figure with kohl-adorned eyes. 'He really liked my look. I was into the beatnik thing – loads of black clothes and make-up. I even used to iron my hair so I could get that really straight effect!'

Sartorio remained a lifelong friend, and back in the early 60s served as Fulcher's life subject. 'I walked into the sitting room one day and Lorry was reclining naked on the sofa,' recalled brother-in-law Brian Jewiss. 'He was sat there nonchalant as you like, and carried on sketching her.'

Fulcher maintained an interest in all aspects of the visual arts. In a detailed series of letters to fellow student Roy Burge, he outlined in storyboards and maps his idea for a 'ton up' movie with a sequence featuring a leather-clad biker racing 'his machine' along the Chertsey Bypass, which ran beside Twickenham College.

At this time the locale was the seedbed of the burgeoning British beat boom which spawned the groups and pop stars who dominated the 60s and beyond.

Many – including Eric Clapton, John Mayall, Rod Stewart, Jimmy Page, Mick Jagger and Keith Richards – cut their teeth at local venues such as the dilapidated Eel Pie Hotel on the tiny Eel Pie Island, and the Crawdaddy Club, just across the Thames at the Station Hotel in Richmond.

In July 1963 the Rolling Stones were booked to play the end-of-year 'Twickenham Design College Dance' and Fulcher's poster – effectively his first piece of commercial art – for the event has become one of the rarest items in the rock band's history. Because it occupied a special place in his work, Fulcher designed a frame for the poster 20 years later as part of a presentation for music agency boss Derek Savage.

On leaving college an opportunity arose for Fulcher to design a pamphlet for Fleetway Publications. He was keen to incorporate the fashions of mods and rockers, the teen groups whose stylistic rivalry and beach-front skirmishes were then preoccupying the British media. This was an extension of a project on the subject Fulcher had developed at college, where he produced watercolours of a blonde Ton-Up girl and The Beatles' George Harrison as examples of the two contrasting looks.

Fulcher was also intent on Twickenham College's resident R&B

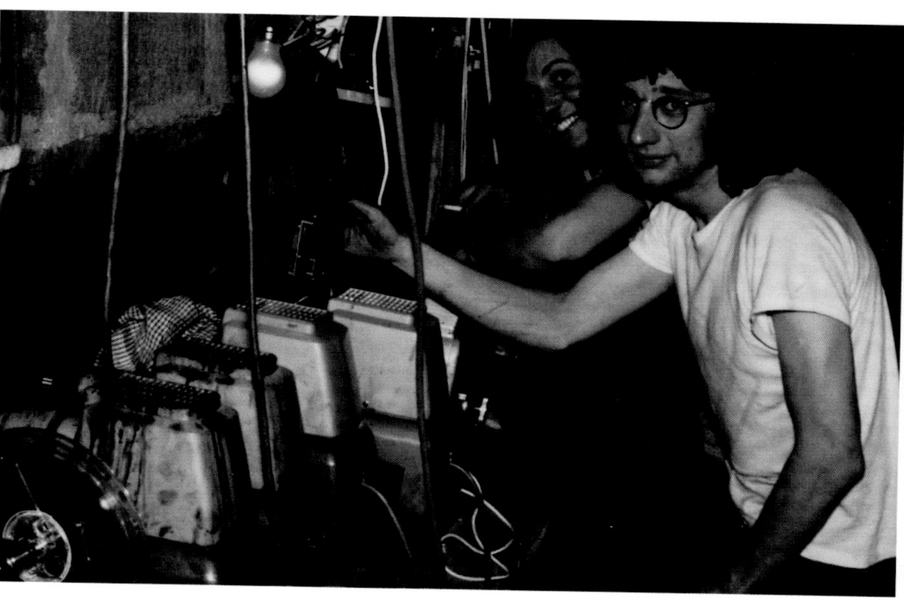

TOP LEFT (from left): Unknown, Colin Fulcher, Stafford Cliff. 1966.

TOP RIGHT: The Barney Bubbles Light Show, Drury Lane Arts Lab, Covent Garden, London. 1967.

group The Muleskinners being a reference point in the Fleetway project, since he was friendly with their keyboard player Ian McLagan (who went on to become a member of 60s mod band the Small Faces and 70s bar-room rockers The Faces).

McLagan described Fulcher – who toted his 12-string guitar around the college halls – as 'one of the coolest people at Twickenham. He was a huge fan of Big Bill Broonzy and could play pretty good gut-string guitar in that folk blues style. He had a ready grin and, when he laughed, he laughed from his long nose to his toes, as if Gerald Scarfe had drawn him. He was like a cartoon character.'

Fulcher conducted a photo session in the living room of his parents' house with Sartorio modelling for him as a 'mod girl teen queen.'

Fulcher had already outlined the shoot in a letter with instructions and sketched options for four poses. 'He draped a white sheet as a backdrop,' said Sartorio. 'I was as nervous as hell; you can see it in some of the photos. He seemed so much more sophisticated than me, but his direction was very encouraging.'

Fulcher supplied his own denim jacket and a white T-shirt to which he had applied in black dry transfer lettering the phrase: 'Them Mule Skinners Knockout R+B Here Tonight'. An encircled love heart appeared between the first two words.

The Fleetway project appears to have been abandoned but Fulcher used one of the stills to produce a striking Muleskinners poster, using acetone to expose the dot screen, backing it with a blue wash and isolating the lettering in white and red.

R&B Here Tonight became Fulcher's first publicly recognised work, receiving a British Poster Design Award in 1965. Describing it as 'a good hard-hitting poster', the judges noted in *Design* magazine's issue of August that year: 'The design is exactly suited to its subject matter; lively, up-to-date, youthful and vigorous; excellent use of colour.'

Other work Fulcher produced for The Muleskinners included a ticket with Cyrillic script for a Cossack-themed gig on Eel Pie Island (rechristened 'Eelpiland') in December 1963.

By this time Fulcher had embarked on his first full-time employment as an assistant at Michael Tucker + Associates, whose modern commercial design studio was on the fourth floor of Artist's House at 14–15 Manette Street – the Soho thoroughfare which links Charing Cross Road to Greek Street.

Tucker had been a star graduate of the London College of Printing, and designed the geometric book jacket to Penguin's 1962 reissue of the 30s self-help book *Meet Yourself As You Really Are* before working for leading post-war British designer Ian Bradbury and then setting up his own practice.

The team was small: three assistants, a secretary and Tucker, with a client list including the tyre-maker Pirelli. At 25, Tucker was not that much older than Fulcher, though a strict taskmaster, insisting on the use of Graphos German mapping pens rather than the more popular Rotrings. With fixed nibs, Graphos pens were more commonly used in architectural drawing and achieved finer lines, though required absolute concentration and precision.

'That's how rigorous it was at Tucker's,' says Brian Webb, who worked there later in the decade. 'I don't remember leaving before 7pm most nights, and every Tuesday and Thursday we were expected to work until 10pm. Rather than Helvetica, Mick insisted on its forerunner, Neue Haas Grotesk from the Swiss Haas foundry. And an unsaid rule was that we had to wear American-made button-down shirts. Anything not Ivy League was frowned upon.'

Many years later, in his only published interview, Fulcher described Tucker's approach: 'Very Swiss; very hard; unjustified; very grey. He taught me everything about typography. It was a great apprenticeship!'

In March 1965, Fulcher joined Roy Burge and David Wills in renting a mansion block flat in the inner London neighbourhood of West Kensington. Within a few hundred yards was the Olympia exhibition and concert hall. Flat 1a Leigh Court in Avonmore Road W6 soon became a hive of activity.

Music, fashion, art, design and photography naturally ruled the lives of the young art graduates. Regular parties were held at Leigh Court, where Burge, Fulcher and Wills came up with the informal alliance 'A1 Good Guyz' (taking part of the name from their address).

In keeping with the gang ethos, Fulcher produced nicknames for the members: Wills became 'Wöll' and Burge 'Bump'. For himself, Fulcher first settled on Maximillian and then Barnstaple, which was soon shortened to Barney. Thus, the seeds of

THIS PAGE: Colin Fulcher. west London, 1966.

ABOVE: Cover. *Nova*. December 1967.

Fulcher's creative persona were being sown.

At Tucker's, the workload increased with the departure of a colleague. 'The jolly old boss MT has bad news. We have to work every night and weekend for one month at least to catch up,' he complained in a letter to Sartorio. 'I'll be going to Chessington (in Surrey) for a week on one project alone.'

Shortly thereafter, Fulcher left Michael Tucker for the design department of the business run by British design guru Terence Conran, who had recently opened the first Habitat outlet in Fulham Road, Chelsea. Modernity was the watchword and the company's unique range, from furniture to homewares, launched the concept of 'lifestyle' as Britain boomed and London swung.

On Fulcher's first day as senior graphic designer at the Conran offices at 5 Hanway Place, where Oxford Street meets Tottenham Court Road, he was introduced to another new recruit, Virginia Clive-Smith (now Storey).

'He was such a sweetheart,' says Storey. 'The first lunchtime we went to a local Italian café, which supplied as a matter of course a slice of buttered white bread cut in half. Barney picked up each piece and held them to his ears, saying, "You see, I even look glamorous in these!"'

The Conran studio's task was to service and supply designs for interiors, retail outlets, restaurants and exhibitions, creating brochures, catalogues, packaging and corporate identities. Storey says that among their first duties were designs for the new shop. 'I think Barney even did window-dressing for Habitat in the early days,' she adds.

'Conran Design was one of the first multidisciplinary design companies in the UK, if not the world,' says Stafford Cliff, who joined the company in 1966. 'Terence was a retailer and design entrepreneur. He wasn't a graphic, product or interior designer himself, but bridged those divisions by creating this company. He had a furniture factory and a fabric manufacturer and sold their products not only through Habitat but also to other contractors, shops and offices.'

Recently arrived from Adelaide, Cliff was effectively the office junior, though the design team only consisted of three or four people under director Ron Baker. 'Barney was my mentor,' says Cliff, who went on to become creative director of the Conran Group and is now an interiors and lifestyle author.

'Working there was heaven, like going to art school. Barney had a kind of magic and extraordinary charisma. There was a lot of mystery to his personality, which made him all the more engaging. But he was too modest to ever let you think, "this is one of the greatest graphic designers of all time".'

Cliff was himself going through a period of adjustment. 'It was one of those moments when your antennae are out,' he says. 'London was bubbling over with creativity and here was I, fresh from Australia and working at one of the most interesting companies in the world.'

Among Fulcher's commercial logos was the Norman archer for H.P. Bulmer's popular Strongbow cider label, which was used in a slightly modified form for many years. The name and retail concept for Strongbow were created by poet Gavin Ewart, then an advertising copywriter working on the Bulmers account and aiming to attract younger consumers to this traditional drink.

Lettering was one particular area of Fulcher's excellence; he supplied it for a game produced by David Wills on a freelance basis for Habitat. Entitled Inspector Burge Investigates, this faux-20s mystery is solved using illustrated cards. In 1966 he also revisited Michael Tucker's offices as a freelancer himself, supplying lettering for a poster for the short Pirelli-backed film *The Tortoise & The Hare*, an early directorial effort by film-maker Hugh Hudson with opening credits on moving vehicles by Robert Brownjohn.

'He was always very chirpy,' says Brian Webb, later a multiple D&AD winner and visiting professor at the London University of the Arts. 'By that stage Tucker's was doing well – having designed the cover of the 1966 D&AD Annual – and Colin and Mick were on extremely good terms. The film poster was excellent: green and yellow 20in x 30in with his lettering in a block serif font which rose and subsided along the top.'

And Fulcher adopted Tucker's exacting attitude to work. 'While he was warm and generous, he could also be demanding and impatient if you didn't get it right because his own work was of such a precise and neat standard,' says Stafford Cliff.

And the Conran studio was an even tighter ship. 'We had deadlines which usually required one all-nighter a week,' says Cliff. 'Ron Baker would say, "We have a project delivery first thing Thursday morning so you, you and you, cancel everything on Wednesday night". We'd work through. There would be no excuses.'

In those days of hot-metal print production, staff hand-drew each job before it was sent for typesetting. 'Every line would be drawn; that could run to several pages,' says Cliff. 'If there was a single mistake Barney would tear it up and make me start again. That teaches you certain standards.

'One was also swept up by his ethic, which was based around the flat in Avonmore Road. There were happenings there all the time. I only worked with him for two years, but it seems like five because we packed in so much.'

The A1 Good Guyz also held events for students from their former college at their West Kensington flat, the result of their continuing friendship with Twickenham teacher Wentworth Shields (nicknamed 'Uncle' by Fulcher).

'They were invited to come along and make things out of coloured wool and film it,' says Cliff. 'Barney wasn't interested in getting them to do something as workaday as make a letterhead. It was much more multimedia.'

Cliff was swiftly seduced into this world of creativity. 'I think of Barney as a frustrated musician,' he says. 'If there was a moment of pleasure or something went well in the office, he would grab his T-square and do an air-guitar fill. A lot of the events he organised were of a musical nature or from the point of view of a pop group.'

An example of this was the poster for an imaginary group called The Image. In contrasting yellow and blue, this featured the A1 Good Guyz and their friends adopting various positions in stars framing a silhouetted rocker with a guitar.

In a David Wills photo from the period, Fulcher wears a bright yellow jacket as a member of another faux band, The Erections (with Pete Brown from The Muleskinners in a one-off group logo T-shirt).

'He'd engage people, because he was so easy-going and charming,' adds Cliff. 'If the plan was to get a crowd of people gathering at dawn on Hampstead Heath to be filmed dressed as elephants, they would be there. You would be swept along. The end result might be slightly tacky, but it would always have a certain magic.'

In 1966 Fulcher recorded a Christmas message at a record booth at Waterloo station which he copied and distributed to

A1GGZ David Wills Colin Fulcher Roy Burge A1 Leigh Court Avonmore Road West Kensington London W14 01 603 5137

Dear

Sounds Good Evening

We have been asked to give a lecture on what we thought about Graphic Design.

However, none of us are any use when it comes to talking out loud, we go red and mumble, especially in the cold hard atmosphere of our old classrooms - so we decided to invite you up our way and give a party. But a party to which you contribute.

What we will do is to provide you with the time, space, excitement, dancing girls, balloons, films, wooden boxes, pink string etc. What happens is that you take over from us and develop these elements and finish up with something good. We have thought of some happy ways of getting you to work which you will enjoy.

You probably wonder how we found excuses for giving a party instead of a lecture, well, the way we persuaded Mr.Shields to sponsor 'Sounds Good Evening' went something like this:

We think that art direction, design, typography and all the mod stuff like Nova, Beano and the Sunday Times is part of our everyday ordinary life. We can easily identify with it and we feel free and easy in its presence. Design is fun and real.

By inviting you to the flat out of the restrictive atmosphere of the art school we hope you will experience some of the excitement we get out of the graphic scene. You will have the fun of a party, while at the same time you will work together towards the culmination of the evening in a show of all the work done.

At the end of 'Sounds Good Evening' we will talk about the evening's work and see if we can think of anything else to do the next time we meet - when we show the film of the evening, which as a group you will make. One idea we had was that you could give us the jobs and get us to work.

The only condition of your return to A1 to see the film is that you bring something brightly coloured with you.

Look forward to seeing you on Tuesday.

DAVID WILLS COLIN FULCHER ROY BURGE

friends and family, packaged in what is his first realised record sleeve; a pink and red pop-lettered circular logo printed on the front of a 14in x 7in folded sheet of paper.

Among the recipients was Virginia Storey, who departed Conran that year. Her replacement was John Muggeridge (who became Storey's partner).

'I greatly admired Barney – he was very efficient and knew exactly what he was doing,' said Muggeridge. 'He would have a conversation with Ron (Baker) about what a client wanted and as Ron talked he would already be drawing it out.'

Muggeridge said that the quality of the work is what kept the team together. 'They may have screwed you for the money, but the experience was invaluable,' he adds. 'I took over an account – I think bathroom fittings – and the client would deal directly with me. We had access to the best photographers and models.'

Yet Fulcher bristled at the slog. Says Cliff: 'You have to remember that his work was extraordinarily thought-out and innovative, and generally speaking, clients in the 60s weren't into innovation.

'There was an ongoing difficulty in that he would produce brilliant work, which drew on his resources of concentration and visualisation, but the client would reject it on a whim or because, maybe, his wife didn't like it. Barney found that difficult to tolerate and became quite angry.'

Muggeridge recalled the all-nighters as 'hard work. One night we went for fish and chips in Tottenham Court Road. There were these amazing lights and sounds coming out of a building – it was Pink Floyd getting together at UFO (the club opened in the basement of 31 Tottenham Court Road on 23 December 1966, by British underground mainmen Joe Boyd and John 'Hoppy' Hopkins). Of course we dropped in and then went back to the office and worked until 8.30am.'

Fulcher precision engineers

Fulcher precision engineers

Fulcher precision engineers

Fulcher precision engineers

TOP LEFT: A1 Good Guyz party invite. 350mm x 225mm. 1967.

TOP RIGHT: A1 Good Guyz letter to Twickenham College students. 1965.

ABOVE: Headed paper for Fred Fulcher's business. 1967.

LEFT: Christmas single sleeve design. 1966.

ABOVE AND RIGHT: Cards and pack. Inspector Burge Investigates game. Habitat. 1966. Design/concept: David Wills. Lettering: Colin Fulcher.

MIDDLE (right): Logo. Justin de Blank. 1968.

BELOW: Logo. Strongbow. 1966.

BOTTOM: Packaging. Bees Ltd. 1971.

The UFO visit provided Fulcher with a possible escape route from Conran. As London's psychedelic scene gathered momentum, he attended more performances and happenings, and was struck by the possibility of launching a light show.

'This again was all about him wanting to be part of the music scene,' says Cliff. 'Barney bought four heavyweight old projectors and suggested we mix coloured inks with oil sandwiched between heavy glass slides.' The lights heated the mixture, creating a 'bubble' effect when screened on to walls and backdrops behind the performers.

Fulcher touted the light show around the new music venues, though Cliff recalls that initially there was some resistance from the elite running the capital's new-style nightlife.

'That was a struggle and I know he found it very frustrating when they didn't want to know, because the show was far superior to what was being done by other people.'

Yet his determination won through, and the light show was booked by Jim Haynes' Arts Lab in Covent Garden. Soon enough Bubbles, Cliff, and others were spending every Saturday night projecting at psychedelic clubs such as Middle Earth.

Spurred on by the acquisition of an 8mm camera, Cliff rented a series of movie classics – Busby Berkeley and Lon Chaney among them – to throw into the mix.

'We melded multimedia visuals into a programme which we could manipulate to match the music,' says Cliff. 'I'd move the projector around so that Fred Astaire and Ginger Rogers swirled through the bubbles at the appropriate moments. Barney's fingers would be covered in ink because he was busily mixing the next slides as soon as the first ones peaked.'

By the second week, Fulcher had a name for the projections: the Barney Bubbles Light Show. 'Eventually he morphed into Barney Bubbles, which I've always aligned with his wish to become a pop star,' says Cliff. 'It was a fantasy identity which he used to escape from reality.'

The contrast with the environment at Conran could not have been more marked; in Cliff's words the light show was 'colourful, ephemeral, free-form and sensual. Of course there was pot smoking, but I didn't indulge because I've always found that deeply boring.' Cliff also filmed a Bubbles-planned happening where the gang dressed in the spirit of *Alice In Wonderland* and frolicked in Hyde Park.

In October 1967, Wills and Barney Bubbles – as he was now known outside of Conran – worked a stint in the art department of Britain's first style magazine, *Nova*, where they made useful contacts with other young designers freelancing for the magazine, including John Dove and Molly White.

'Molly was a furnishing textile designer and I was a struggling sculptor living off my illustration work,' says Dove, who went on to found rock'n'roll clothing labels Wonder Workshop and Kitsch-22 with White.

'I'd been working at *Nova* for about a year with (photographer/designer) Harri Peccinotti, his assistant Sue Wade and (art director) Bill Fallowell. Bill was away on holiday so Barney and David Wills stood in for him for the December issue.'

On the afternoon of Friday, 22 December, 1967, Dove and White visited 1a Leigh Court. 'We heard familiar sounds drifting across from Olympia,' says Dove. 'It was The Who sound-checking.'

The band was preparing to headline the last major underground event of the year, an all-nighter entitled Christmas On Earth Continued. Though the line-up included Jimi Hendrix Experience,

Eric Burdon, Pink Floyd and Soft Machine, the gig had been inadequately publicised. The temperature dropped below freezing. Dove remembers wandering around the vast hall with Bubbles and about 50 others. The Who, disgruntled at the poor attendance, didn't even perform.

'There was a movie wall of Warhol films and a funfair including a classic carousel,' says Dove. 'Eventually the venue filled a bit and we spent the evening with Barney. We started to meet up regularly to swap comics, since we both collected Marvel, particularly *Fantastic Four* and *Silver Surfer*.'

As a result, Dove became a member of the team Bubbles and Wills assembled in the winter of 1967 to produce issue 12 of underground magazine *Oz*.

They had been commissioned by art editor Jon Goodchild to conceive, design and deliver two double-sided poster sections which folded into double-sided 'pages'.

Published in May 1968, *Oz* 12 consisted of inserts and these two fold-outs, one side of which was originally intended to carry the cover: a photograph of a wild celebration featuring Bubbles, Wills and their friends in bizarre outfits.

However, this was rejected and replaced by classifieds and advertising – for an Incredible String Band album and the Cockell & Johnson fashion outlet – as well as two Martin Sharp illustrations, one of which, two naked females in a bathtub on a stormy sea, became the cover.

In the introduction, the reader of this 'fun & games *Oz*' is told that the issue is based on 'the great Buddhist Liberation, or the method of realizing Nirvana through knowing the mind'. A sarcastic aside reveals that 'the fourth side – and thus the fourth truth – had to be dropped because of extra advertising. But don't worry. The advertisements promise you Nirvana too'.

The three remaining sides are tagged 'a', 'b' and 'c' and named after the Buddhist precepts Existence Is Unhappiness, Unhappiness Is Caused By Desire Or Craving and Desire Can Be Destroyed.

The posters combined grids, games, symbols and codes, cut-out postcards, astrology, rock'n'roll and eastern religions, effectively drawing together the various strands of current hippy imagery. The 3D colour effect was achieved by gluing images on to Kodatrace film in register, with trichromatic colours allocated as the work progressed.

There are puerile elements – notably a seduction game called 'A Touch Of The Sex Jollies' – recipes for hash brownies and a diagram tracing The Beatles' musical heritage. These are overshadowed by the poster Existence Is Unhappiness, a geometric puzzle dominated by a beatific face above a karmic circle. This was, in fact, a photograph of former Twickenham classmate Dave Palmer, who himself has another imprinted on his forehead with the words 'The symbol of the happy circle' surrounding a Masonic handshake.

One element is a pencil drawing by John Dove of female breasts. 'This was supposed to be a poster of 20 pairs of breasts montaged, painted and sketched, with a drawing of a Kellogg's Rice Crispies box with a cut-out puppet of Roger Moore as a jester,' says Dove. 'Barney was assembling the layouts and we were all sticking stuff up on the separate film layers to be printed. The piece which was eventually printed was a smaller vignette; I was disappointed.'

There were also contributions from illustrator and fellow Twickenham alumnus Chris Higson, and Bubbles' father Fred Fulcher appeared among the credits, with Wills assuming the pseudonym 'Eric Stodge'.

ABOVE: Drawing for Justin de Blank. 1968.

The back cover featured a multiple Xerox of yet another naked female advertising an '*Oz* Benefit Concert' at Middle Earth with attractions including the 'Sexy Barney Bubbles Light Show'.

Californian musician Paul Olsen visited 1a Leigh Court when Wills and Bubbles were completing the endeavour.

'They were sprawled out on the floor surrounded by scalpels and tins of Cow Gum,' recalls Olsen. 'The temperature was close to zero, but they were dressed in several layers of clothing and unaffected by the gripping cold, which cut me to the bone. Barney lit up the place with his infectious smile and his constant giggles: "Cold? What cold?!" This was to be my introduction to British pluck, Barney Bubbles-style.'

Cliff, who contributed drawings and a Krishna wallchart, believes that the issue was Bubbles' bid to score regular work at *Oz*. 'He wanted a job there and persuaded them while the art director was on holiday,' says Cliff.

'He saw it as a big opportunity because he knew he could handle the design far better than it had been up to that point. When they rejected the cover he became disillusioned because it was the same crap that he'd experienced from the corporate-identity arseholes. That makes him sound impatient. He wasn't. He didn't tolerate fools gladly because he was so sure of his work.'

In the spring of 1968, Bubbles left Conran. 'He'd wanted out for some time, and when he did go he left quite a big hole in the department,' said Muggeridge. 'The day he handed his notice in, he said to me: "You've got to get out as well. When you do, come and work with me."'

By this time Bubbles had met 18-year-old Giana Cioffi, who moved into Leigh Court with him as he set about raising funds for a trip to San Francisco. Here he hoped to find the true spirit of the counterculture.

As part of a fund-raising effort, Bubbles worked with Wills – who had stayed at *Oz* – under the banner O.K. Designs ('24 hour interpretations with a smile'), providing an invitation to the opening of fashion designer's Thea Porter's West End shop in the form of a five-inch Hand of Fatima on silver card.

They also oversaw the redesign of Knightsbridge Publications' hobbyist magazine *Motor Racing*. The relaunch issue, unveiled

in the same month as *Oz* 12 – May 1968 – brought the title into step with the 60s by introducing sans serif typography, improved photographic quality, humorous captions and images of scantily clad females.

During this period Bubbles maintained a presence in the mainstream by acting as freelance art director/chief designer for former Conran director Justin de Blank.

'I had been at Conran for about a year, and during that time recognised that, as well as being a very nice chap, Barney was extremely talented, hard-working and always spot-on,' said de Blank. 'I rated him very highly so, when I left, he handled designs for my clients: wine labels, packaging for Jackson's of Piccadilly tea and seed packets.'

In 1968 de Blank launched his own up-market provisions company which included a retail outlet in Elizabeth Street, Knightsbridge, which utilised Bubbles suggestions in its design. The pair didn't socialise, though they maintained a solid working relationship for several years. 'He was already quite a hippy by this point but we always found common ground,' said de Blank, who prized among his possessions a portrait of a reclining female Bubbles drew for him in the style of Goya.

The Justin de Blank shop, grocery range, restaurant, recipe books and flower delivery service soon attracted a clientele (which included younger members of the royal family) avidly seeking out goods carrying Bubbles' distinctive circular logo.

Such commissions provided the necessary funds for Bubbles to buy his ticket for the trip to San Francisco in the summer of 1968.

After a farewell gathering at 1a Leigh Court on Saturday 13 July, Bubbles set off to the US for a six-week trip during which he stayed with Olsen in Haight-Ashbury.

There Bubbles associated with the new hippy stars such as Janis Joplin and later claimed to have met his psychedelic art heroes Alton Kelley and Stanley Mouse. In a letter to Cliff from the US in early August, Bubbles was enthusiastic, informing his friend of the new argot, including such buzzwords as 'far out' and 'outstanding'.

'The whole of San Francisco is on an intimate scale,' he wrote. 'You make friends easy and, if you want to, can grab a large slice of scene… we ride around on a motorbike sightseeing and all eat hamburgers and ice-cream then take in four horror movies for $1.'

He informed Cliff that he was earning $250 a night operating light shows for bands such as Moby Grape at the Fillmore West and Pink Floyd at the Avalon Ballroom: 'I've seen Howlin' Wolf, Steppenwolf, Country Joe and Jeff Beck, all far out and outstanding. Our light show is better than anything these guys do.'

With plans to visit Yosemite, Disneyland and Los Angeles, Bubbles' upbeat mood in the fully illustrated letter to Cliff (which included a drawing of the correct way to throw a peace sign) was maintained in a 25 August card to Lorry Sartorio as he prepared his return to the UK.

Recounting how he had hiked from LA ('which is neither as nice nor as intimate as San Francisco') Bubbles announced his intention to revisit SF to live for a minimum of six months: 'In fact, I'm definitely coming back. I find SF in particularly (sic) very fulfilling. People place and climate is (sic) near to my heart.'

In another letter to Sartorio, meanwhile, Bubbles hinted at feeling overwhelmed by the experience: 'America is even more than I expected. More bigger, more bolder, more food, everything is everything but more (if you see what I mean).'

On his return, Bubbles moved back to his parents' home in Whitton. Giana Cioffi lived with him there for periods as he embarked on a freelance career, retained by de Blank and picking up piecework with Wills, including illustrations for the Spectator Publications cookery title *The Book Of Egg Cookery* (where his credit was 'Barney Fulcher').

It's indicative of Bubbles' enigmatic nature that those close to him view the effect of his California visit in contrasting terms to the cheerfulness of his correspondence.

'I don't know what went on there, but he came back almost a different person,' said his sister Jill. 'He totally lost self-confidence. After America his work went from what I call "normal" to containing lots of weird shapes. There was always a monster in the picture.'

Storey agrees. 'Barney hated America,' she sighs. 'It was too much for him. He told me that when he got back to the airport in London, he burst into tears he'd been so overwhelmed.'

In contrast, Paul Olsen, with whom Bubbles stayed, depicts his trip as 'an odyssey. He was in heaven and floated through his holiday, eyes wide open and totally amazed at everything American in that beautiful city, at that psychedelic time. It was pure magic to him.'

John Muggeridge confirmed that the West Coast trip marked a change in Bubbles' nature: 'Before he went he was a hippy in his mind. Having been there, right in the middle of the scene at its peak, he became one for real.'

There is no doubt that Bubbles' experiences on the Californian sojourn set him on the path towards realising his first substantial body of work, one which picked up the artistic gauntlet thrown down by the West Coast graphic practitioners. Although he was, for the time being, back in suburban Whitton, Bubbles was also infused with the personal freedoms and camaraderie experienced in San Francisco.

With income from freelance work and a spreading network of contacts throughout London's underground, Bubbles determined at the end of 1968 to set up his own creative commune in the London neighbourhood which most resembled The Haight: Notting Hill Gate.

ABOVE: Stills. Photoshoot for *Oz* 12. 1968.

RIGHT: Front and back. Postcard. 1968

THIS PAGE: Poster. The Image. 760mm x 560mm. 1966.

finished effect. Nevertheless, painting
is still 9/10 inspiration and no amount
of mechanical formulae can destroy
the fact, the artist's vision is his own
and that aesthetics are as important
as life THESE NOTES ARE WRITTEN
IN THE MOMENT, IN THE PRESENT,
INTOXICATED BY THE CREATIVE ENERGY
OF THE ATMOSPHERE AROUND THIS
ROOM. THEY ARE INTENSELY PERSONAL,
AND ON RE-READING THEM, ARE PROBABLY
JUMBLED. PATHS LEAD OFF AND COME BACK
TO CROSS AND RUN BESIDE FOR A TIME, THEN
THOUGHTS DISAPPEAR JUST AS QUICKLY.
Words are delicious, delicious is a meaty
word. Music can inspire and evoke a whole
mood, writing gets quicker and the rhythm
written to 1812 overture.
margin and
outside world is suddenly insignificant
For once I am terribly important and the
universe revolves around the record player.
It is now 9.30 in the evening and we
have decided to go up the pub. Margaret
and me. If anyone should ever read these
notes they should not sniff and say what
bad drawing or what terrible handwriting
(as they undoubtedly will) but rather think
of it as a rather insignificant emotional
report on art. A small, minute, molecular
ripple in the enormous world of paintings
9.35 The end of an experiment, I am exhausted
and feel unaccountably wet and hollow
I have put my coat on and taken the umbrella
as it is raining.

OPPOSITE AND THIS PAGE: Pages from Colin Fulcher's Twickenham College sketchbooks. 1962–4.

I cannot write back again this week as I will be pretty busy so when you reply put in where you can do it, when you will do it and what your fee is. I'll just turn up with the camera.

* Thanks for the letter I got this morning, pretty pictures and all. When I woke up Ian Brown was sleeping in the bed with me and Chris was curled up on top of the wardrobe. And a girl came in with our breakfasts. This is dead true. Apparently (she said) we were all pretty drunk on Sunday night and picked up these two girls on a back of bus and all went back to my house. Fantastic story eh! try explaining that to your mother when she wakes up. The last thing I remember was walking over Eel Pie Island bridge.

TOP: Letter from Colin Fulcher to Lorry Sartorio. 1964.

THIS PAGE: Contacts from photo session in Whitton. Middx, 1964.

OPPOSITE: B+W version of 'Knockout R&B Tonight', winner, British Poster Design Award 1964–5.

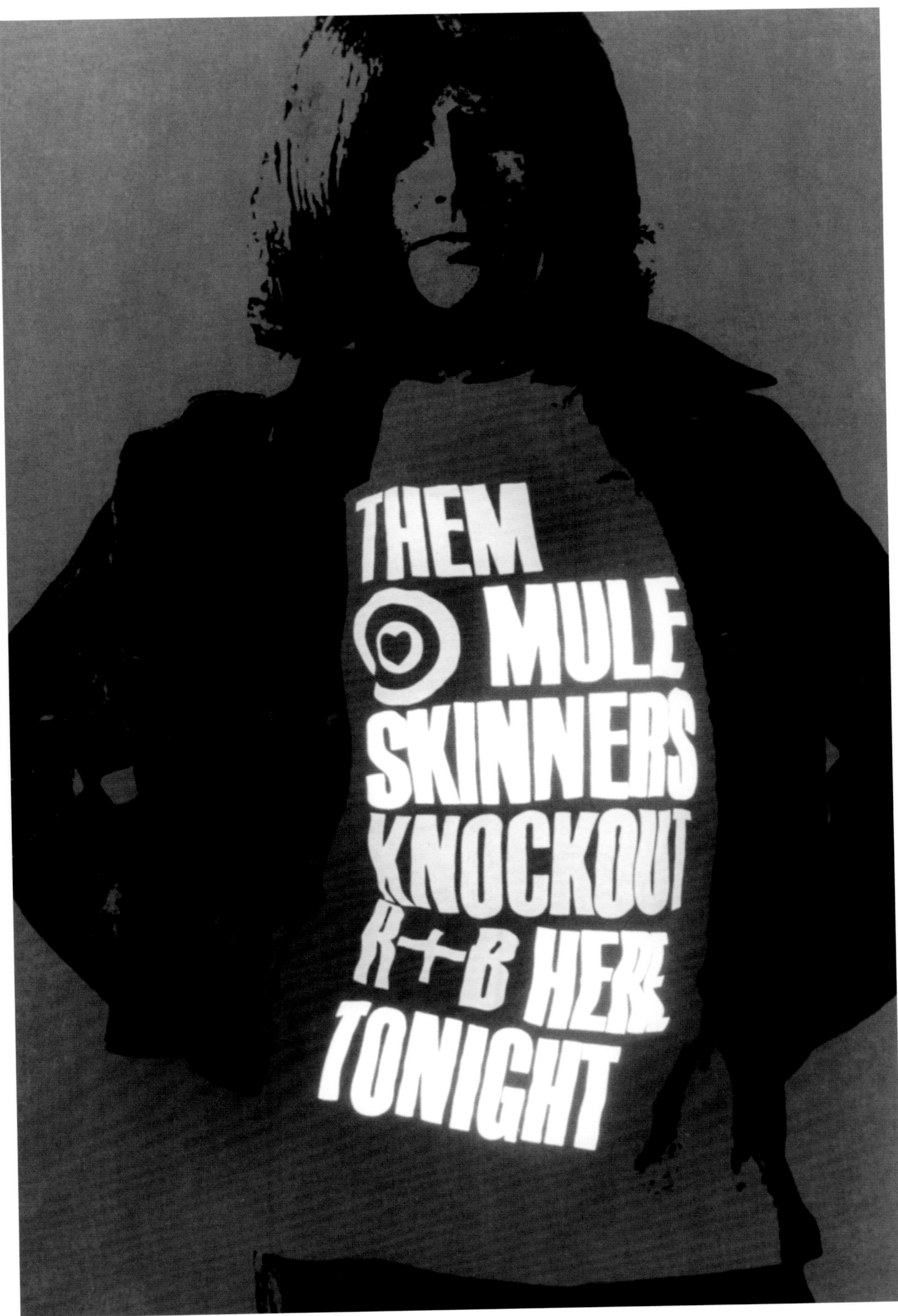
THEM
MULE
SKINNERS
KNOCKOUT
R+B HERE
TONIGHT

OPPOSITE PAGE: Portrait for 'Rockers & Mods' project. Pen, ink, watercolours. 250mm x 230mm. 1964.

THIS PAGE: Portrait for 'Rockers & Mods' project. Pen, ink, watercolours. 360mm x 230mm. 1964.

Existence is unhappiness
a
This is a fun & games OZ. The pullout sheets are based on the Great Buddhist liberation, or method of realising Nirvana through knowing the mind. Three out of the four poster-sides represent three out of the four truths which comprise Buddhism. The fourth side—and thus the fourth truth—had to be dropped because of extra advertising. But don't worry. The advertisements promise you Nirvana too.
TASMANIAN ORCHARDISTS AND PRODUCERS
HOBART, TASMANIA
ROYAL
I'M A HOPPY POPPY
CIVIL DEFENCE
1
2
3
4
5
6
7
8
9
10
11
12
A
B
C
D
E
F

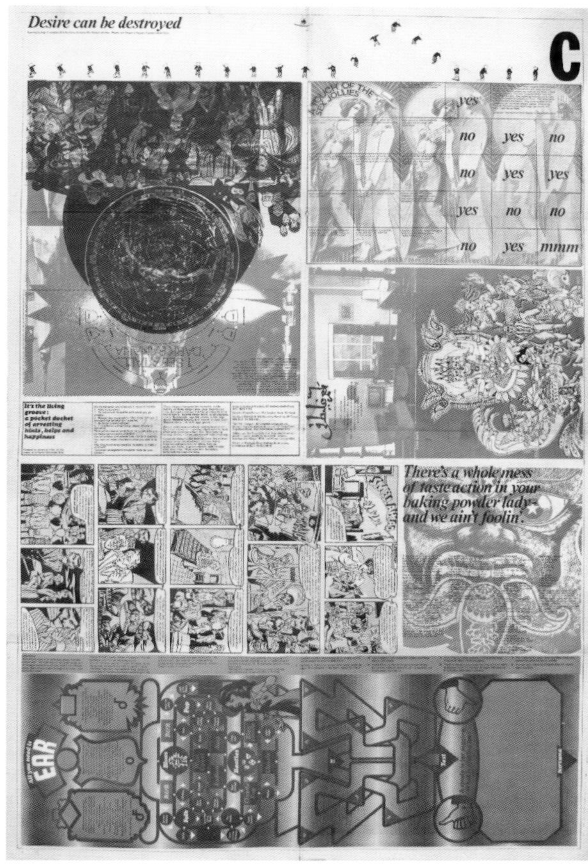

LEFT: Existence Is Unhappiness, *Oz* 12. 900mm x 600mm. 1968.

ABOVE: Desire Can Be Destroyed, *Oz* 12. 900mm x 600mm. 1968.

CREDIT: 'Summer *Oz* supplement rainbow designed by Eric Stodge (David Wills) and Barney Bubbles in co-operation with Onederland Productions. A1 Good Guyz gratefully acknowledge Chris Higson, Stafford Wiley Cliff, John Dove, Nanook Bunker, Fred Fulcher, Gary and Carol Russof, Paul Olsen, Dave Pether and Peter Brown, without whose help it would have been a bleak winter.'

RIGHT: Pen and ink self-portrait. October 1968.

In Search Of Space 1969–1972

ABOVE: Barney Bubbles, west London. 1970.

At the beginning of 1969, Barney Bubbles once more left the family home in Whitton and took a lease on the three-storey building at 307 Portobello Road in Notting Hill, west London.

With a retail space on its ground floor, this remains at the northern end of the thoroughfare which has contained a weekly street market since the 1870s. After the Second World War, rag-and-bone men moved in to sell junk and were followed in the early 1960s by antiques traders who drew tourists in large numbers. By the end of the decade, the availability of cheap housing and the attraction of sources of marijuana from the local Caribbean community had transformed Portobello into a countercultural hive.

Bubbles was dead-centre of the action: 293 Portobello Road was the head shop Forbidden Fruit (where the celebrated drug smuggler Howard Marks later operated), while 305 housed the junk/antiques emporium Much Ado About Nothing.

Visitor Paul Olsen describes Bubbles' new abode as 'a fantastic duplex, right in the middle of where the music scene was happening in London. Barney wanted it to become a creative commune for friends to live and work in.'

Bubbles converted the ground floor into a studio for his new company, Teenburger Designs. Over the next 18 months, the house became a crash-pad for the wilder local elements: hippies, musicians, drifters, draft dodgers and all manner of like-minded individuals.

The first raft of residents included Bubbles' girlfriend Giana Cioffi, her friend Donna and a Scottish painter and decorator named Colin Ramsay Elder.

The top floor was occupied by an individual known as 'Record John', who ran a record stall in alternative retail haven Kensington Market. This was John Cowell, half-brother of music mogul and *The X Factor* creator Simon Cowell, who is now a marketing millionaire.

'Barney was a real hippy, always one to shun self-publicity', says Cowell. 'I miss him so much and think of him often.'

On the middle floor was US draft dodger Rod Baker, 'a guy called Mexican Dave and a girl, Suzi from California', says Cioffi. 'People came and went – including Kathy Moon who sometimes worked with Barney. There were always six or seven people living there'.

A regular was hippy doctor Sam Hutt, later to benefit from Bubbles' designs in his persona as parody country and western star Hank Wangford, and visitors included Australian musicians Phil 'Shiva Shankar' Jones and Ron 'Raja Ram' Rothfield, whose new band Quintessence rehearsed in the basement. All the while Bubbles continued his association with Justin de Blank, designing everything from ex libris notes and postcards to headed paper and adverts.

On 14 April 1969, Bubbles received a visit from an ebullient entrepreneur named Edward Molton and his younger partner Stephen Warwick, who knew Bubbles from the west London art school scene (they had mutual friends in fellow Twickenham student Chris Higson and Barnes resident John Eichler).

On the lookout for a business address from which he and his partner could operate, Molton had been alerted to Bubbles by the company insignia he had recently designed for Warwick's Breydon Films. Struck by Bubbles' commercial potential, Molton reached an agreement with the designer: in return for use of the address, he offered to chase Teenburger invoices (for a ten per cent commission) and promised to open the horizons for all manner of design work.

Just over a week later, on 22 April, 307 Portobello Road was registered as the new address of Breydon Films and, on 8 May, Bubbles (signing as C. Fulcher) witnessed the registration at his address of another company, Sea Tribe Ltd, whose directors were Molton, Warwick and his wife Patricia.

As detailed in Will Birch's definitive pub-rock history *No Sleep Till Canvey Island*, Bubbles became Molton and Warwick's key to unlocking the west London hippy scene with a view to exploiting its commercial potential via a series of hair-brained schemes. These included the filming for general release of a celebrity bridge tournament starring Omar Sharif and the launch of a pirate radio station on a Second World War fort off the Essex coast.

Soon Teenburger Designs became subsumed into Molton and Warwick's new umbrella organisation which took its name from a suggestion of Bubbles: Motherburger. It is this name which Bubbles emblazoned on an illustration of 307 in a letter to Lorry Sartorio in mid-May 1969. Bubbles depicts himself watching Quintessence rehearse and describes 307 as a 'groovy scene... with lots of hard work and fun play'.

That summer Bubbles participated with David Wills in a photo-shoot for neighbour Phil Franks for the recently launched UK edition of *Rolling Stone*.

The pair were photographed painting the naked body of Notting Hill scenester Nikki with a fiery red, green and yellow motif. A member of a local coven, Nikki was preparing for a celebration of a change in the UK law governing the performance of magic ceremonies. This was held later that day in the distinctly unmagical surrounds of the Classic cinema in north-west London suburb Hendon (a couple of years later one of Franks' photographs from this shoot appeared in cheesy British soft-porn magazine *Curious*, where Wills was employed).

In June 1969, Molton moved in next door to Bubbles at 305 Portobello Road and, buying out a partner in Much Ado, added the antiques business to the Motherburger portfolio. By this time Bubbles had produced his own distinctive livery for Teenburger: squares of yellow burger bun-wrapping paper with a brown pop-art hamburger on the back. With work coming in, he recruited former Conran colleague John Muggeridge as his assistant.

'Molton was definitely bad news but did have the contacts, even arranging for us to pitch for the titles to (Ken Russell's 1969 movie) *Women In Love*,' said Muggeridge. 'We didn't get the job, but there was a refusal fee. I clearly remember Ted being paid £500 for that, but don't know whether we saw any of it.'

The atmosphere at Teenburger was 'totally haywire but very exciting', added Muggeridge. 'Molton would come rushing in and we'd be working non-stop while all these wild characters tramped in and out of the building. Anybody and everybody came because it was the happening place to be.'

Among the designs and promotional material supplied by Bubbles was headed paper for another Motherburger protégé, young film director Jodi Routh, the son of the late Jonathan Routh, at that time a major British celebrity as the main man of TV show *Candid Camera*. Jodi Routh – like many who fell under Molton and Warwick's spell – smarts to this day about his association with them.

'I remember I was very pleased with the headed paper, but upon reflection I realised I was being used as a pawn to pave contacts to obtain money from (Shell heiress) Olga Deterding and publicity through my father,' says Routh.

And so, while Bubbles toiled, Molton and Warwick dodged creditors by moving the Motherburger funds between the bank accounts they controlled, Bubbles' included.

Though the financing may have been shady, Teenburger was quickly established as a key location on the map of alternative London, from where Bubbles made his mark in record sleeve design. The first commission was sparked by his friendship with Quintessence, for whom he was by now creating light shows, notably at a benefit at Notting Hill's All Saints Hall for the King's Road restaurant and magazine *Gandalf's Garden* (for the final edition – number 6 – he also contributed layout and a Quintessence poster).

Bubbles' light show was a feature of Quintessence gigs at the Sunday evening Implosion events at north London's The Roundhouse, where he also contributed to performances by hard-rockers The Gun.

After just a couple of months on the live circuit, Quintessence were snapped up by the local Island Records in the summer of 1969 and set about recording their debut album In Blissful Company for release in November of that year, trailed by a single, their paean to the neighbourhood ('Everything's great in ...') Notting Hill Gate.

In Blissful Company is the first record release to feature the Barney Bubbles design credit, while Muggeridge is billed as 'J. Moonman'. The luminescent front cover portrayal of a Buddha is backed by a multi-hued mandala (both by Gopala, a member of the Quintessence crowd).

Stitched into the inner gatefold photograph of the Quintessence cover was a 12-page, 12sq in black and white booklet which offered a very different proposition to the outer sleeve. Amid photographs of the individual members in full flight during recording and performance, Bubbles placed repeated, multiple ellipses. He also die-cut triangles, circles and squares into the centre of six of the pages, creating a geometric puzzle to be enjoyed by stoned listeners craving a visual accompaniment to the music.

The first album to feature the Teenburger Designs credit was the February 1970 eponymously titled debut by Scottish five-piece Cressida. This was one of the first releases from Vertigo Records, launched by the major label Philips in late 1969 to capitalise on the burgeoning interest in progressive rock, which was characterised by multi-instrumental musicality and grandiose concepts.

For Cressida, Bubbles designed the front cover image of a temple with windows through which are viewed a twilit grid of stars. On the back a section of this grid was repeated in five-pointed star shapes, as if in close-up. Flying among them was a winged statue – possibly Cressida from the Trojan myth – which also appeared in the monochrome inner gatefold. This presented a sepulchral interior, with the stars on the horizon. The contemplative space was dominated by the forbidding faces of the Cressida band members.

Early in 1970, the next Teenburger commission arrived via Famepushers, the artist management wing of Motherburger which had been installed in 305 Portobello Road. Famepushers was run by one-time Jimi Hendrix road manager Dave Robinson. He had engaged the interest of new breed A&R man Andrew Lauder, then transforming the old-fashioned Liberty label into United Artists Records – into signing his charges Brinsley Schwarz.

At the Teenburger studio, Robinson spotted a 50s Western paint-by-numbers portrait of a native American brave, which Bubbles psychedelicised so that the figure appeared to be observing the Earth through alien skies. Bubbles also added

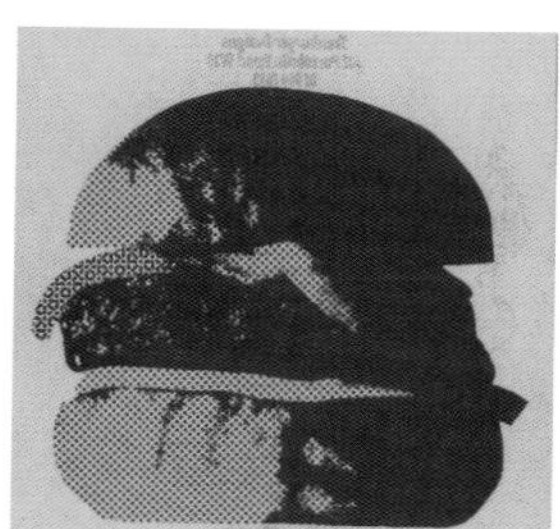

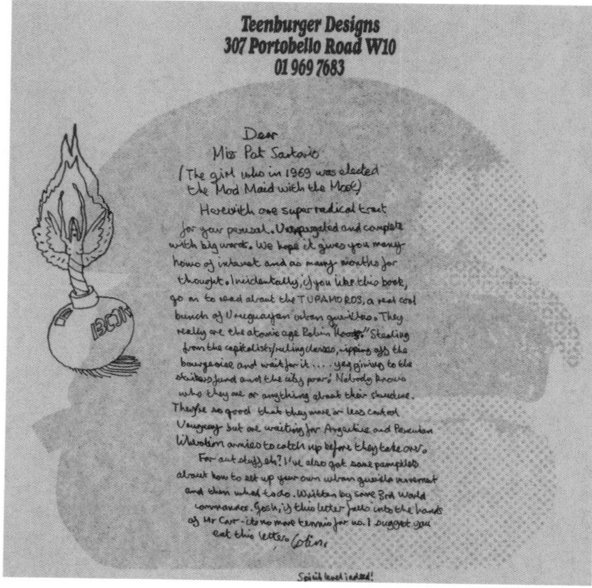

Teenburger Designs
307 Portobello Road W10
01 969 7683

Dear
Miss Pat Sartorio
(The girl who in 1969 was elected the Mod Maid with the Most)
Herewith one super radical tract for your perusal. Unexpurgated and complete with big words. We hope it gives you many hours of interest and as many months for thought. Incidentally, if you like this book, go on to read about the TUPAMOROS, a real cool bunch of Uruguayan urban guerillas. They really are the atomic age Robin Hoods." Stealing from the capitalists/ruling classes, ripping off the bourgeoisie and wait for it.... yes giving to the strikers fund and the city poor! Nobody knows who they are or anything about their structure. They're so good that they more or less control Uruguay but are waiting for Argentine and Peruvian liberation armies to catch up before they take over.
For out stuff eh? I've also got some pamphlets about how to set up your own urban guerilla movement and then what to do. Written by some 3rd World commander. Gosh, if this letter falls into the hands of Mr Carr - its no more tennis for us. I suggest you eat this letter. Colin.

Spirit level indeed!

Conran Fabrics Limited

C Information Sheet

As with most things my love, the funky things are the best things. That being the rule (at least for this dear postie) please excuse hurried biro and strange quality paper. I have been intending and now I am intended. At last the love me love u Larry letter. First. Our new address is 307 Portobello Road and our telephone number is 969 7683. Second. [illegible] in fact - Rod (American cheeseburger manufacturer). John (of long hair record fame) and Jan (back again). Colin Ramsay Elder (Scottish decorator). Donna (Moroccan explorer). Assorted hippies in the basement and me. Third. I am writing to you now as a happy settled person. We have a groovy scene operating from here with lots of hard work and fun play. Four. Thank you for your extremely settling talk sometime in the past. Five. Please come and share our hospitality as soon as possible. We're living pretty rough, until the decorating is completed but I want very much to talk some more to you as I felt our conversation didn't quite finish. So if you can come sometime this Whitsun I would be happy. Could you phone me at above number with a yeah or nay. P.S. I apologise for formal structured letter. Love and kisses Barney Bubbles (better known as Barney). PEACE.

TOP: Bubbles (standing centre) with other residents of 307 Portobello Road, among them John Cowell (standing, second right) and Giana Cioffi (between Bubbles and Cowell). 1969.

MIDDLE: Back and front of letter to Lorry Sartorio on Teenburger Designs livery. 200mm x 210mm. Summer 1969.

BOTTOM: Back and front of letter to Lorry Sartorio on Conran Designs livery. 297mm x 210mm. Spring 1969.

a distorting effect by horizontally stretching the image. 'Barney was quite cheap and none of us had any money,' says Robinson. 'The painting was propped against the wall. It was a really impressive, singular image, so we struck a deal and I bought it from him.'

It is said that Bubbles was forever disgruntled with Robinson for writing the name of the band on the lower right-hand corner of the artwork just before it was sent to be printed as the gatefold cover to the band's April 1970 release.

Nick Lowe, Brinsley Schwarz vocalist and songwriter, chortles at the memory. 'When Robbo scrawled on it with his biro it was just the worst,' he says. 'Whenever a dog-eared copy is stuck under my nose to sign, I always think: "Oh no, how could you have done this?"'

The album release was overshadowed by Famepushers' disastrous attempt to hype Brinsley Schwarz into stardom with a doomed voyage to New York for a special performance at the Fillmore East (also covered in Birch's *No Sleep Till Canvey Island*). The impact of this was to drive the musicians away from their mellow meanderings into becoming a founding force of the pub-rock movement.

The Brinsley Schwarz gatefold cover was, in fact, a reject, which is why it had been left on display, propped against the studio wall. Not long before Robinson's visit, executives at Fontana Records had rejected it as the sleeve for the release of the eponymous debut by Yorkshire blues-rock ensemble Red Dirt.

Instead, Fontana plumped for an alternative, cheaper option put forward by Bubbles; the monochrome two-sided envelope sleeve which packaged Red Dirt when it was released in the same month as Brinsley Schwarz, April 1970.

The back and the front of Red Dirt each featured a brutal crop of a native American warrior roughly enlarged to the point of image degradation and dominated by half-tones in the manner of a Wild West 'Wanted' poster.

The front cover of the Apache chief Geronimo presented the only colour: the band's name was studded as if by bullet holes on the heavy brow and blood-red drips trailed along the ridges of the face.

The primary reference shared by Red Dirt and Brinsley Schwarz chimed with the contemporary usage of Native American portraits as symbols of rebellion; in a different context, Nigel Waymouth, co-founder of the Chelsea boutique Granny Takes A Trip (which presented at different times two such images on its facade), has said: 'They represented everything that we as hippies looked for.'

And Bubbles' design for Fontana further resonated since Geronimo was buried at Fort Sill in Oklahoma in 1909 in a region renowned for the presence of soil known as 'red dirt'. It is believed that only 200 copies of Red Dirt were circulated for sale and, as of 2021, original copies fetched £2,750-plus in online auctions.

By the time of the release of these records, serious cracks were appearing in Molton and Warwick's empire, though Motherburger's credibility had at least been propped up by the leasing since late 1969 of two floors of 305 Portobello Road to the underground magazine *Friends* (which had grown out of the UK version of *Rolling Stone* and was edited by Alan Marcuson).

'When *Rolling Stone* America pulled the plug we had to find new offices,' says the magazine's news editor Jonathan Green, whose oral history of the period, *Days In The Life*, contains the definitive account of the *Friends* saga.

'Somehow Alan had became involved with Steve (Warwick) and

Eddie (Molton). One of them was fat and the other thin. I don't remember which way round it went, but what's important was that they turned out to be pretty bent. The story was they had a cheque for £10,000 which they routinely shifted around ten different bank accounts.'

Since the magazine's arrival at 305, Bubbles had contributed art direction and layout, with girlfriend Cioffi typing up copy and Phil Franks taking photographs.

'It was clear Barney was a proper designer but he was also a complete hippy, with the hair and the tie-dyes, having studied at the feet of Stanley Mouse, so legend had it,' says Green. 'We frequented the Mountain Grill, a greasy spoon in Golborne Road which sold steak and chips for fuck all. Barney would occasionally sprinkle hash on his. He would also go off for weekends, taking acid, and come back having cleaned his mind out, or maybe having blown it.'

Despite this continued appetite for hallucinogens, Green believes Bubbles was not as actively involved in the counter-culture as the *Friends* staff. 'He was much more of a service industry, which is really how it should have been because he was so evidently talented,' says Green. 'Pearce Marchbank, who worked alongside him, was always a great admirer because the design standards of the underground press were so low.'

Still, Motherburger's chickens were coming home to roost as spring 1970 turned to summer. By June, Bubbles was actively looking for an out, placing an ad in *Friends*: 'Boss penciller Barney Bubbles, Bumper Bundle Bonus of fun, poor but honest, urgently requires unfurnished pad in Gate or Grove area, lousy with smiles, phone 969 7683.'

'The crunch came when Molton arrived at Teenburger and announced his doctor had told him he was suffering from a severe heart condition which meant that he had six months to live,' recalled Muggeridge. 'Of course it was pure hype. He had spent all the money we had earned. Soon after, he disappeared and that was it. Teenburger was over, the studio shut down and Barney left 307.'

Molton and Warwick trailed many unpaid creditors in their wake, and the precariousness of Bubbles' financial situation snowballed with the arrival of a tax demand which he was unable to settle. This was to plague him for years.

'There is always a fantasy side to Barney's life and work,' says Stafford Cliff. 'On the one hand his design was very practical but on the other there was a constant fantasy aspect. The two things don't marry up too well when it comes to things like paying tax or getting paid. He was a trusting soul and when people ripped him off by not paying invoices, or made him wait, he found it hurtful.'

Bubbles moved with Cioffi into a council flat in Octavia House, on a housing estate in Ladbroke Grove, sharing with their friend Kathy Moon.

The last release to bear the Teenburger credit was another project for Vertigo, the August 1970 self-titled debut by London band Gracious!

This is known as the 'Exclamation Mark' album, due to Bubbles' placement of a giant punctuation mark on the white cover in raised black dots, which give it a reptilian quality. The inner gatefold is designed to provoke an exclamation of shock: a flouro-pink suspenders-and-stocking-clad female form executed in the manner of 60s pop artist Tom Wesselmann bears down on a tiny collaged muscleman who is either flexing his muscles or shaking his fists.

'I don't believe we were told Barney was involved,' says

Gracious! band member Alan Cowderoy, later to work alongside the designer at Stiff Records. 'Vertigo said the inside was going to have a 3D effect like that of (the Rolling Stones') Their Satanic Majesties Request. Next thing we knew, the budget had run out so we'd better be happy with what we got. And I must say we were. It's stunning.'

In November 1970 the *Sunday Times* published an exposé of Motherburger's dodgy dealings and Molton subsequently disappeared without trace.

Teenburger was over, and Bubbles' finances may have been reeling from the association, but his reputation was firmly established in music industry circles. As John Muggeridge said, 'Barney could capture what the client wanted, whether it was a "straight" job like Justin's or a street band like Quintessence. He wouldn't change his appearance or attitude, but would go into meetings as a hippy with long hair and scruffy clothes. He was so well-known for having "it" that business people put their preconceptions to one side.'

In 1971, Bubbles' design energies took a new direction as he became absorbed into west London musical collective Hawkwind. The group's gangly blond saxophonist, Nik Turner, became a particularly close friend. From the coastal town of Margate, Turner's childhood friend, the poet Robert Calvert, had drawn him to Hawkwind and also to *Friends*, where Calvert was a contributor along with the sci-fi writer Michael Moorcock.

'It was Robert who introduced me to Barney,' says Turner. 'We hit it off immediately. He had very long and unkempt henna-ed hair and obviously had a handle on light shows, having operated them on the West Coast. He seemed a very friendly, off-the-wall creative person.'

Turner was to live intermittently with Bubbles, Cioffi and others at Octavia House over the next couple of years as their friendship matured into a working relationship, and their circle included not only Calvert and Moorcock but also Hawkwind founder Dave Brock, roadie Gerry Fitzgerald, dancer Stacia Blake and manager Doug Smith as well as scenester John Trux (who oversaw *Friends'* mutation into *Frendz* in May 1971).

Hawkwind's street-theatre biker rock provided a rambunctious antidote to the pomposity of the progressive music scene and the excesses of the stadium bands. And their extended and

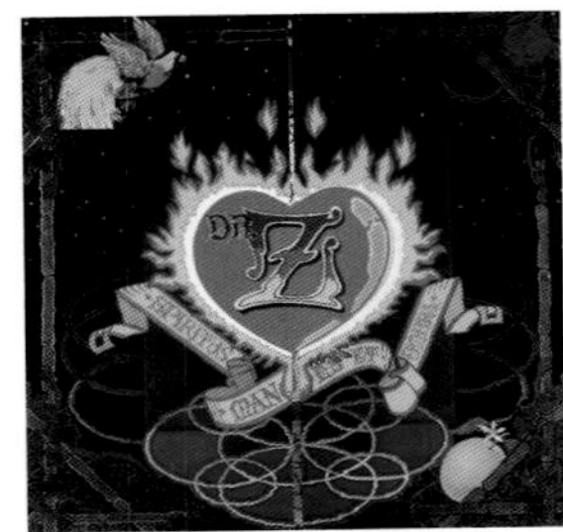

TOP: Front and back cover. Red Dirt, Red Dirt, Fontana. 12in album. 1970.

CREDIT: Teenburger.

ABOVE: Front cover and inner sleeve. 3 Parts To My Soul, Dr Z, Vertigo. 12in album. 1971.

CREDIT: Barney Bubbles.

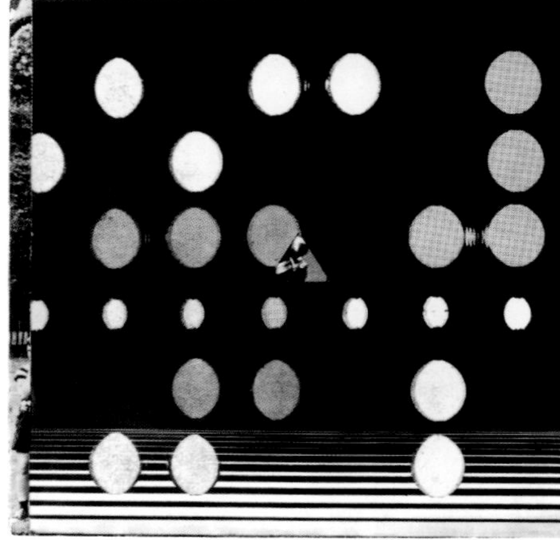

ABOVE: Three sections from inner booklet. In Blissful Company, Quintessence, Island Records, 12in album. 1969.

CREDIT: Barney Bubbles/J. Moonman Esq.

ever-changing line-up meant that Hawkwind's tentacles spread throughout the British underground, bolstered by appearances at benefits and free gigs. 'We had credibility because we appealed to people at a grass-roots level,' says Turner, reminiscing in the barn/recording studio at his farm in a remote corner of Wales from where he conducts an active musical career which includes membership of at least three different bands.

When Calvert joined as frontman/singer in June 1971, Hawkwind evolved into a poetic multimedia space-rock outfit aligned in certain ways with the German 'Krautrock' groups of the early 70s; Dave Brock provided the sleeve-notes to the first UK release by the movement's founding group, Neu!

With the addition of Stacia Blake and other naked dancers – whom Bubbles adorned with body-paint – and a stunning light show operated by Jonathan Smeeton (known as Liquid Len), Bubbles blazed a trail as the first graphic designer to handle every aspect of a single rock group's visual identity, combining record sleeves, posters, stickers, badges, painted equipment and even stage directions into a coherent package.

'Barney fitted in very well, although quietly in the background,' says Doug Smith. 'That's where he preferred to be, though in many ways he was another member of the band because his contribution was so important.'

Producing the sleeve design and packaging for the group's second album, X In Search Of Space (released in October 1971), Bubbles cemented a visual sub-genre defined in recent years by designer John Coulthart as 'cosmic Art Nouveau'. While revivalism in graphics circles had been addressed for more than a decade, rarely had a commercial artist of such talent and imagination been afforded this level of direct access to the youth market.

Defining Hawkwind's sci-fi self-mythologising, the X In Search Of Space sleeve enabled Bubbles to once again challenge received packaging practice. The front locked together via die-cut serrated edges, and when unfolded displayed, in the shape of a cruciform, the outline of a hawk featuring the credits, photographs of the musicians and their milieu (including Bubbles and Cioffi), and band logos. Also included was a 24-page paper booklet, The Hawkwind Log, put together by Bubbles and Calvert.

'We were just stunned when he brought in the artwork,' says Smith, who had himself worked in interior design in the 60s and would spend many hours poring over Art Deco, Nouveau and other art history books with Bubbles. 'The thing about Barney is that he created a visual vocabulary for Hawkwind and the other bands he worked with. That's why I say he was the most important artist of our generation.'

Just a month after the release of X In Search Of Space, another Bubbles' cover die-cut was given more limited exposure with the issue by Vertigo of London prog trio Dr Z's ultra-rare album 3 Parts To My Soul.

This is reputed to have been pressed in a run of just 80 copies. This figures, since 3 Parts To My Soul was likely to have been an extremely expensive investment for an unknown act. The full-colour heavy-duty card sleeve is again bisected on the front with two panels into which is cut a central flame-edged shape. These opened onto a blood red medieval sacred heart imposed over a ghostly figure and framed with barbed wire.

This evoked the concept underlying the music: that the human soul is divided into 'the spiritus' (inherent good); 'the manes' (the underworld); and 'the umbra' (the ghost). Bubbles' design effetctively anglicised the work of the West Coast psychedelic pioneers with heraldic and folkloric devices.

This was to be Dr Z's only release. As a result, 3 Parts To My Soul has become one of the all-time vinyl collectibles, much bootlegged and rarely heard.

By contrast, X In Search Of Space benefited from promotion by one of the hardest gigging bands around, and soon began to sell in large numbers.

'In Search Of Space is to this day the most influential piece of work on my life,' says British designer Malcolm Garrett. 'It coincided with me finding my feet as a teenager, discovering girls, drugs, rock'n'roll and art.'

Garrett (who first made his mark on the British music scene with designs for Buzzocks in 1977 and went on to become designer of choice for such international acts as Duran Duran) believes that the scene from which Bubbles sprang was the model for punk.

'Barney was effectively a member of the collective, being responsible for the visuals,' says Garrett. 'I drew reference from that for what I saw as my role as Buzzcocks developed. I was working very closely with them, not hired by a record company once they'd been signed. I was on the ground and they were part of the life I was living. And so In Search Of Space is to blame for everything I've done since.'

With Hawkwind's wordsmith and theoretician Robert Calvert, Bubbles and Turner developed a shared interest in abstruse subject matter, from cosmology, astrology, astronomy and cryptography to pagan ritual, Weimar imagery, ley lines, space travel and pyramid theory.

On a more personal level, Bubbles and Calvert shared common ground as sufferers of bipolar depression, symptoms from which became marked in both men as the 70s progressed.

During such bouts, Calvert would absent himself from the Hawkwind circle, spending time in institutions and receiving medication. Calvert was outspoken about his condition, even mentioning it in press interviews. In contrast, Bubbles was taciturn; his friends became used to his unexplained absences.

Typically, Calvert and Bubbles collaborated in creative bursts, resulting in such fully illustrated tracts as the 'Hawklog' and the detailed proposals for live performance, staging and direction.

When the Calvert-composed track Silver Machine became a hit single in the summer of 1972 (sung by bassist Lemmy), it arrived in a Bubbles silver-printed blue sleeve, a relative rarity since only albums were deemed worthy of non-standard covers.

Meanwhile, Bubbles' design for the band's November 1972 album Doremi Fasol Latido identified the sci-fi conceptualising in the form of the Hawkwind 'gateway' shield on the gatefold sleeve which, in its original form, was silver foil overprinted in black.

The rear cover, inner sleeve and 'Star Rats' poster contained within were illustrated with futuristic warriors, and Bubbles and Calvert expounded in the sleeve-notes on a 'Pythagorean concept of sound' with the universe as 'an immense monochord, with its single string stretched between absolute spirit and at its lowest end absolute matter. Along this string were positioned the planets of our solar system.'

To chime with Doremi's themes, Bubbles produced a set of graphic posters to accompany the so-called 'Space Ritual' tour promoting the album's release.

As noted by John Coulthart (who himself designed three album sleeves for Hawkwind later in their career), these illustrations reflected the influence of cinematic comic book hero creator Jack Kirby. One, Fanon Dragon Commando, lifts the central figure from a strip by French artist Philippe Druillet and adds a new

TOP: Front cover. Cressida, Philips. 12in album. 1970.

MIDDLE: Inner gatefold. Cressida, Philips. 12in album. 1970.

BOTTOM: Back cover. Cressida, Philips. 12in album. 1970.

CREDIT: Teenburger.

ABOVE AND RIGHT: Booklet. The Hawkwind Log. 280mm x 200mm. X In Search Of Space, Hawkwind, UA. 1971.

background and several embellishments (and was to be used in a Bubbles ad promoting Hawkwind's MC5-like single Urban Guerilla the following year). According to Doug Smith, the posters failed to sell in any quantity because there was no overt link between them and the album.

'None of us realised at the time how great his work was,' says Smith. 'Barney executed it with such wit and certainty. Hawkwind would not have sounded the same with anybody else's designs.'

Although he was a dedicated member of the Hawkwind family, Bubbles continued to work for other sympathetic clients. Wayne Bardell, Doug Smith's former partner in concert promoter Clearwater Promotions, called upon Bubbles' services for the sleeve of the debut album by the Scottish folk-rock siblings he managed, Iain and Gavin Sutherland.

'Wayne took us along to meet Barney; we liked him and what he had to say,' recalls Gavin Sutherland. 'A couple of days later he came to a session at Island's studios in Basing Street to hear the tunes we were working on and get a feel for our music. A week went by, we met up and he explained his master plan. Barney had seen a battered fruit box in the street and liked the way the damaged logo looked.'

With their go-ahead, Bubbles painted a portrait of the brothers on a piece of plain wood he acquired from a local joiner's yard (whose Mr Winton received a sleeve credit). For the back cover, Bubbles chose a band photograph, which he subjected to his own method of weathering. 'He folded it up and put it in the arse pocket of his famous red dungarees for a week or so, until it looked bad enough for the job,' says Sutherland.

Having completed the cover painting in the style of the image from the pack of a favourite cigarette brand, Capstan Full Strength, Bubbles invited the brothers back to Octavia House. 'We all agreed it looked fab as it lay on his kitchen table,' says Sutherland. 'Then came the moment we'd been waiting for. Barney picked up a hammer and smashed it to fuck before our very eyes. Awesome! We said nothing more, shook hands and called a cab. The best sleeve we ever had.'

Soon the Sutherland Brothers were to join forces with another London band, Quiver, for whom Bubbles also designed. For the sleeve of their mid-1972 release Gone In The Morning, he placed the band name on a banner over an Art Nouveau painted glass portrait with heraldic tulips and poppies sprouting from a marquetry frame. The inner bore tinted images of the group members (including future Elvis Costello And The Attractions bass player Bruce Thomas) set against the fine wood veneer.

'Barney was a splendid chap,' says Quiver guitarist Tim Renwick. 'I had the painted piece of glass which was a mock-up of the Quiver artwork he did for us. Unfortunately, it suffered an accident a few years back and broke into a thousand shards. Barney also painted a bass drum head for (Quiver drummer) Willie Wilson which he has kept rather safer than my glass artwork.'

In August 1972, Bubbles' partner Giana Cioffi gave birth to their son Aten (named after an ancient Egyptian deity). A few months later they took a cottage on a friend's farm in Clovelly, Devon.

This planned long-term departure to the West Country was, to say the least, short-lived for Bubbles. Cioffi depicts him as 'a workaholic' who had become obsessed with leaving the capital but couldn't commit to a rural existence when it became a reality.

'There had been all this talk about getting away from it all and living a simple life without any pressures,' she says. 'So we were driven down by our friend Pat Synge, but the very next morning

FINGERING THE ENVIRONMENT

GLASS

LETTER FROM AMERIKA 2

JOURNEY BOKABOK INTO SPACE THOOM KERWHUMP WRAK...

Barney announced he had to go back to London! He said he had a load of work to do. I stayed down there with Aten for about a year and Barney came and saw us occasionally.'

Earlier in 1972, Bubbles had been contracted as house artist at Revelation Enterprises, the company founded by *Friends* music critic John Coleman to help pay the debts accrued by the previous summer's music festival Glastonbury Fayre.

Attendance at this event had been severely hit when the Grateful Dead, for contractual reasons, were prevented from headlining by their record company. The organisers, including Winston Churchill's niece Arabella, conceived a plan for a compilation to pay creditors. To make this as attractive as possible to consumers, it was decided – by Churchill, Coleman, scenester/DJ Jeff Dexter and others – that it should be a triple album with the added value of an elaborate sleeve.

In addition to live performances from the festival, the album contained songs donated by the likes of Pete Townshend, David Bowie, Marc Bolan and the Grateful Dead, whose live version of Dark Star recorded elsewhere occupied the whole of one side.

Bubbles – who had been drafted in at Revelation on the recommendation of his friend, Mighty Baby's Martin Stone – produced a simple packaging solution: the three records were housed in 2ft x 3ft folded pieces of paperboard sealed in clear vinyl envelopes onto which was printed title and credits in comic book font ridden by a Silver Surfer figure.

When unfolded, one side created a six-panel poster of the pyramid stage at Glastonbury aglow at night, while the other carried a monochrome daytime image of the crowd. The theme was driven home with small paper cut-out fold-outs: one a pyramid to be constructed from two black and silver printed loose leaves, the other a tiny Buckminster Fuller/*Whole Earth Catalogue* geodesic dome.

There are also two booklets, one black and white and containing musings and artwork by underground figures, and the other brown, green and marijuana leaf-adorned, providing track-listing and credits.

Glastonbury Fayre was released in a pressing of 5,000 copies, retailing at £3.99 each, inexpensive by the standards of the day when a single album was priced £1.50 or so. In adverts designed by Bubbles for *Frendz*, he reprised the 'Earth family' from the Doremi tour posters with a pyramid-shaped order coupon. These days the album is a collectable, with pristine copies fetching several hundred pounds.

Bubbles' residency at Revelation led to the design of the record company's only other release, Kings Of The Robot Rhythm by Chilli Willi And The Red Hot Peppers (at this stage Mighty Baby's Martin Stone and his friend Phil Lithman with backing from sundry musician friends including members of Brinsley Schwarz).

Again Bubbles opted for an organic approach; the sleeve's stock brown card is printed with earthy greens and reds and the cover is an illustration of a 30s island girl. The inner places band photographs on a repeated cartoon duck image while the reverse of the lyric sheet (which bears the watermark of the paper stock Glastonbury Wove, thus cross-referencing Revelation's other album) is a line-drawn portrait of a cowgirl against the sun's rays. This is delivered with a typical Bubbles maneouvre to engage – the record buyer is exhorted to colour it in, using such hues as 'Acapulco gold' and 'Guano brown'. There is also a cut-out-and-keep bow tie. Such throwaway items helped Chilli Willi connect with their audience.

ABOVE AND LEFT: *Friends*. 13 September 1970.

ABOVE: Inner gatefold. Gracious!, Gracious!, Vertigo. 1970

OPPOSITE: Front and back cover. Gracious!, Gracious!, Vertigo. 12in album. 1970.

CREDIT: Teenburger Designs.

'I traced around it and made "bow-ties" for me and my friends to wear to all the Willis' gigs,' says Tom Sheehan, then working at Sheffield parks department but soon to become one of Britain's most highly rated music photographers (supplying images for Bubbles' sleeve designs later in the decade).

Among Chilli Willi's fans was Andrew 'Jake' Jakeman, a former mod from north-west London looking for a scene which reflected his interests in rock'n'roll, country and soul.

In the 60s, Jakeman had tried his hand at bands (including one with schoolmate Felix Dennis of *Oz*) and advertising. He had even dipped his toe in the underground by selling candles in Kensington Market and coincidentally at the so-called Friends Market, a jumble of stalls which occupied the ground floor of 305/7 Portobello Road for a period.

By 1972 he had become a driver for prog band Darryl Way's Wolf. One evening, Jakeman turned up at west London pub the Kensington to catch a performance by Brinsley Schwarz. When he found out that their PA had developed a fault, he offered the gear from his van.

'My boss – who was a bit of a twit – found out and tried to read me the riot act,' grins the man who later became Jake Riviera over lunch at his comfortable club in Chiswick. 'I delighted in telling him that, not only had I lent it to the band, but I hadn't charged them either. Then I told him to stick it. That night I mentioned to the Brinsleys I had lost my job. They recommended me to Martin Stone and I threw my lot in with Chilli Willi.'

Soon after, Riviera dropped in at Revelation's offices above Compendium Books in Camden Town, to pick up copies of Kings Of The Robot Rhythm.

There he found Bubbles, surrounded by unfolded Glastonbury Fayre sleeves. 'He was packing them together one by one,' says Riviera. 'I thought it unfair to leave him to do it all on his own. So I said: "Look, if you get the records and the bits together, I'll do the folding, and we can speed things up."

Soon, the pair had shared a lot of their experiences and much about their dreams. The man who would help Barney Bubbles realise many of his had entered his life.

VERTIGO
Gracious!

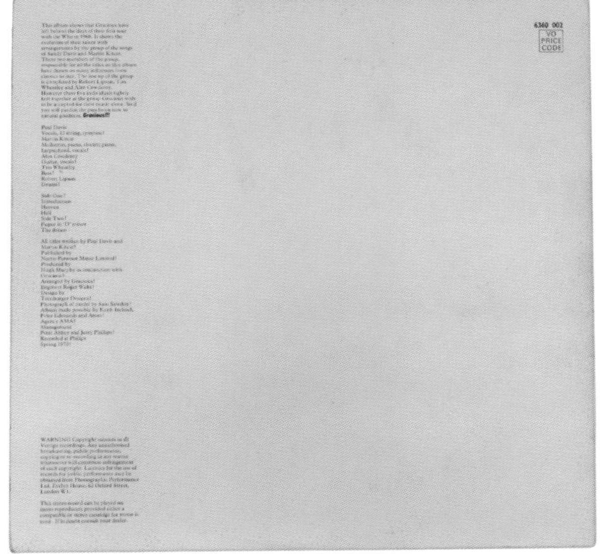

stereo
also playable mono

ABOVE: Outer gatefold. Brinsley Schwarz, Brinsley Schwarz, UA. 12in album. 1970.

CREDIT: Teenburger Designs.

IN SEARCH OF SPACE
HAWKWIND

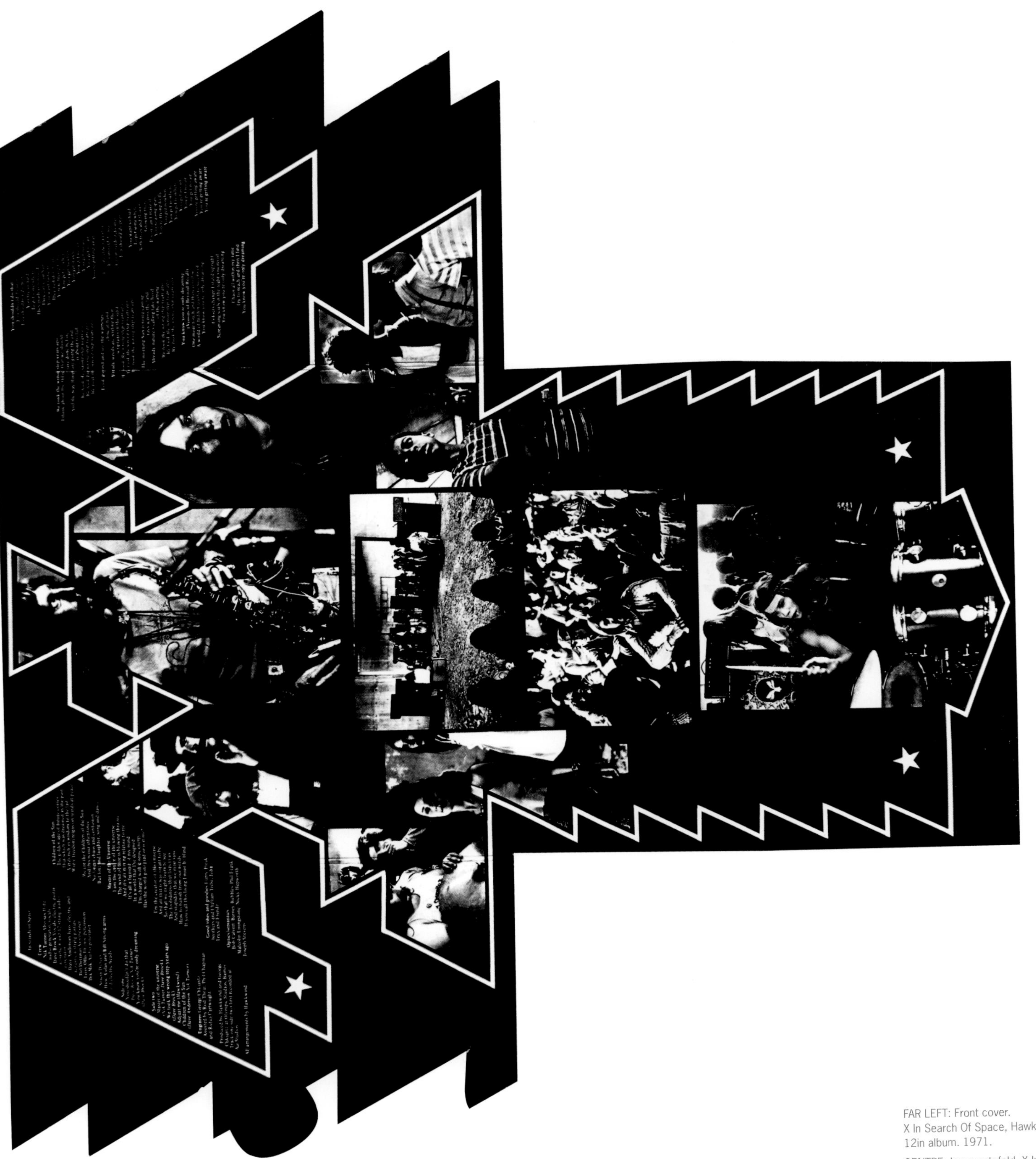

FAR LEFT: Front cover. X In Search Of Space, Hawkwind, UA. 12in album. 1971.

CENTRE: Inner gatefold. X In Search Of Space, Hawkwind, UA. 1971.

THIS PAGE: Full gatefold. X In Search Of Space, Hawkwind, UA. 1971.

CREDIT: Optics – Barney Bubbles.

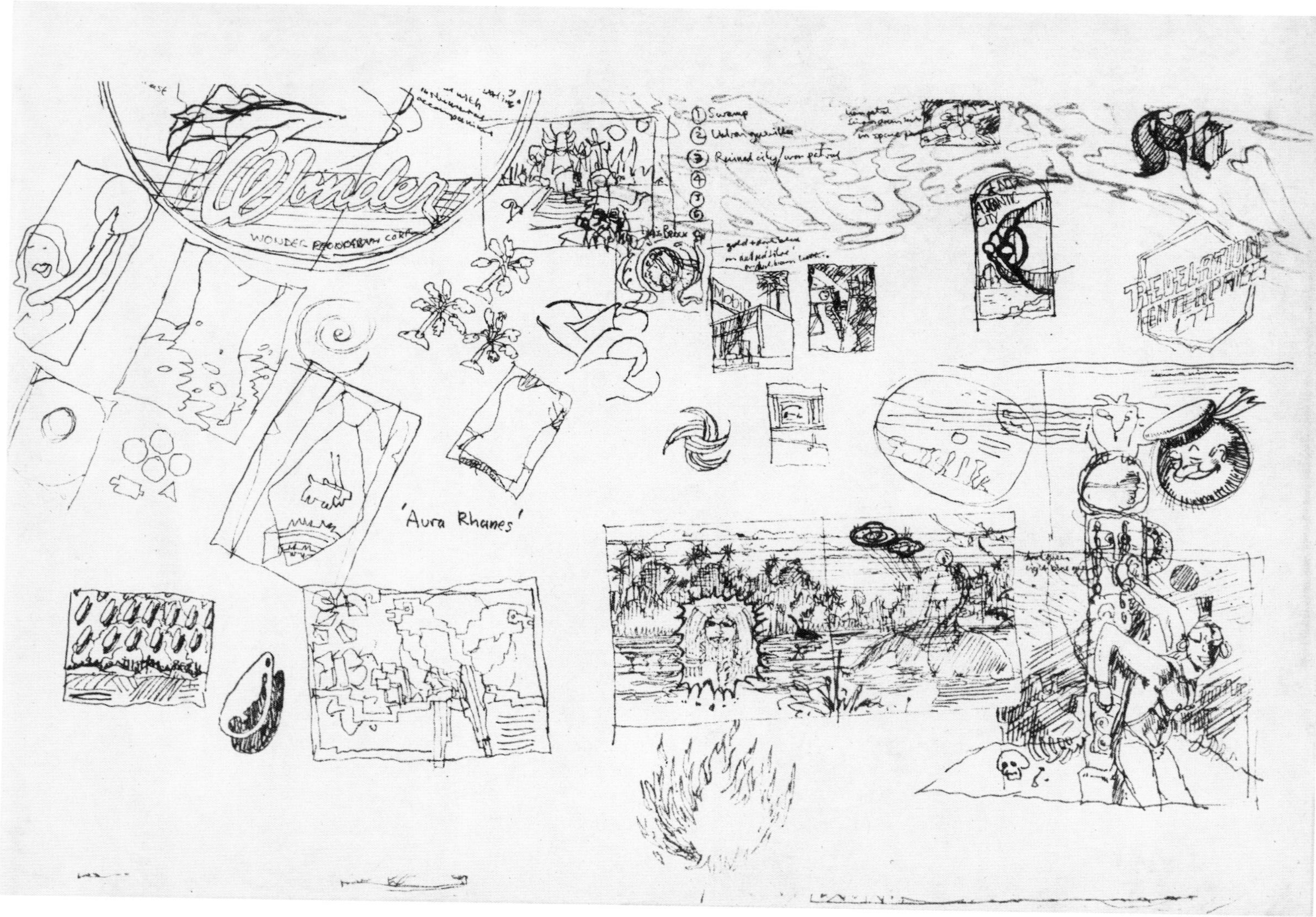

'Aura Rhanes'

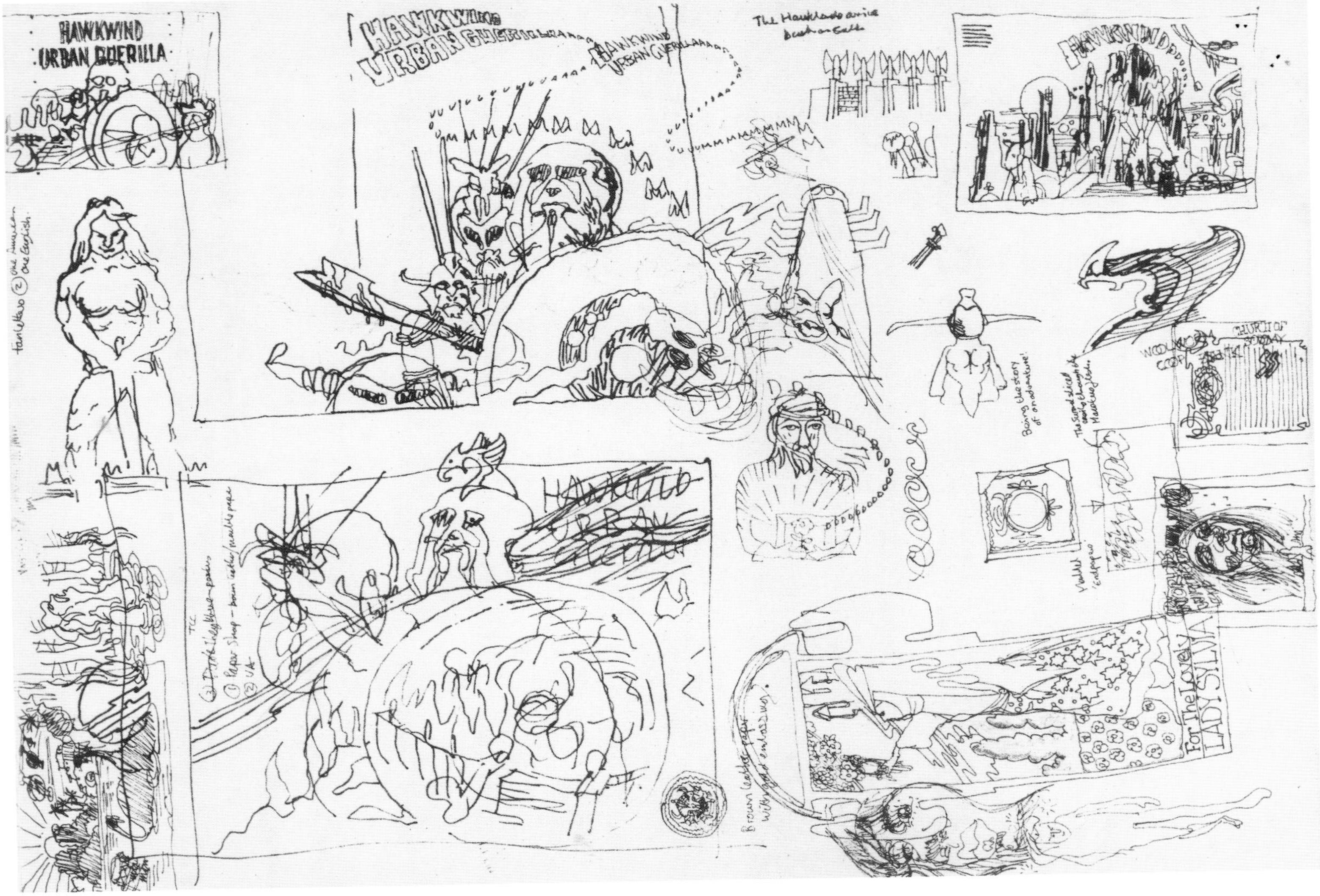

OPPOSITE AND THIS PAGE: Working sketches. Hawkwind projects. 1972/3.

Hawkwind
DOREMI FASOL LATIDO

OPPOSITE AND THIS PAGE: Front and back cover. Doremi Fasol Latido, Hawkwind, UA. 12in album. 1972.

CREDIT: Barney Bubbles.

THIS PAGE, OPPOSITE: 4 x posters. 370mm x 470mm. 1972.

ABOVE: Prince Minsky's chopper.

OPPOSITE TOP: Earth family.

OPPOSITE MIDDLE: Fanon Dragon Commando.

OPPOSITE BOTTOM: The Temple Of Hex Peyotl/Atlantis.

Prince Minsky's chopper Hawkwind Barney Bubbles

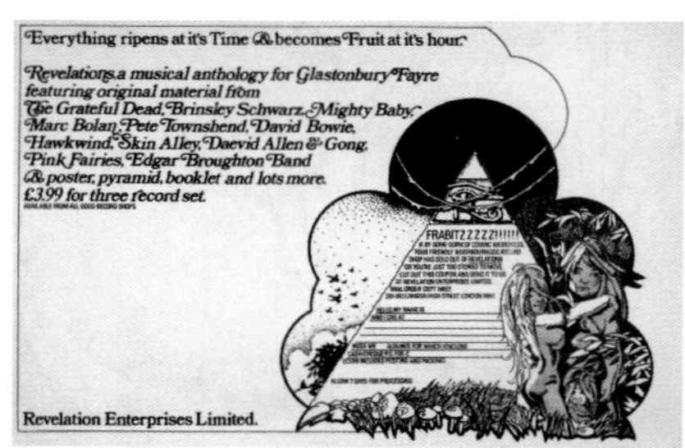

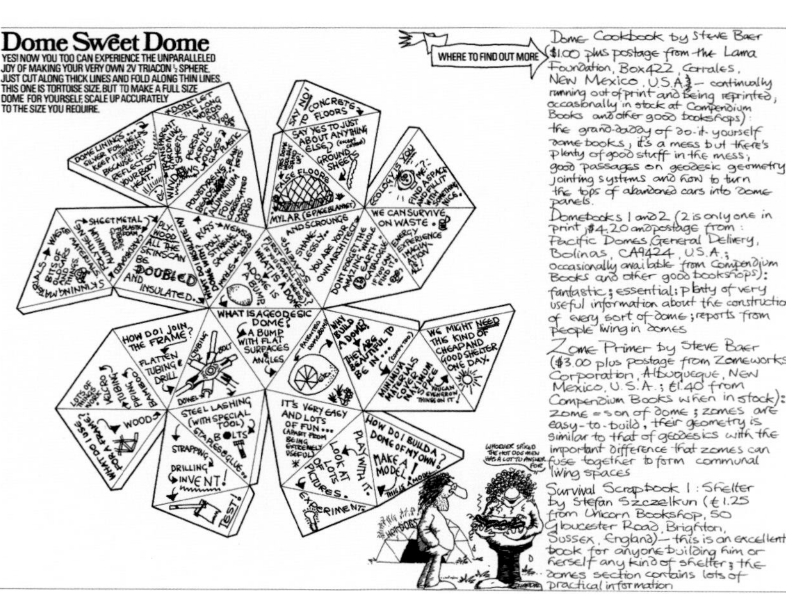

TOP LEFT: Clear vinyl envelope. Glastonbury Fayre, Revelation Records. 12in album. 1972.

CENTRE: Advert. Glastonbury Fayre, *Frendz*. 1972.

LEFT: Insert. Glastonbury Fayre, Revelation Records. 1972.

ABOVE: Six-panel cover. Glastonbury Fayre, Revelation Records. 900mm x 600mm. 1972.

RIGHT: Inserts. Glastonbury Fayre, Revelation Records. 1972.

RIGHT: Poster. Glastonbury Fayre, Revelation Records. 594mm x 841mm. 1972.

TOP: Six-panel inner. Glastonbury Fayre, Revelation Records. 900mm x 600mm. 1972.

FAR LEFT AND LEFT: Booklets. Glastonbury Fayre, Revelation Records. 1972.

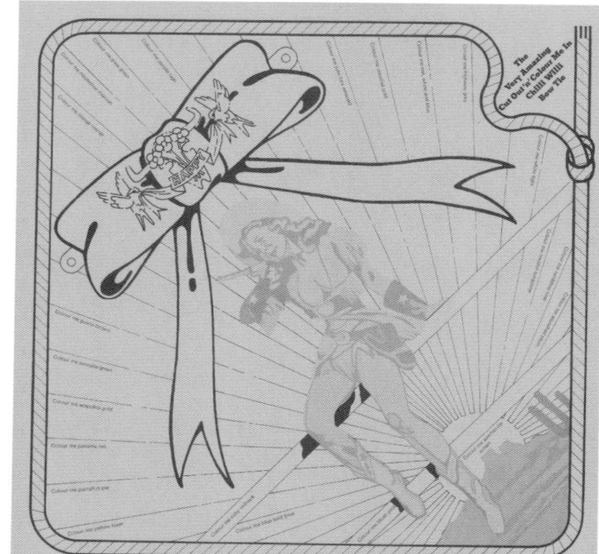
The Very Amazing Cut Out'n'Colour Me In Chilli Willi Bow Tie

Living Out My Suitcase The Ballad Of Chilli Willi Window Pane I'll Be Home Nashville Rag That's All Right Mamma
Drunken Sunken Red Neck Blues Get Your Gauge Up Let Your Love Come Down Happy You Fiddle Dee Astrella From The
Astral Plane Paper Mill A Page In History
Chilli Willi

85987 IT STEREO
The Sutherland Brothers Band
Iain Sutherland
Vocals/guitars/piano/harmonica
Gavin Sutherland
Vocals/guitars/steel guitar/percussion
Kim Ludman
Bass guitar
Neil Hopwood
Drums/percussion
Production by Muff Winwood
Production Engineer Richard Digby-Smith
Recorded at Island Studios
Cover Art by Barney Bubbles
Photograph by David Redom
Wood by Mr Winton
Special thanks to Muff Winwood and Wayne Bardell
Side One
The Pie
Sleeping Dog
Hallelujah
I Was In Chains
Medium Wave
Big Brother
Side Two
Wars Of The Roses
Midnight Avenue
Sunny Street, W14
Where In The World
Long Long Day
Im Ariola-Vertrieb

Chilli Willi
and the Red Hot Peppers
KINGS OF THE ROBOT RHYTHM

THE SUTHERLAND BROS.' BAND

THIS PAGE: Gone In The Morning, Quiver, Warner Bros. 12in album. 1972.

CREDIT: Barney Bubbles.

OPPOSITE PAGE
LEFT AND FAR LEFT: Back and front cover. The Sutherland Bros' Band, The Sutherland Brothers, Island. 12in album. 1972.

CREDIT: Barney Bubbles.

TOP LEFT: Insert. Kings Of The Robot Rhythm, Chilli Willi And The Red Hot Peppers, Revelation Records. 12in album. 1972.

TOP RIGHT: Front cover. Kings Of The Robot Rhythm, Chilli Willi And The Red Hot Peppers, Revelation Records. 1972.

CENTRE: Back cover. Kings Of The Robot Rhythm, Chilli Willi And The Red Hot Peppers, Revelation Records. 1972

CREDIT: Barney Bubbles.

THIS PAGE: Aura Rhanes. Initiate keeper of Queen Thoras' Weyrling. 370mm x 470mm. 1972.

So It Goes 1973–1976

ABOVE: Barney Bubbles with Giana Cioffi and their son Aten, Devon. 1973.

Barney Bubbles spent the early months of 1973 preparing designs for the project which captured him and Hawkwind at the height of their combined powers: the double album Space Ritual Alive In London And Liverpool.

The music was recorded on the final dates of the 28-venue Space Ritual tour at the close of 1972, when – with fortunes turned around by the success of the single Silver Machine – the group and their designer realised a set of extravagant musical and presentation ideas to back up a complement of new songs.

The resultant 'Space Rock Ritual' was a heady mixed-media concept exploring the interests of Bubbles, Robert Calvert et al: time and space travel, astrology, Pythagorean geometry, Teutonic and Egyptian legends, Norse mythology and the findings of radical psychoanalyst Wilhelm Reich.

The music was for the most part hard-edged; songs such as Orgone Accumulator matched the aggression of Iggy & The Stooges' album Raw Power (released the same year), while electronic mood pieces underlined the group's Krautrock affiliations. 'Hawkwind was an early version of trance music,' says Malcolm Garrett. 'Their performances were total: lights, dancers, set design, these insistent, almost tribal, rhythms. It was an amazing experience.'

With a light show by Jonathan Smeeton and his team (in the guise of Liquid Len & The Lensmen), and costume designer Debbie McNeedles and dancers – including Stacia Blake, 'Miss Rene', *Friends* journalist John May and mime artist Tony Carrera – at his disposal, Bubbles applied himself to every aspect of the show, positioning the musicians according to their astrological signs, decorating equipment in ultraviolet, light-sensitive paint and flying specially made heraldic banners from the lighting rig. Nik Turner's featured a swan and five stars to align him with Lohengrin, the medieval 'swan knight' of Wagner's opera.

Bubbles produced copious and fully illustrated notes in mathematical detail and designed equipment such as horned speaker cabinets with Hawkwind's in-house boffin, former telephone engineer Gerry Fitzgerald.

'Barney included suspension in his designs for the stacks so they would respond to the high and low frequencies and literally move,' says Fitzgerald. 'I think the idea was that hopefully they would levitate. The first cabinets we produced were so heavy we couldn't shift them, so we visited a specialist shop in Notting Hill which stocked a new, much lighter material – MDF. I reckon we were among the very first people to use it.'

On release in May 1973, the Space Ritual sleeve marked the beginning of Bubbles' gradual withdrawal into absolute anonymity. He is credited with 'packaging' while the art direction is attributed to 'Pierre' (Tubbs, UA's in-house designer). This at least confirms Bubbles' application of his ingenious six-panel Glastonbury Fayre format, again with the outer in full colour and the inner duochrome.

'Both designs make maximum use of the size of card,' says Garrett. 'Barney understood the technical parameters, so proposed a large folding sleeve which did not require glue.'

Once folded, the Space Ritual cover was dominated by a portrait of Stacia Blake presiding over snarling tigers' heads, identified by designer John Coulthart as having been executed in the style of Alphonse Mucha's L'Emeraude. Mucha – a strong source of inspiration during this period – similarly 'favoured a combination of illustration with hard graphics', as Coulthart has pointed out.

This was an abiding influence during this period; Bubbles'

design for the Hawkwind poster Love & Peace the following year was based on another of the Czech Art Nouveau artist's work, the Moët & Chandon advertisement Champagne White Star.

Space Ritual's 12in records were housed in waxed paper bags decorated with an Islamic tessellated pattern in yellow on orange, which combined to present the by-now familiar triangular pyramid shape, and the unfolded outer panels featured scenes from the band in performance, as well as images of deep space and cosmic/sonic/brain-wave forms.

To these are added song titles and quotations while the inner cross-references maternity and the symbolic power of circles – an embryo floating in outer space, a giant nipple as a planet, black holes, the moon, mandalas and more quotes, from William Blake among others.

The first panel (at top right on the inner) contains the tracklisting and credits around an image of a vintage photograph of a bare-breasted kneeling female draped in necklaces and clutching a rose; this image would have been familiar to Bubbles since it also formed the basis of a 1967 poster by Californian psychedelic artist Victor Moscoso.

A couple of Space Ritual tracks were written and performed by sci-fi novelist and poet Michael Moorcock, who occasionally deputised for Robert Calvert when the frontman's spells of depression forced him to withdraw from the scene. Moorcock had previously hoped to attract Bubbles' layout talents to the sci-fi magazine *New Worlds* so was gratified to be part of a project steered by the designer.

'We'd met at the usual places like (Ladbroke Grove café) the Mountain Grill, offices of magazines, gigs, the Global Village,' says Moorcock down the line from his home in Texas. 'Barney was very shy and often out on a job of some kind, but he and I got on because we weren't super-sociable.'

Moorcock recognises that Bubbles' working experiences of the 60s were crucial in conveying the personality of Hawkwind and their music to a wider public. 'Barney and I understood the world of commercial magazines and both of us wanted to bring our expertise to something more idealistic and interesting,' he says. 'It was his understanding of branding which was important.'

Moorcock's preoccupations were present in the fold-out black-and-white Space Ritual tour programme conceived by Calvert and designed by Bubbles. In the manner of the text in 1971's The Hawkwind Log, this threaded a tale of the fictional futuristic exploits of the band members.

In the same month as UA released Space Ritual, Bubbles' artwork also adorned Oora, the final album on EMI's specialist prog imprint Harvest by the Edgar Broughton Band.

Oora marked a move by the London-based festival favourites away from basic boogie into complex rock territory with backing vocals from top session singers Madeleine Bell and Doris Troy and synthesisers courtesy of arranger David Bedford. Working to a design by EMI in-house staffer Chris Smith with contributions from band member Steve Broughton, Bubbles packaged the vertical gatefold in a clear vinyl envelope, like that for Glastonbury Fayre (though unsealed). This was printed with the reversed-out faces of the musicians.

These, the album title and the band's name (both in the same computer font as used on Space Ritual) frame a grinning skull-like visage, against the backdrop of the album cover, a glowing, geometrically woven sphere in the style of the Hungarian optical artist much in favour in the 60s, Victor Vasarely.

Using the same vivid colours against a black background, the back cover mirrors this with a pair of swooping eagles in another reference to an enigmatic and ancient meta-American civilisation. As such, these conform to Vasarely's theory that there is an 'internal geometry' to the known world, waiting to be uncovered.

On the inner were placed two basic outlines – a heart shape and a circle – as well as a three-tiered block of hand-drawn capital lettering which reads: WEMEENIT. This was also provided as a black-and-white sticker.

The Oora designs contrasted greatly with Bubbles' sleeves for two albums by The Sutherland Brothers & Quiver. The two groups joined forces just after the release of the Scottish siblings' second album Lifeboat (which was reissued with an amended credit in 1973). On this, Bubbles' lettering complemented the cover painting plucked from the Royal National Lifeboat Institution archive: Bernard Gribble's storm-tossed Pride Of Our Isles. For the follow-up 'Dream Kid', also released in 1973, Bubbles' fantastical depiction of a child venturing forth from his room was washed in pastel blue which recurred on the inner as the backdrop of a painting of a seagull in flight. Using cinematic titles, the 'Dream Kid' cover compacted a number of references; tracks on the album included the title song as well as Bluesy World and Seagull/Lonely Love.

While The Sutherland Brothers & Quiver ploughed a folk rock path which would score them moderate success (and provide Rod Stewart with a Number One in the form of their song Sailing), progressive rock was beginning to recede, with imprints such as Harvest calling time. So the demand for Bubbles' elaborations began to thin out. In the summer of 1973 an opportunity arose for a more pared-down approach at Richard Branson's recently launched Virgin Records, at that time based just off Portobello Road.

This came via photographer friend Phil Franks. Uncredited, Bubbles handled the layout of Franks' photographs of singer-songwriter Kevin Coyne for the gatefold sleeve of his first solo album, Marjory Razorblade. As well as hand-lettering the credits, Bubbles also rendered a green and orange logo – a hatchet-faced Marjory Razorblade – for the double album's September 1973 release.

All the while, Bubbles maintained his position as Hawkwind's art director, operating a studio as Hawk Graphics from Westbourne Park's Great Western Road, producing the Germanic double-headed hawk insignia which became increasingly favoured over the 1972 'gateway' logo.

He also dedicated more time to Chilli Willi And The Red Hot Peppers. The group's line-up had stabilised around a quintet including future Attractions drummer Pete Thomas and Jake Riviera's assumption of the managerial reins from Revelation's John Coleman had steered the Willis (as they were known) into a packed diary of live work on the by-now flourishing pub-rock circuit.

Working on Chilli Willi allowed Bubbles and Riviera to indulge their shared affinity for wordplay, visual jokes, rock'n'roll, art, design and pop culture. In the guise of the porcine Vinyl Mogul, the caustically witty Riviera became a goldmine of wise-cracking slogans and wind-ups, and Bubbles set about creating posters and stickers for the band, headed paper for Riviera's company Downhill Management and the group's fanzine newsletter, *Up Periscope*.

Chilli Willi's bespoke guest-list paper was always designed by Martin Stone, and Bubbles and Riviera came up with such gimmicks as band postcards and even cardboard toilet roll covers for journalists.

TOP: Logo. Marjory Razorblade, Kevin Coyne, Virgin Records. 1973.

MIDDLE: Front cover. 'Dream Kid', The Sutherland Brothers & Quiver, Island. 12in album. 1973.

BOTTOM: Inner sleeve. 'Dream Kid', The Sutherland Brothers & Quiver, Island. 12in album. 1973.

CREDIT: Barney Bubbles.

WATCH OUT! FIRST TIME EVER!
NON STOP REAL MUSIC COMING YOUR WAY AT 1000 SMILES AN HOUR!

KOKOMO
DR. FEELGOOD
CHILLI WILLI

UK75

ALL THE TURNS ARE PLAYING SETS OF EQUAL TIME BUT THE PLAYING ORDER WILL CHANGE NIGHTLY. SEE THE NAUGHTY RHYTHMS UK'75 TOUR AT

JANUARY
11 BRISTOL UNIVERSITY
12 GUILDFORD CIVIC HALL
28 WATFORD TOWN HALL
29 BIRMINGHAM TOWN HALL
30 MANCHESTER FREE TRADE
31 PENZANCE WINTER GARDENS
FEBRUARY
1 PLYMOUTH GUILDHALL
2 YEOVIL JOHNSON HALL
5 SHEFFIELD CITY HALL
7 LONDON UNIVERSITY BALL
8 EWELL TECHNICAL
13 CHELTENHAM TOWN HALL
15 RAINBOW LONDON
21 CARDIFF UNIVERSITY
22 EASTBOURNE WINTER GARDENS
23 CHANCELLOR HALL/CHELMSFORD
25 LEICESTER DE MONTFORT
28 NORTH LONDON POLYTECHNIC

NAUGHTY RHYTHMS

MM ½ PAGE AD. REVERSE BLACK TO WHITE. LINE. POS.

TOP: Press advert. Naughty Rhythms tour. 1975.

ABOVE: Roundel. Naughty Rhythms tour. 1000mm diameter. 1975.

Among his earliest commissions was the sticker bearing a repeated image of a cartoon dog. This announced that the band are 'Real Sharp', while the dog's head and distinctive ears were also seen among the silhouetted crowd in Bubbles' artwork for the '1999' Party poster to promote the spring 1974 tour of the US by Hawkwind and Welsh boogie merchants Man.

This wily approach to placement appealed to Riviera. 'He had a tremendous eye and the details take a while to sink in; Barney's work kind of creeps up on you,' says Riviera. 'For the stickers, we printed 1,000 in two colours – because we didn't have any money – and covered phone boxes, lamp-posts, everything. It was a bit like graffiti, getting the band's name out there. In the end fans would ask for them at gigs.'

Riviera became increasingly aware of the wealth of experience on which Bubbles drew. 'The fact that he had created the wonderful Justin de Blank logo and the Strongbow packaging was really impressive,' says Riviera. 'We were such fans that, when Bulmer announced they were changing the Strongbow logo, me and the Willis went out and nicked a load of pub ashtrays featuring Barney's design.'

Yet Bubbles wasn't always around. In May 1974, in yet another attempt to drop out of the rat race and concentrate on his relationship with Cioffi and their son Aten, he bought a three-room cottage in need of repair in a far-flung part of Mayo, on Ireland's west coast.

Bubbles drew up plans on building work and costed out the move, yet his increasing struggle with depression precluded settlement away from the security of London, and in particular Whitton.

'He was there for about a week and then announced that he couldn't stay and went back to London,' says Cioffi, who settled and raised Aten in Mayo, acquiring the property from Bubbles with her new partner a couple of years later.

Back in England, Bubbles discovered that Chilli Willi's healthy live workload ('one year we played 370 gigs', says Riviera proudly) had resulted in a record deal with Mooncrest, a division of Charisma Records.

The sleeve he created for their August 1974 release Bongos Over Balham continued the wry retro feel of the band's debut, furthering his investigations away from Nouveau and Deco into 20th-century ephemera: the kitsch, the comical, the surreal and the mundane.

On the front of Bongos Over Balham, a couple of swells, from an illustration in a 30s children's annual, float in a dustbin in a sewer, surrounded by an audience of cartoon rats observing their absurd encounter with a suave gent in a catsuit. In the background the cosmic circles from his work with Hawkwind have become underground tunnel rivets ferrying sewage.

'We spent all the budget on the cover, so, for the back, Barney took an Osram ad from an old magazine of mine and then spiced it up,' says Riviera.

Bubbles embellished the pink credit panel with two tiny illustrations. 'The album was recorded with Ronnie Lane's mobile studio at my friend Sue's watermill in Cornwall. We called it Lucky Abattoir and Barney came up with the logo of a skull inside a horseshoe,' says Riviera.

Next to his design credit (the first appearance of 'Big Jobs Inc'), Bubbles drew a smiling chap with his thumbs up declaring

'Hello Chums!', while the cover features the stamp 'Bohemian Revivalist Series Volume II'.

'You could look at it as just a couple of stoned hippies having a bit of fun,' says Riviera. 'But rather than just talk about it, Barney delivered. His artwork carried no sense of the time and effort which went into it.'

The press release did not adopt the music industry staple approach of typewritten sheets of A4. Instead, Bubbles positioned the Chilli Willi logo in the favoured colours of red on yellow on one side of a sheet of paper measuring 11.5in x 14.5in.

Folded vertically into three, the other side presented a photograph of the band in performance and a biography by *ZigZag* journalist Andy Childs.

Determined that the advertising for the album would differ from publication to publication, Riviera tapped into Bubbles' boundless imagination.

With Vinyl Mogul portrayed as a cigar-chomping pig declaring that the band 'is not a frozen food… it'll look good in your fridge', the Bongos Over Balham sleeve is propped up by a series of objects apparently thrust through a hole in the poster. In one is a mannequin's hand, in another a trotter and in a third (for *Let It Rock* magazine) a dildo.

'The record company hated us because it meant more work, but we were on a mission,' says Riviera. 'We had that "collect-the-set" mentality.'

Bubbles' growing alignment with Riviera and Chilli Willi's approach – and concomitant disaffection with the sturm und drang of Norse legends and space fantasy – may be detected in his work for Hawkwind's October 1974 album Hall Of The Mountain Grill. One side of the inner sleeve makes plain use of contact strips of the band on a children's climbing frame. The other has Phil Franks' photograph of the Mountain Grill café with a lyric bracketed in Chilli Will-style 'From The Legend Of Beenzon Toste'.

Bubbles did not provide the back cover – a predictably executed alien planet landscape by David Hardy – but his air-brushed depiction of the band's crash-landed spaceship on the front spoke to the lack of direction and internal dissent brewing within Hawkwind.

By the time of Mountain Grill's release, Bubbles was planning the visual aspects of the 60s-style package tour Naughty Rhythms, which Riviera had cooked up in the face of the lack of ambition within the pub-rock movement, as manifested by the fact that Bongos Over Balham had only shifted 16,000 copies.

'People weren't exactly banging down the doors,' says Riviera. 'I realised that, to survive, we had to get out of the pubs.'

With financial backing from Dr Feelgood's label boss Andrew Lauder, Charisma owner Tony Stratton-Smith and Pink Floyd manager Steve O'Rourke (who had recently signed the soul-funk ensemble Kokomo to CBS) the Naughty Rhythms tour rolled out across the UK in January 1975.

Each night the lead slot was rotated between Dr Feelgood, Chilli Willi and Kokomo. All had albums to promote and the exercise was backed by a promotional hook-up with the *NME*. This was a sophisticated marketing campaign enlivening the

TOP LEFT: Poster artwork. Chilli Willi And The Red Hot Peppers. 1974.

ABOVE: Stickers. Chilli Willi And The Red Hot Peppers. 1973–5.

gloomiest days of the post-war British music business.

Bubbles was called on to provide a coherent visual package, which he based around a cheeky logo of a scarved 40s moll springing from a banana skin. Press ads and concert posters took the form of concert ticket stubs straplined: 'First time ever! Real non-stop music!'

Organiser of the Naughty Rhythms tour was Paul Conroy, booking agent for Chilli Willi and Dr Feelgood. Conroy was later to handle marketing at Stiff Records and embark on a career at major UK labels including the running of Virgin Records and signing of such acts as the Spice Girls.

'Barney did these huge posters and also flyers and badges, so it was a total package which suited the spirit of the tour,' says Conroy, sitting in the garden of London club Home House. 'The woman coming out of the banana had these words accompanying her, "Wud Wud", which was so Barney.'

Simultaneously, Bubbles was called upon to redesign independent music monthly *Let It Rock* by incoming editor John Pidgeon.

'I had known Barney since he did the Sutherland Brothers' first album cover and loved the story that he had shot holes in the wooden artwork with an airgun,' said Pidgeon, a leading broadcast journalist who later nurtured comedy talent at the BBC. 'I immediately discovered we had mutual friends in Ian McLagan and (Bubbles' Twickenham College contemporary) Mick Finch.'

Bubbles arrived at Pidgeon's flat in Clapham, south London, with ten pages of pencil-sketched artwork, some on his father's company headed paper.

These included several options for a masthead: one used 'cacti' lettering, as in his drumhead for Chilli Willi And The Red Hot Peppers, another substituted the 'o' in 'Rock' with a spinning reel of recording tape.

There were also single-page and double-page spread layout samples, one a Bob Dylan feature for direction on photography and text placement.

Presenting a subheading 'The world's greatest rock read', Bubbles listed the magazine sections – Oldies, Singles, Album Reviews, News and Letters – providing the last with its own ident: a bobbysoxer writing fan mail.

Pidgeon opted for one masthead which was completed by Bubbles with the addition of a lightning bolt decoration.

The redesign was introduced in the magazine's January 1975 issue. 'For the catchline I amended "greatest" to "best",' said Pidgeon. 'It was a typically brilliant Barney Bubbles slogan.'

The publication of the redesigned *Let It Rock* coincided with the Naughty Rhythms tour, which brought mixed blessings for its participants. The victors were Dr Feelgood, whose ferocious attack won audiences over nightly, while Kokomo settled into a middling career; their Brit-soul would not come into fashion for a few years.

As for Chilli Willi, time was up. The band called it a day in February 1975 and Riviera threw in his lot with Dr Feelgood as tour manager. For Bubbles, commissions started to thin out. His next, UA's March 1975 release of New Worlds Fair by Michael Moorcock and his backing musicians The Deep Fix (mainly Hawkwind members including Dave Brock and Nik Turner), was for a curio which had been recorded over the previous couple of years.

Moorcock's songs – part poetry incantation/part space boogie – tied together a concept pinned to the notion of a post-apocalyptic fairground.

For the front cover photograph, Bubbles had constructed and painted a wooden fairground booth a couple of years before. 'It was knocking about Barney's studio for some time afterwards before it disappeared completely,' says Moorcock. 'I wonder what happened to it? I loved that cover.'

The fact that Bubbles was now straddling two opposing musical worlds – space-rock and roots/pop music — was driven home when Naughty Rhythms tour organiser Paul Conroy brought him on board to design for the young act he managed, the Kursaal Flyers.

Conroy had signed the Southend quintet to the indie label UK Records, run by now-disgraced maverick pop star and music business executive Jonathan King. Their album Chocs Away was being readied for release in May 1975.

'Paul Conroy shared a flat with Adrian Boot (the photographer who took the shots for the Chocs Away cover) and Barney and Jake were on the fringes of our scene,' says Will Birch, the Kursaal Flyers' drummer and latterly Ian Dury's biographer.

'I can honestly say I'd never heard of Barney Bubbles. I was aware of this "art guy" who had done the Hawkwind stuff, but that was way beyond our frame of reference. It wasn't what we listened to.'

For his credit on Chocs Away, Bubbles chose 'Grove Lane', the street in Kingston upon Thames, south-west London, where Conroy roomed with Boot (and Bubbles occasionally stayed in stints away from Whitton).

An obvious visual pun formed the cover design: a chocolate aeroplane melted as it flew too close to the sun. The back appropriated out-of-step commercial imagery by presenting the band members as the Fry's 5 Boys.

These had appeared on the confectionery company's milk-chocolate packaging since 1902 (and were removed in a marketing overhaul the year after Chocs Away came out). To underline the album title reference, the Fry's logo on a chocolate bar was reinterpreted as 'Fly'.

'For the summer of 1975 this was absolutely fabulous work,' says Birch. 'We were knocked out. The seed of this concept may have been Paul Conroy – of course, he went on to succeed at Stiff using nostalgic visual puns with Madness and the rest – but the execution and the impact were down to Barney.'

As musical fare, however, Chocs Away was distinctly lightweight. A European support slot for the long-past-their-sell-by-date Flying Burrito Brothers didn't help matters. The Kursaal Flyers were dropped by UK Records and jumped to major label CBS, where they eventually scored a Top Ten hit a couple of years later with the single Little Does She Know.

Pub rock's failure to deliver on its promise was symptomatic of the moribund state of the British music business. Meantime, Bubbles' association with Hawkwind started to fray.

He did not design the tricksy mask-and-shield sleeve for their May 1975 album Warrior On The Edge Of Time, though he was responsible for the illustrations in the style of the Doremi posters which frame the credits and song titles on the inner bag. The album design was attributed to the 17th-century French soldier, the Comte Pierre d'Auvergne (again UA art director Pierre Tubbs).

In this period Bubbles' productivity lay relatively fallow, as depression forced him to disappear from the scene for sustained periods. Cioffi believes he mostly resided with

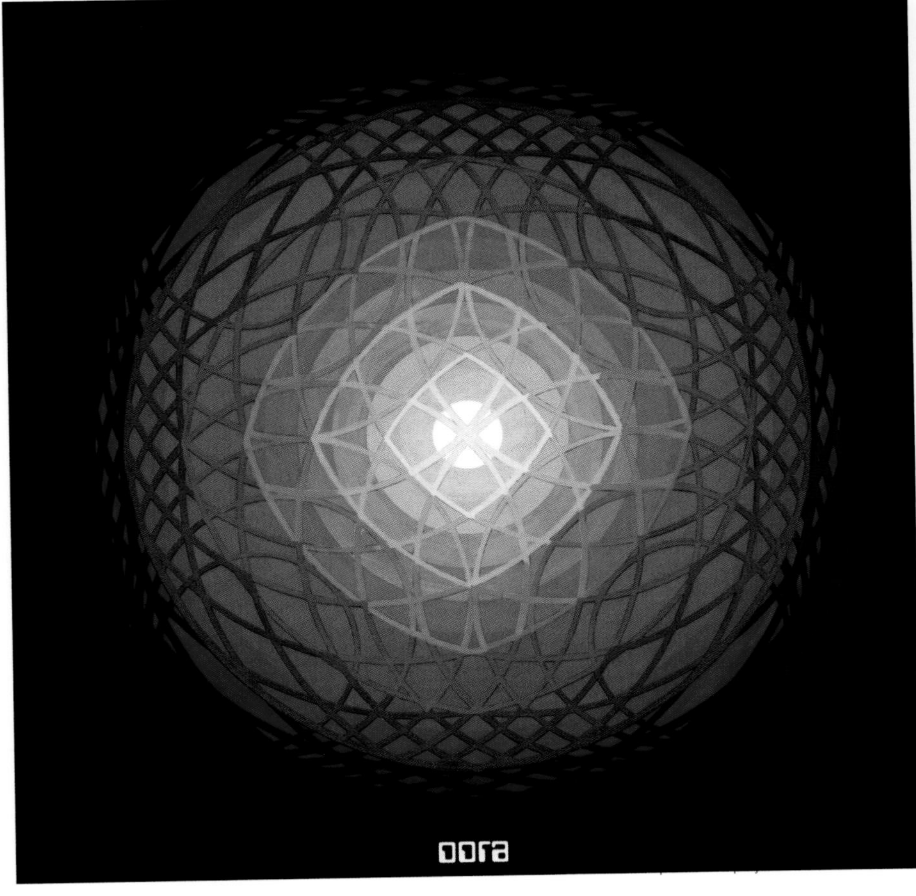

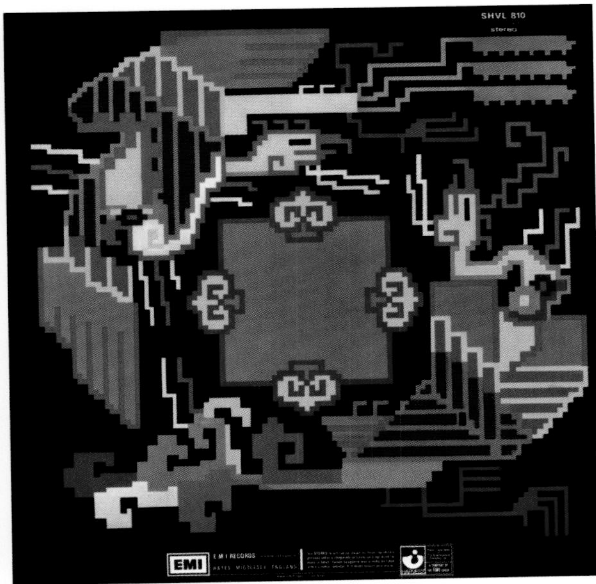

TOP LEFT: Front cover with overlay. Oora, Edgar Broughton Band, Vertigo. 12in album. 1973.

TOP RIGHT: PMT (photomechanical transfer) of Oora artwork. 1973.

LEFT: Front cover. Oora, Edgar Broughton Band, Vertigo. 1973.

ABOVE: Back cover. Oora, Edgar Broughton Band, Vertigo. 1973.

CREDIT: Barney Bubbles.

ABOVE: Front cover. Hawkwind tour programme. 1974.

TOP RIGHT: Lohengrin banner. Space Ritual tour, Hawkwind. 1400mm x 900mm. 1972.

CENTRE: Front cover. Hall Of The Mountain Grill, Hawkwind, UA. 12in album. 1974.

CREDIT: Barney Bubbles.

RIGHT: Sticker. Hawkwind. 1972.

FAR RIGHT: Sticker. Hawkwind/Man '1999' Party US tour. 1974.

his family at Whitton, which is borne out by contemporary correspondence.

At one stage Bubbles told acquaintances that he had rejected design altogether in favour of stacking supermarket shelves.

'Barney often absented himself without warning,' says Jake Riviera. 'The black dog would descend and he wouldn't answer the phone. There would be no, or very little, contact. I've always thought that was one of the best things about him, he would never burden anybody with his moods or problems. I wish now that he had.'

In April 1976, a Bubbles painting of a hell-bound locomotive driven by a skeleton – executed in the same airbrush style as the Chilli Willi poster By Night And Day Here Those Weirdoes Come To Play and intended as a Hawkwind tour poster – was adapted for the gatefold cover of the band's holding-pattern compilation Roadhawks (and included as a poster in the initial run).

That the Roadhawks sleeve was in fact a rendition of Bubbles' artwork by artist Bob Searles was a symptom of the series of schisms rocking the Hawkwind set-up. Bass player Lemmy, for many fans a key member, had been dismissed and then Doug Smith was ditched in favour of music agent Tony Howard.

Howard's partnership with Jeff Dexter enabled Bubbles to briefly reconnect with the DJ and one-time promoter of Implosion at The Roundhouse, where Bubbles had worked his light show for Quintessence and The Gun.

Aside from his involvement in Hawkwind's management, Dexter was working with a new group called Alfalpha. 'One day I called Barney up and said I needed a logo for them,' says Dexter.

Bubbles' ident spelt out the band's name in a serpentine pink on black line, intended for use on badges, T-shirts and other promotional paraphernalia. The image did not progress beyond prototype stage; out of step with the times, the only album by the long-haired Alfalpha (whose ranks included the future Dream Academy frontman Nick Laird-Clowes) was subjected to delays and finally released in 1977 with a cover photograph taken by David Hockney.

Meantime, Tony Howard negotiated a new record deal for Hawkwind with Charisma, which released their Astounding Sounds Amazing Music in August 1976. Bubbles handled art direction and Nik Turner's artist friend Tony Hyde was commissioned to produce the 'Astounding' side of the sleeve: a pastiche of the front page of a 50s sci-fi comic.

In a letter to Hyde published on Hawkwind website aural-innovations.com, Bubbles – who opted for the Grove Lane credit – intended the 'Amazing' side to consist of his painting of an omniscient lupine visage wreaking havoc across a cityscape (this was inspired in part by the Hermann Hesse novel *Steppenwolf*, also the name of a nine-minute track on the release).

Writing from his parents' house in Whitton, Bubbles was explicit in his instructions to Hyde: 'To make the word HAWKWIND stand out from all the other lettering and painting (which after all is the whole point of the exercise) it should print as white.

'Therefore AMAZING MUSIC should be in coloured tones i.e. lettering in red, shadow on lettering in yellow, for example. To get the period style correct I'm doing the artwork in watercolour. When the order and the final tracks are ready I'll Letraset all the copy and paste it on an overlay.'

But his 'Steppenwolf' design was rejected (and the painting given to Hawkwind manager Doug Smith). In its place appeared one of Bubbles' most imposing works: a monolithic hawk statue in black and red, evoking Nazi Germany's Wehrmacht eagle set amid Albert Speer-like 'cathedrals of light'. For the first pressing this was printed as the front cover; on subsequent issues the two designs were reversed so it was relegated to the back.

Bubbles' withdrawal to Whitton occurred as the music scene hit a low. 'There was something else out there, but I didn't know what it was,' Nick Lowe told Will Birch in *No Sleep Till Canvey Island*. 'I felt the music was about to change. Things were certainly getting faster.'

For a short spell in the spring of 1976, Lowe joined Riviera as a member of Dr Feelgood's road crew on a US tour.

During downtime on the road, Riviera visited record shops, buying singles released by obscure independent record companies. 'In places like New Orleans you could pick up sharp little songs on wonderful labels like Jin and Swallow,' he says.

'I loved the Feelgoods but realised that I wanted to do my own thing when I got home. I mentioned this to (Dr Feelgood's dynamite frontman) Lee Brilleaux. He wrote me a cheque there and then for £400 to start my own label. I never cashed it.'

Back in London, Riviera joined forces with former Brinsley Schwarz manager Dave Robinson, by then overseeing Graham Parker & The Rumour, and formed independent label Stiff Records.

Based on the ground floor of management company Blackhill Enterprises' building at 32 Alexander Street in Paddington, Stiff combined the irreverence and streetwise attitude of the emerging punk scene with savvy and sardonic marketing.

Proclaiming themselves 'undertakers to the music industry', Riviera and Robinson ensured Stiff sleeves made tongue-in-cheek claims that the music had been 'Electrically Recorded' in 'Mono-Enhanced Stereo'.

Installed as in-house producer and the label's first signing, Lowe emerged as a charming jack-of-all trades with an ability to recycle familiar hooks and rhythms into fresh composites.

Designer Chris Morton created Stiff's first label font and oversaw artwork to the initial run of single sleeves, with contributions from illustrator Edward Barker, PR man Pete Frame and even Riviera himself.

'The idea was really the biggest part of Stiff,' says Robinson. 'And that's why we needed Barney. Chris Morton did an OK job but Barney was much more cutting-edge.'

By the time of Stiff's first release, Nick Lowe's So It Goes on 14 August 1976, an aggressive wave of new groups were asserting themselves; within a month the Sex Pistols, The Clash and The Damned played the Punk Rock Festival at Oxford Street's 100 Club.

The latter act were snapped up by Riviera and their furiously paced track New Rose scored the label a publicity coup as the UK's very first punk rock single, released on 22 October 1976.

This underlined the need for Bubbles' presence on the team. 'There was never an argument about who would be Stiff's resident artist,' says Robinson. 'Jake and I, who pretty much couldn't agree on anything, were in absolute agreement on the two key ingredients: the producer would be Nick Lowe and the designer would be Barney Bubbles.'

As 1977 loomed, Bubbles finally responded to a message of Riviera's. The friends struck a deal: in return for joining Stiff as art director and providing an album sleeve design a month for free, Bubbles would be given studio space in the grotty basement of 32 Alexander Street.

Clearly, Bubbles was refreshed, as re-energised as British music and ready to return to the fray.

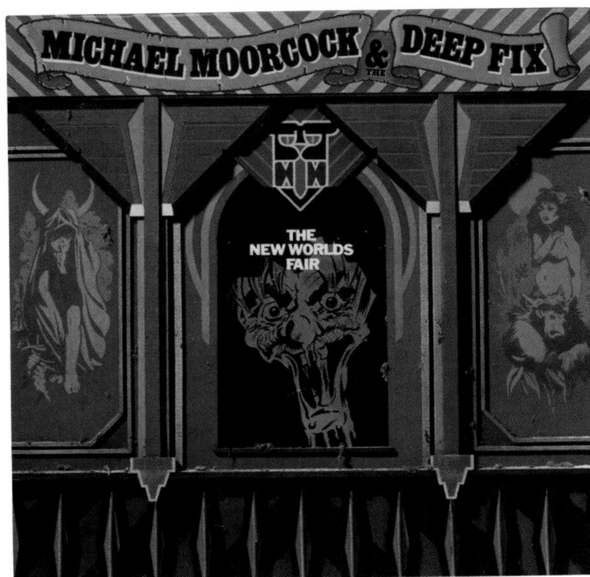

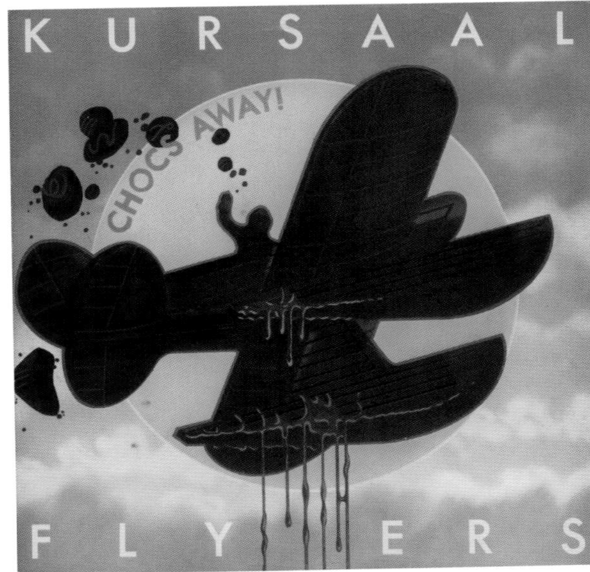

TOP: Front cover. The New Worlds Fair, Michael Moorcock & The Deep Fix, UA. 12in album. 1975.

CREDIT: Barney O'da Bubbles.

CENTRE: Front cover. Chocs Away, Kursaal Flyers, UK Records. 12in album. 1975.

CREDIT: Grove Lane.

BOTTOM: Back cover. Chocs Away, Kursaal Flyers, UK Records. 12in album. 1975.

CREDIT: Grove Lane.

ABOVE: Alfalpha logo, badge. 3.5mm diameter. 1976.

Recorded live at Liverpool Stadium & Brixton Sundown
SPACE RITUAL
HAWKWIND
Flying is trying is dying
Brainstorm here we go
We were born to go as far as we can fly; Turn electric dreams into reality...
Master of the Universe

OPPOSITE PAGE: Six-panel front cover. Space Ritual, Hawkwind, UA. 900mm x 600mm. 1973.

THIS PAGE: Six-panel inner. Space Ritual, Hawkwind, UA. 900mm x 600mm. 1973.

CREDIT: Barney Bubbles.

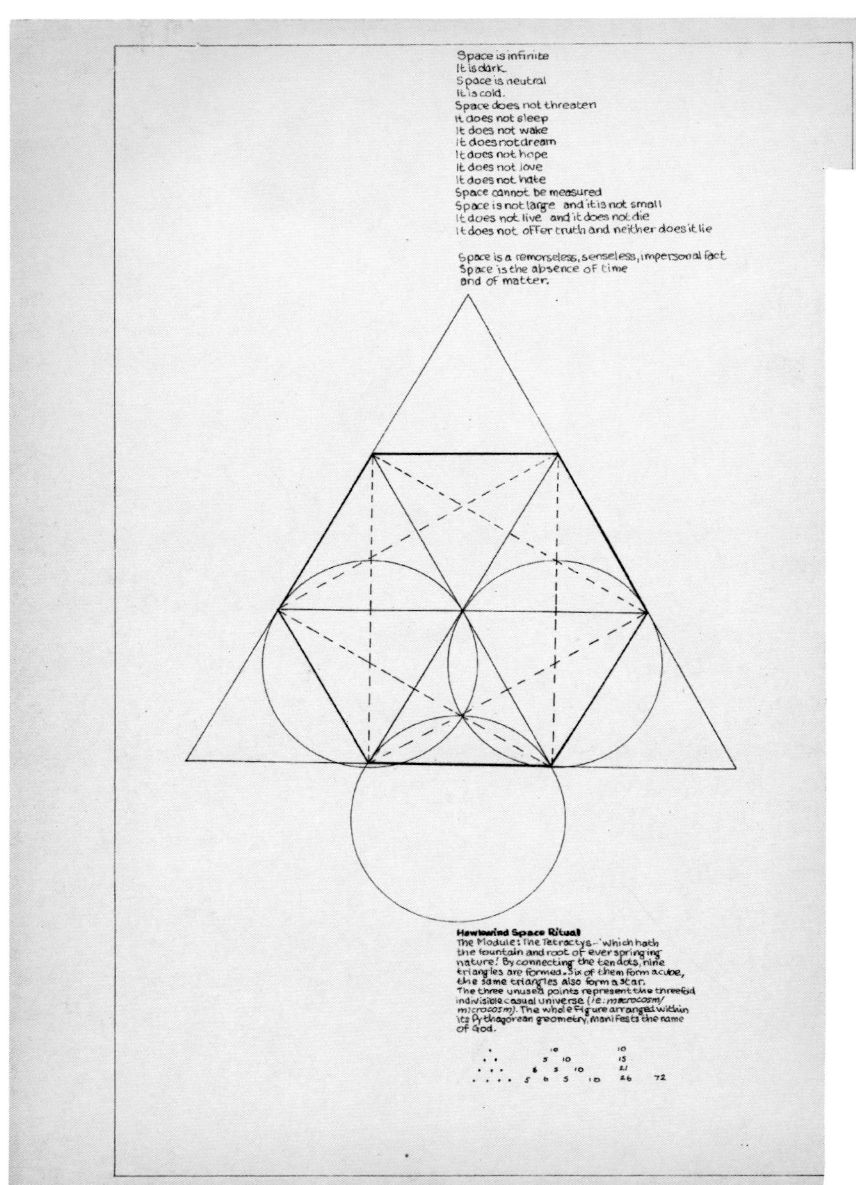

CONCEPTION 1

Space is infinite
It is dark.
Space is neutral
It is cold.
Space does not threaten
It does not sleep
It does not wake
It does not dream
It does not hope
It does not love
It does not hate
Space cannot be measured
Space is not large and it is not small
It does not live and it does not die
It does not offer truth and neither does it lie

Space is a remorseless, senseless, impersonal fact
Space is the absence of time
and of matter.

Hawkwind Space Ritual
The Module: The Tetractys – 'which hath the fountain and root of ever springing nature.' By connecting the ten dots, nine triangles are formed. Six of them form a cube, the same triangles also form a star.
The three unused points represent the threefold indivisible casual universe (*ie: macrocosm/microcosm*). The whole figure arranged within its Pythagorean geometry, manifests the name of God.

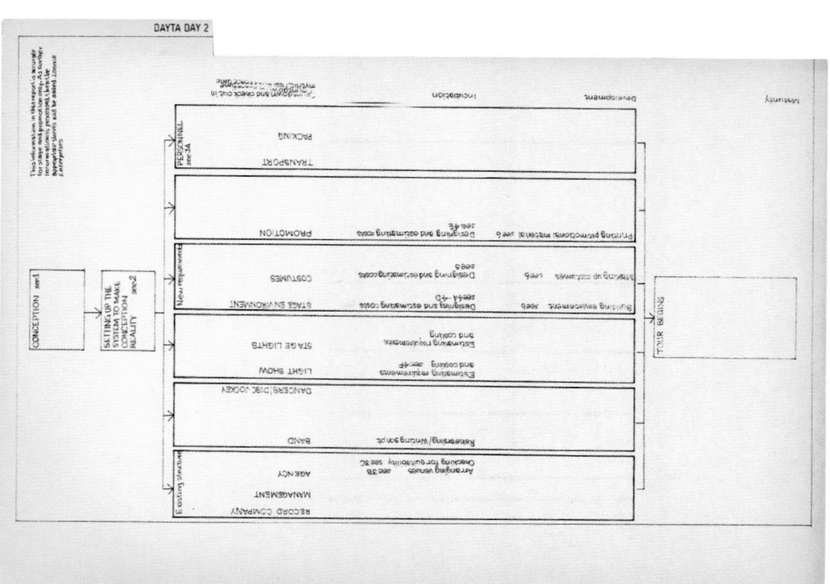

DAYTA DAY 2

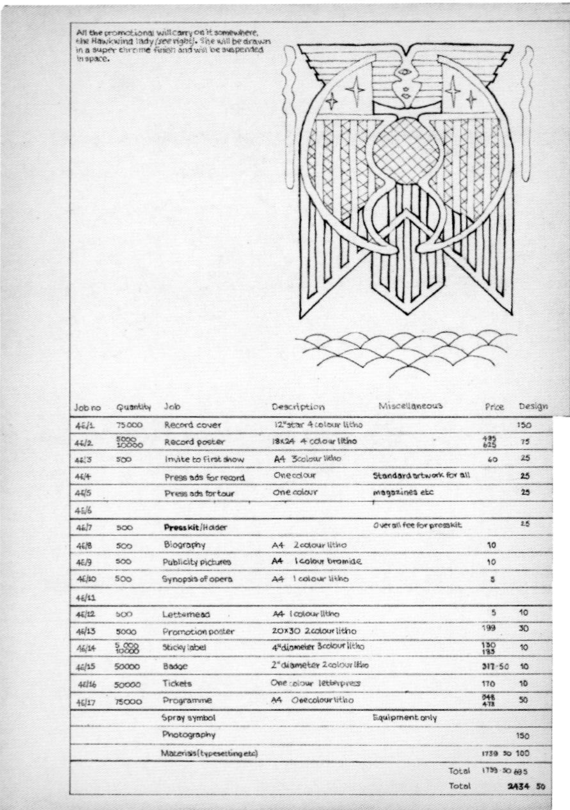

PROMOTION 4E

All the promotional will carry on it somewhere, the Hawkwind lady (see right). She will be drawn in a super chrome finish and will be suspended in space.

Job no	Quantity	Job	Description	Miscellaneous	Price	Design
4E/1	75000	Record cover	12"star 4 colour litho			150
4E/2	5000 10000	Record poster	18x24 4 colour litho		485 625	75
4E/3	500	Invite to first show	A4 3colour litho		60	25
4E/4		Press ads for record	One colour	Standard artwork for all		25
4E/5		Press ads for tour	One colour	magazines etc		25
4E/6						
4E/7	500	Presskit/Holder		Overall fee for presskit		25
4E/8	500	Biography	A4 2colour litho		10	
4E/9	500	Publicity pictures	A4 1colour bromide		10	
4E/10	500	Synopsis of opera	A4 1 colour litho		5	
4E/11						
4E/12	500	Letterhead	A4 1colour litho		5	10
4E/13	5000	Promotion poster	20X30 2colour litho		199	30
4E/14	5 000 10000	Sticky label	4"diameter 3colour litho		130 185	10
4E/15	50000	Badge	2" diameter 2colour litho		317·50	10
4E/16	50000	Tickets	One colour letterpress		170	10
4E/17	75000	Programme	A4 Onecolour litho		548 478	50
		Spray symbol		Equipment only		
		Photography				150
		Materials (typesetting etc)			1739 50	100
				Total	1739·50	695
				Total		2434 50

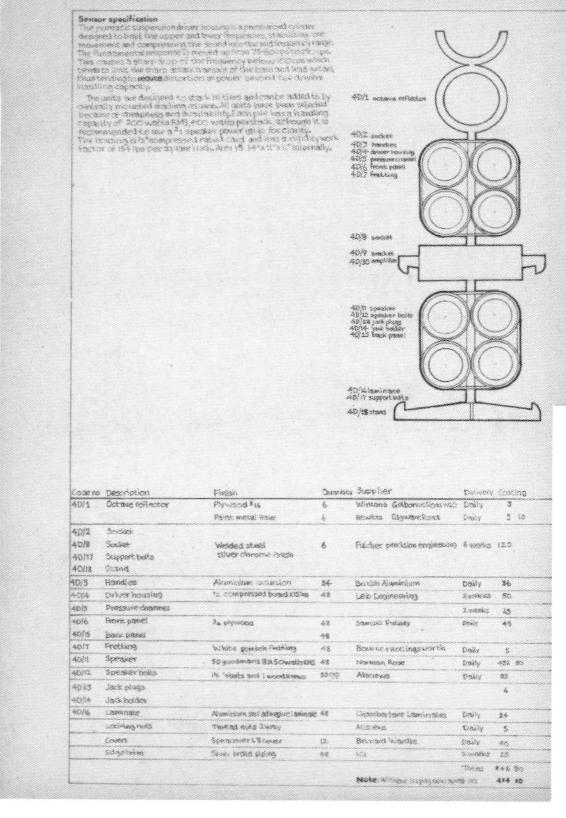

SENSORS 4D

Sensor specification

Code no	Description	Finish	Quantity	Supplier	Delivery	Costing
4D/1	Octave reflector	Plywood 3/16	6	Wintona Golborne Road W10	Daily	3
		Paint metal flake	6	Hewitts Edgware Road	Daily	5 10
4D/2	Socket					
4D/8	Socket	Welded steel silver chrome finish	6	Fulcher precision engineering	6 weeks	120
4D/17	Support bolts					
4D/18	Stand					
4D/3	Handles	Aluminium extrusion	24	British Aluminium	Daily	36
4D/4	Driver housing	½ compressed board X15lbs	48	Leb Engineering	3 weeks	50
4D/5	Pressure channel				2 weeks	15
4D/6	Front panel	¾ plywood	48	Samuel Putney	Daily	45
4D/5	Back panel		48			
4D/7	Fretting	White gaelich fretting	48	Bourne + Hollingsworth	Daily	5
4D/11	Speaker	50 goodmans 8Ω 50watts RMS	48	Norman Rose	Daily	432 80
4D/12	Speaker bolts	[illegible]	2500	Allscrews	Daily	25
4D/13	Jack plugs					6
4D/14	Jack holder					
4D/16	Laminate	Aluminium self adhesive laminate	48	Chamberlains Laminates	Daily	24
	Locking nuts	Thread nuts 2way		Allscrews	Daily	5
	Covers	Spencover L3 cover	12	Bernard Wardle	Daily	46
	Edgetrim	[illegible]	48	ICI	2 weeks	25
					Total	846 80
				Note: Without buying new speakers		414 10

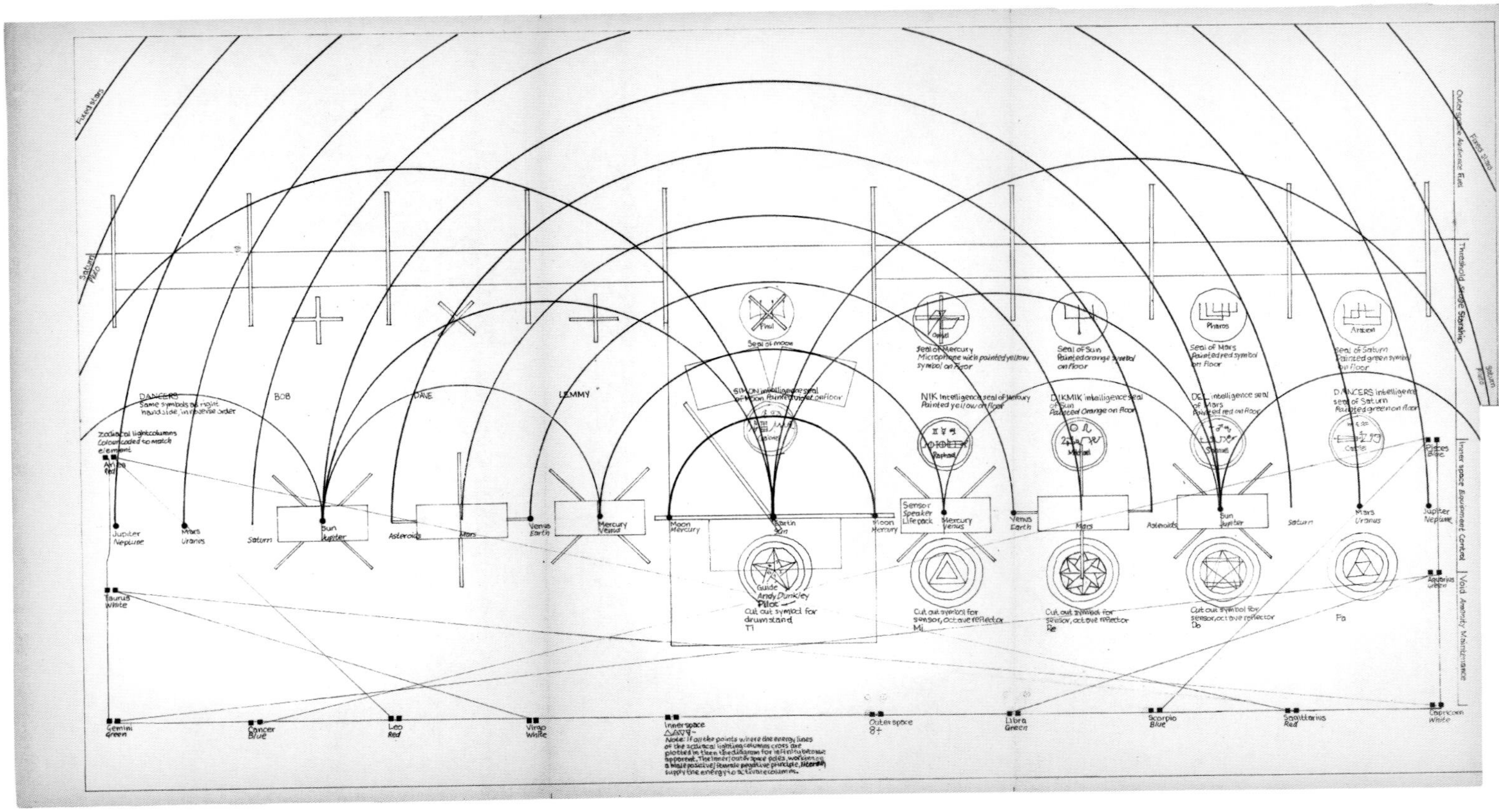

CIRCUITRY 4B

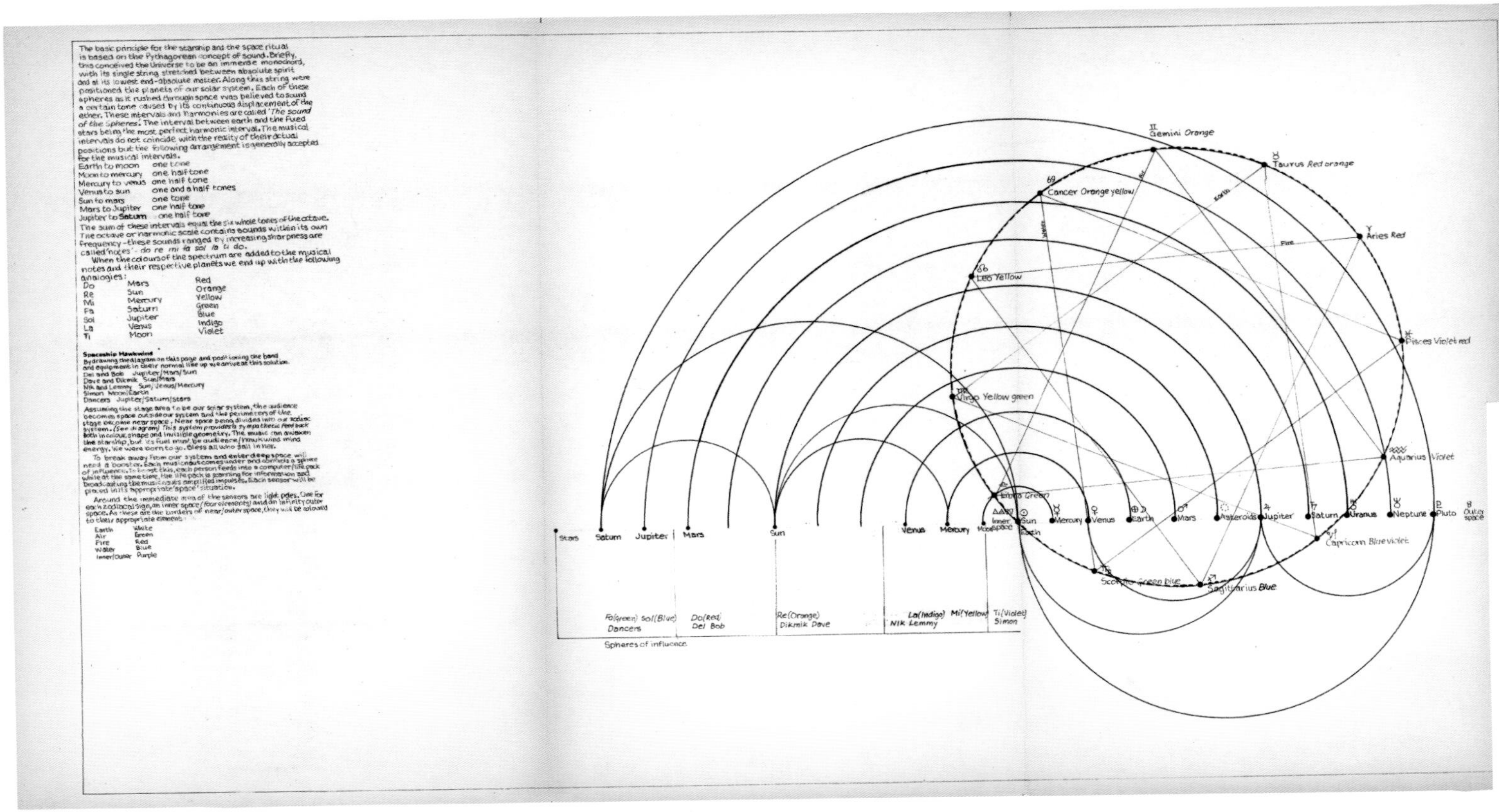

STARSHIP 4A

The basic principle for the starship and the space ritual is based on the Pythagorean concept of sound. Briefly, this conceived the Universe to be an immense monochord, with its single string stretched between absolute spirit and at its lowest end-absolute matter. Along this string were positioned the planets of our solar system. Each of these spheres as it rushed through space was believed to sound a certain tone caused by its continuous displacement of the ether. These intervals and harmonies are called *'The sound of the Spheres'*. The interval between earth and the fixed stars being the most perfect harmonic interval. The musical intervals do not coincide with the reality of their actual positions but the following arrangement is generally accepted for the musical intervals.

Earth to moon	one tone
Moon to mercury	one half tone
Mercury to venus	one half tone
Venus to sun	one and a half tones
Sun to mars	one tone
Mars to Jupiter	one half tone
Jupiter to **Saturn**	one half tone

The sum of these intervals equal the six whole tones of the octave. The octave or harmonic scale contains sounds within its own frequency - these sounds ranged by increasing sharpness are called 'notes' - *do re mi fa sol la ti do*.

When the colours of the spectrum are added to the musical notes and their respective planets we end up with the following analogies:

Do	Mars	Red
Re	Sun	Orange
Mi	Mercury	Yellow
Fa	Saturn	Green
Sol	Jupiter	Blue
La	Venus	Indigo
Ti	Moon	Violet

Spaceship Hawkwind

By drawing the diagram on this page and positioning the band and equipment in their normal line up we arrive at this solution.

Del and Bob Jupiter/Mars/Sun
Dave and Dikmik Sun/Mars
Nik and Lemmy Sun/Venus/Mercury
Simon Moon/Earth
Dancers Jupiter/Saturn/Stars

Assuming the stage area to be our solar system, the audience becomes space outside our system and the perimeters of the stage become near space. Near space being divided into our zodiac system. *(See diagram) This system provides a sympathetic feed back* both in colour, shape and invisible geometry. The music can awaken the starship, but its fuel must be audience/hawkwind mind energy. We were born to go. Bless all who sail in her.

To break away from our system and enter deep space will need a booster. Each musicnaut comes under and controls a sphere of influence. To boost this, each person feeds into a computer/life pack while at the same time, the life pack is scanning for information and broadcasting the musicnauts amplified impulses. Each sensor will be placed in its appropriate 'space' situation.

Around the immediate area of the sensors are light poles. One for each zodiacal sign, an inner space (four elements) and an infinity outer space. As these are the borders of near/outer space, they will be coloured to their appropriate element.

Earth	White
Air	Green
Fire	Red
Water	Blue
Inner/Outer	Purple

OPPOSITE AND THIS PAGE: Tour notes and stage directions. Space Ritual tour, Hawkwind. 1972.

it

LEFT: Poster. Hawkwind. 750mm x 1050mm. 1973.

THIS PAGE: Poster. Love & Peace, Hawkwind. 900mm x 530mm. 1974.

THIS PAGE: Artwork. Poster/back cover image for The New Worlds Fair, Michael Moorcock & The Deep Fix. 800mm x 450mm. 1975.

THIS PAGE: Artwork.
The '1999' Party, Hawkwind/Man.
800mm x 450mm. 1974.

THIS PAGE: Painting. Proposal for cover of Astounding Sounds, Amazing Music, Hawkwind. 450mm x 450mm. 1976.

RIGHT: Artwork for poster. Used as basis for Roadhawks, Hawkwind, UA. 12in double gatefold. 1976.

WIND
H·A·W·K·S

RIGHT: Front cover. Bongos Over Balham, Chilli Willi And The Red Hot Peppers, Mooncrest. 12in album. 1974.

TOP LEFT: Inner sleeve. Bongos Over Balham, Chilli Willi And The Red Hot Peppers, Mooncrest. 1974.

BOTTOM LEFT: Artwork. Bongos Over Balham advert. 1974.

BOTTOM RIGHT: Back cover. Bongos Over Balham, Chilli Willi And The Red Hot Peppers, Mooncrest. 1974.

CREDIT: Big Jobs Inc.

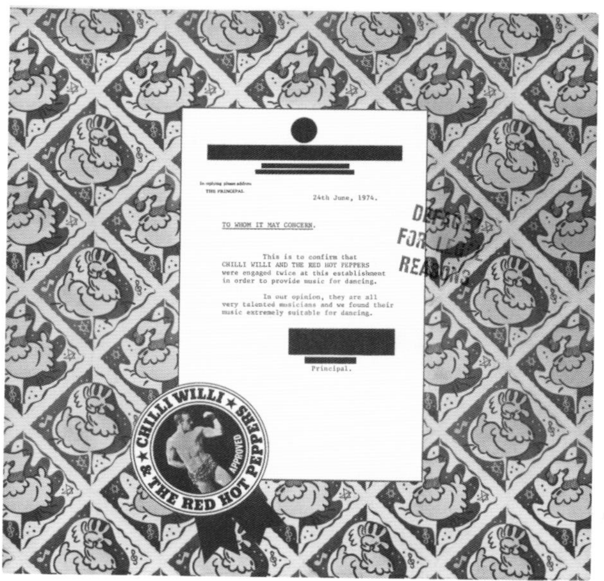

In replying please address
THE PRINCIPAL.

24th June, 1974.

TO WHOM IT MAY CONCERN.

This is to confirm that CHILLI WILLI AND THE RED HOT PEPPERS were engaged twice at this establishment in order to provide music for dancing.

In our opinion, they are all very talented musicians and we found their music extremely suitable for dancing.

Principal.

CREST 21 STEREO

How pretty I look in the glass tonight

In the gentle glow of that Pink Pearl light!

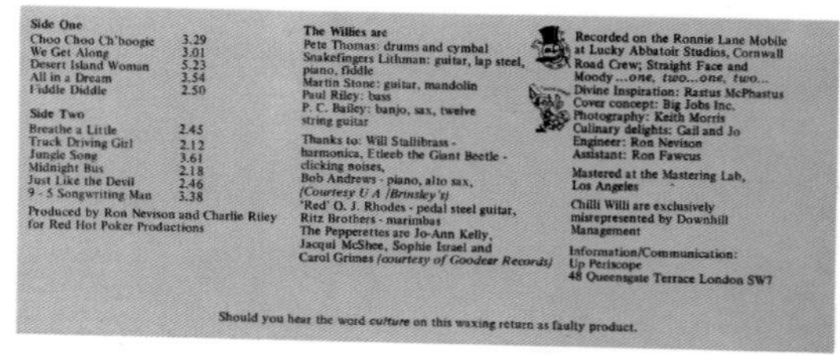

Side One
Choo Choo Ch'boogie 3.29
We Get Along 3.01
Desert Island Woman 5.23
All in a Dream 3.54
Fiddle Diddle 2.50

Side Two
Breathe a Little 2.45
Truck Driving Girl 2.12
Jungle Song 3.61
Midnight Bus 2.18
Just Like the Devil 2.46
9 - 5 Songwriting Man 3.38

Produced by Ron Nevison and Charlie Riley for Red Hot Poker Productions

The Willies are
Pete Thomas: drums and cymbal
Snakefingers Lithman: guitar, lap steel, piano, fiddle
Martin Stone: guitar, mandolin
Paul Riley: bass
P. C. Bailey: banjo, sax, twelve string guitar

Thanks to: Will Stallibrass - harmonica, Etleeb the Giant Beetle - clicking noises,
Bob Andrews - piano, alto sax, *(Courtesy U A /Brinsley's)*
'Red' O. J. Rhodes - pedal steel guitar,
Ritz Brothers - marimbas
The Pepperettes are Jo-Ann Kelly, Jacqui McShee, Sophie Israel and Carol Grimes *(courtesy of Goodear Records)*

Recorded on the Ronnie Lane Mobile at Lucky Abbatoir Studios, Cornwall
Road Crew; Straight Face and Moody ...*one, two...one, two...*
Divine Inspiration: Rastus McPhastus
Cover concept: Big Jobs Inc.
Photography: Keith Morris
Culinary delights: Gail and Jo
Engineer: Ron Nevison
Assistant: Ron Fawcus

Mastered at the Mastering Lab, Los Angeles

Chilli Willi are exclusively misrepresented by Downhill Management

Information/Communication:
Up Periscope
48 Queensgate Terrace London SW7

Should you hear the word *culture* on this waxing return as faulty product.

MARKETED BY B & C RECORDS, LTD, 37 SOHO SQUARE, LONDON, W.1.

Printed and made by the E. J. Day Group, London and Bedford

ORDER

No. 538

F. FULCHER (PRECISION ENGINEERS) LTD.

76 Tranmere Road, Whitton, Middlesex

POPesgrove 8604

M..........

..........19..........

Please supply:

Your Ref.:

LEFT: Masthead options and design sketches for *Let It Rock*. 200mm x 140mm. 1974.

ABOVE: Launch issue of redesign. *Let It Rock*, January 1975.

THIS PAGE: Poster. Hawkwind Astounding Sounds 1976. 750mm x 500mm. 1976.

My Aim Is True 1977–1978

ABOVE: Photo-booth shots from Stiff day out. Barney Bubbles with (top left) Cynthia Lole and Pauline Kennedy. 1977.

Settled in the basement of 32 Alexander Street at the dawn of 1977, Barney Bubbles hit the ground running by providing sleeves for The Damned's debut album Damned Damned Damned and second single Neat Neat Neat, both released on 18 February.

'I gotta studio (a mouldering basement overlooking a garden) in Paddington,' Bubbles wrote to his friend Lorry Sartorio. 'The building is shared with a punk rock record company called Stiff. I really enjoy it there. Lotsa people dropping in all day. Everyone seems committed (even the accountant) and the energy level is extremely high.'

The person primarily stoking this atmosphere was Jake Riviera (in his letter Bubbles reminded Sartorio she had described Riviera after a recent encounter as 'a public school type', given his penchant for severe short-back-and-sides haircuts and formal suits).

He and Bubbles set about reaffirming their creative relationship with intense brainstorming sessions. 'To get away from the phones we'd walk round and round the block, past Porchester Baths,' says Riviera. 'We must have trodden miles of that same bit of pavement, chatting about music, art, design, cinema, old TV shows, comedy, magazines, anything to inspire us. Later we visited exhibitions, not to nick ideas but to get the cogs whirring.'

Once they had reached agreement on a theme, Bubbles roughed out options in small boxes in his neat script. When the proposal was sanctioned, Bubbles beavered away, briefing photographers, finalising proofs and readying finished artwork for printers.

At once the cheery scrappiness of the label's visual identity was replaced by a dextrous and informed approach, not only to design and typography, but also concise layout and sharp photographic placement, key elements of punk and post-punk visuals.

'Barney opted not to emulate the ripped and torn ethic of the Pistols and The Clash,' says Billy Bragg, a Stiff fan who collaborated with the designer a few years later. 'Punk was all about reacting against the music and the look, including the album sleeves, of the overblown mid-70s bands. Barney was a genius at progressing and refining that aesthetic.'

Nick Lowe believes the relationship with Riviera was central to Bubbles' achievements at the record company.

'Jake treated Barney with tremendous respect,' says Lowe. 'He was forever urging Barney onwards: "More, more, further, further". I'd forgotten that I'd even met Barney back in the day. I was pretty young and stupid, and Barney, as everybody knows, wasn't exactly the most forceful of characters, so it took me a while to join the dots. But I do recall Jake clapping his hands and announcing, "Barney's back. Here we go!"'

The Stiff staff included Suzanne Spiro, a fashion stylist who had joined in the early days and was one of the many beneficiaries of Bubbles' professional generosity. He suggested she design spin-off project *The Damned Songbook*, even though she had no experience of layout. 'Barney explained the technical stuff and left me to it,' she says. 'There was no ego with Barney. As much as I got to know him, I never knew his real name and in a way I think it's a shame that it's been revealed. If you asked him he would just shrug his shoulders and giggle.'

While others have speculated that Bubbles' insistence on anonymity stemmed from the tax problems which had plagued him since the Teenburger days, Spiro believes it is best explained by his professional certainty.

'The work speaks for itself,' she says. 'This is art we're talking about – it surpasses design and graphics. Sometimes there is a thin line between humility and arrogance and, in a way, if you don't recognise it's Barney's work then you just don't get it.'

What is certain is that Bubbles maintained a powerful working momentum in the circumstances – drunken visits from The Damned, Wreckless Eric and others, Riviera and Robinson roaring into telephones and the odd cider bottle flying across the office.

Only once did he find the lively atmosphere intolerable. An over-refreshed executive – who may or may not have been Robinson – failed to hit the target in the lavatory on the floor above Bubbles' desk, and ruined artwork with splashes which rained down from the loose floorboards overhead.

'Barney was absolutely hopping mad,' says Glen Colson, the former Charisma press officer who was part of the Stiff crowd and Graham Parker's PR man. 'He came out screaming and shouting about that, and quite right too. But it was very funny.'

Colson describes the environment at Alexander Street as 'manic'. He adds, 'Barney was working at full pelt. I don't know how he did it. If I spent a day there I needed a couple of days off.'

At one point in 1977, Bubbles absented himself for a few weeks, recruiting art student Pauline Kennedy to assist the late Kevin Sparrow in the art department while he was away. Later to become known as a designer in her own right using the nom de plume Caramel Crunch, Kennedy became Bubbles' assistant on his return.

'There was a lot of madness, bitching and back-stabbing,' says Kennedy. 'I don't suppose it helped that we were all on various substances, mainly speed, dope and drink. I was incredibly green. On my first day (The Damned bassist) Captain Sensible was standing in the doorway and greeted me with the words, "Hello, you cunt". That was my introduction to life as a punk rocker.'

For the most part, says Spiro, 'Barney just got on with it, working on intricate little sketches in his notebook. It was like observing an animal nurture offspring; they are utterly involved in the creative act and Barney would be like that, crouched over his desk, totally absorbed in the process. But when it was done he would move on to the next thing, just like an animal once it has reared its young.'

With Stiff motoring critically and commercially, Bubbles was again dead-centre of an extraordinarily fertile scene.

'At that time everybody seemed to have a song, a look, a joke, a slogan, an angle. These were people with serious points of view,' says Lowe of the first 12 months of Stiff's existence. 'They all congregated at that moment in that place.'

And Bubbles was in his element, having moved from Whitton into a west London squat, reconnecting with old friends as a neighbour of former Hawkwind roadie Gerry Fitzgerald, and striking new creative alliances.

'I share (the squat) on a strange basis with a Scots lady called Lynsey,' he wrote to Sartorio. 'We're working on a play together (to be performed in Bristol) and she's introduced me to a whole bunch of odd people.'

Bubbles also related that he was interested in exhibiting artwork on an ad hoc basis and that, as well as making kites, he had been approached to become involved in a new magazine.

But the focus of Bubbles' energies was once again the music industry. Having hacked off his hair and reverted to the utility wear, skinny jeans and monkey boots of his student years, Bubbles introduced to Stiff brutal cropping, stark isolation of images and monochromatic, gritty photo-play, particularly by developing a close working relationship with photographers Chris Gabrin and the late Keith Morris.

Gabrin had met Bubbles a few years earlier when he was stage manager at The Roundhouse and worked with Welsh band Help Yourself, who were labelmates of Hawkwind and managed by Dave Robinson.

'I'd set up my studio in Pancras Way, Camden, and started taking photographs for Stiff,' says Gabrin. 'One day I got a call about some contact sheets and it was Barney. He had such an eye that he could immediately spot which picture was the one to select. I always agreed with him wholeheartedly.'

The printing and processing at Gabrin's studio was handled by former Goldsmiths fine art student Bob Hall, who was nicknamed 'Bob Bromide' since he delivered the bromides (black and white positives or proofs on photographic paper).

'This incredibly shy, thin guy would come along and art direct,' says the affable Hall, reminiscing in a south London pub garden. 'But you wouldn't know he was doing it. He'd just sit quietly in the corner and make sure that his idea was realised.'

At first Bubbles was forced to rely on stockpiled shots, but soon he was providing explicit instructions on what images to take and focusing on presenting the record buyer with an artefact as exciting as (and sometimes more exciting than) the music it packaged. At this time UK seven-inch sales were booming and to achieve a Top Ten chart placing required selling tens, if not hundreds, of thousands of copies.

The immediacy of the single sleeve appealed to Bubbles. Using the 7in frame to communicate Stiff's mix of celebratory sarcasm and wilful eccentricity, Bubbles, Riviera and Robinson were responsible for the return to vogue of the single picture sleeve in Britain after more than a decade.

For The Damned single Neat Neat Neat and parent album Damned Damned Damned, Bubbles harmonised the typography over band photographs by Gabrin and Peter Gravelle respectively. He and Riviera conspired to create a back-cover in-joke on the album to help propel it into the charts.

By arranging at the pressing plant for the initial run of 2,000 copies to feature a photo of Island Records' Eddie And The Hot Rods on the back cover with a bogus erratum sticker apologising 'for any inconvenience caused', they came up with an instant collectible; Riviera had worked out that it was this number of sales which would enable the release to go into profit. He was also aware that this strategy would help test the humour of Stiff's new distributor, Island Records.

And for a select tier of vinyl fanatics, they housed a small number of copies of this 'misprint' in a clear plastic envelope designed by Bubbles to feature the album title in red 'food-fight' title lettering.

The standard issue was impactful in its own right (and all versions credited the design to 'Big Jobs Inc', the pseudonym used for Chilli Willi's 1974 album Bongos Over Balham).

'The lettering on Damned Damned Damned was important,' says the band's drummer Rat Scabies. 'In those days, you had to be able to read the name in the rack, and Barney made us stand out in huge bright yellow letters. He understood that, much as Stiff was a lot of fun, the releases had to have a commercial appeal. At the same time he made it edgy and kind of sinister.'

For The Damned's follow-up album, Music For Pleasure, released in November 1977, Bubbles produced a pastiche of the work of Russian Futurist artist Wassily Kandinsky, and in particular his kinetic Composition VIII.

The frenetic forms of the band members are reduced to lines and shapes; Music For Pleasure is cited as the cover

which embodies the contained energy to be found across Bubbles' work.

By the time Music For Pleasure was ready for release, the band was already splintering and Scabies was soon to leave. 'We were in a state of turmoil and the cover reflected that,' says Scabies. 'We appear to be catapulting off on our own tangents, but are all still identifiable.'

Scabies delightedly describes as 'insanity' one particular Bubbles design for The Damned: a 60in x 40in poster consisting of a monochrome crop of singer Dave Vanian's face in performance displaying giant half-tones. 'He enlarged that from a crop from a 10in x 8in photo,' says Riviera. 'Barney loved working with scale, blowing up a tiny image so it degraded, or bringing down a large image so everything condensed. He would cry: "I want dots the size of golf balls!"'

In a similar move, Bubbles' enlargement of a crop of the face of The Adverts' bassist Gaye Advert for the front cover of their single One Chord Wonders became one of the defining images of the punk era yet, like The Damned poster, harked back to his 1970 Red Dirt album design.

It is interesting to note that Bubbles escaped punk's year-zero intolerance of anyone with hippy associations, or indeed with any musical style preceding 1976.

'If there was a relevant point to be made he wouldn't hide his past,' says Scabies. 'Even though he was a hippy, he was still in tune with the punk ethic about there being no rules. Everything is fair game to get the point across and that's what Barney was about.'

The Stiff style thrust individual acts to the foreground on the front covers, while the reverse side of the sleeves played with the traditional detailing of track-listing and publishing ownership by adding graphic tics, in-jokes and tiny figures. Over a series of single releases, Bubbles placed cut-out 'Stiff single vouchers' which were worthless (though served notice that the design was his).

This first appeared on the back of Whole Wide World, the debut single by Wreckless Eric (aka Eric Goulden) released in the summer of 1977.

The front cover was a crop from a Chris Gabrin portrait which had appeared on the inner of A Bunch Of Stiff Records. This was overlaid with an ident which also appeared on the record label. 'Barney used an office guillotine to cut jagged strips of paper which he put together to make up a logo of my name,' says Goulden.

For the back, Goulden was despatched to a photo-booth and ordered to improvise semaphore signals. Barney then cropped and bleached out one of the frames. 'I'd never seen anything like it; he made it look incredible,' Goulden adds.

Meanwhile, Bubbles' working relationship blossomed, in particular with Stiff's prominent triumvirate Ian Dury, Elvis Costello and Nick Lowe.

Lowe's deftness with a musical quotation and lightness of lyrical touch brought out Bubbles' playful streak. When David Bowie issued his album Low in February 1977, Lowe responded by entitling the EP he released the same month Bowi.

Bubbles set the title in a similar font to that on Bowie's cover, and a Peter Gravelle head-and-shoulders shot of Lowe is backed by an approximation of the Bowie album's burnt orange background.

Lowe's late 1977 Billy Fury cover Halfway To Paradise was rush-released so came in the standard Stiff Records bag. The label was presented as the primary image, bearing a bleached-out shot of Lowe's face and his signature, a take on a fan photo which might have appeared in a 60s pop magazine (as Lowe himself had done as part of beat combo Kippington Lodge).

'I always got the impression Barney didn't really like my music,' says Lowe. 'Though I felt that he liked me and the people I hung around with, I think he thought my stuff was a bit square. He never said anything, but that came across pretty clearly.'

Nevertheless, Bubbles was to maintain a close working relationship with Lowe beyond Stiff, and the musician's aquiline features regularly appeared on the labels of records he designed for him, just as Bubbles created 'bespoke' labels for other artists whose work he treasured.

For example, painter and former member of Kilburn & The High Roads Humphrey Ocean is shown performing the elaborate dance moves for which he was noted on both sides of the label on his Stiff release, the single Whoops A Daisy. These stemmed from a photographic session which was directed by Bubbles and resulted in a segmented promotional poster to be cut into sections to create a flick-book.

Such integrated treatment, where the usually inconsequential label copy is handled with as much care as the cover image, indicated to the Stiff crowd that Bubbles was in full control of the process.

'I was quite surprised at how steely he could become,' says Lowe. 'I did a photo-session with Chris Gabrin directed by Barney. We were all a bit drunk and mucking about and suddenly he put his foot down. He didn't throw a wobbly, just said something which got our attention. I remember thinking: "Bloody hell, Barney. Where did that come from?"'

Gabrin had photographed Elvis Costello from the get-go and Bubbles homed in on certain shots for the covers of his first two singles, Less Than Zero and Alison.

Costello – previously country-rock performer D.P. MacManus – was positioned by Stiff as a twisted outsider, to match the subject matter of his tightly wound songs filled with jealousy and disgust.

Gone was his denim work-shirt, flared dungarees, sensible spectacles and coiffed hair, and in their place a neat quiff, oversized Buddy Holly glasses, a thrift-store jacket with skinny tie, Doc Marten's and drainpipe jeans.

'The idea was that he would be like Buddy Holly on acid,' says Riviera. 'Barney's brief was that we conveyed the minimum of information. No credits, just the song titles. We wanted to intrigue people, get them asking, "Where's this guy from?"'

When it came to the shoot by Keith Morris for Costello's debut album, Bubbles art-directed the session, throwing moves and poses behind the camera to inspire and animate the singer.

'Barney was always into Elvis Presley,' says B. Syme, who became the designer's partner in the late 70s. 'He told me that he did all these Elvis stage moves while Keith took the photos, and that's how they got the shot.'

On the cover Costello is aggressively hunched over his guitar, a vengeful geek surrounded by a chequerboard border which repeats in tiny Letraset letters 'Elvis Is King'. On the back another black-and-white shot from the same session is highlighted by a wash of fluorescent colour, which features the barely discernible song titles and an undulating graphic announcing, 'Surfing The New Wave'.

'Help us hype Elvis' implored an insert with the first pressing. This promised a free copy of the album if consumers sent a letter to Stiff proving they had persuaded a friend to buy one.

ABOVE: A Bunch Of Stiff Records, Stiff. 12in album. 1977.

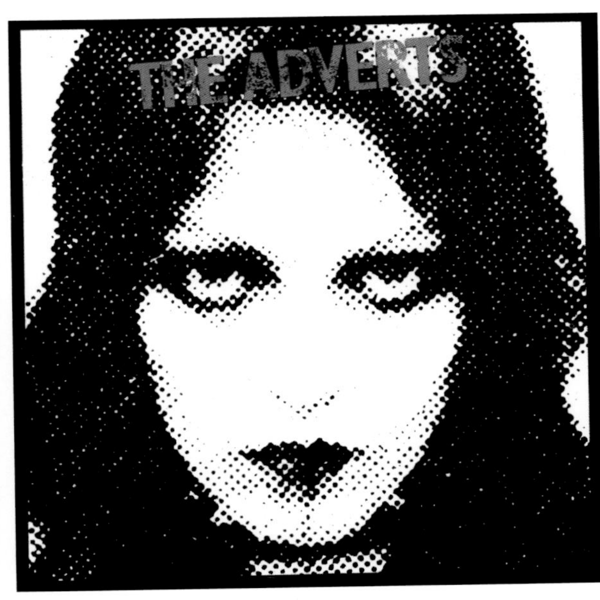

ABOVE: Poster. Larry Wallis, Stiff tour, with Chris Gabrin. 1500mm x 1000mm. 1977.

TOP LEFT: One Chord Wonders, The Adverts, Stiff Records. 7in single. 1977.

MIDDLE: Neat Neat Neat, The Damned, Stiff Records. 7in single. 1977.

FAR LEFT: Less Than Zero, Elvis Costello, Stiff Records. 7in single. 1977.

LEFT: Damned Damned Damned, The Damned, Stiff Records. 12in album promo. 1977.

CREDIT: Big Jobs Inc.

'We wanted to appeal to the pacemakers, those who wanted something different,' says Riviera. 'Our credo was that people are more intelligent than politicians and big business give them credit for.'

The first 10,000 copies placed a bright yellow screen over the image of Costello, and, as sales took off, Riviera was keen to find a way to maintain momentum. For such priority projects, Bubbles attended printing plants to ensure artwork instructions were followed to the letter. Riviera accompanied him on an early visit and discovered that changes to the ink colour would not make any difference to the cost, but would result in many different variations.

'We ended up doing at least 50 versions,' says Riviera. 'I remember Barney came in with a colour-code pamphlet for bathroom tiles, and we instructed the printer to change the ink on every batch of 5,000 according to its colours.'

The centre spreads of weekly music papers *NME*, *Melody Maker* and *Sounds* were booked in late July for Stiff adverts which each featured two panels of a cut-out-and-keep six-piece poster of the front cover shot of Costello.

'We wanted to really engage with fans and, since there were so many papers, why not come up with a collectable series?' says Riviera. 'Better than the same old ad for the latest Genesis album. Hold me back, you know?'

Brevity was the watchword of the My Aim Is True campaign. Some ads presented the album cover with the command 'Buy It' and, specifically for the trade press, 'Stock it'. One states: 'The best record company in the country presents the best artist(e) in the world.'

By contrast, Ian Dury was an elder of British pub rock, and needed no makeover to achieve a unique appearance. Stricken by polio in childhood and garbed in second-hand clothes, Dury (who died in 2000) was a punk inspiration with his savage, institutionalised haircut and facility for gutter-mouthed poetry.

At 35, Dury was street savvy and art smart, having studied under the great British pop artist Peter Blake and taught at various art colleges. At one time he'd also contributed illustrations to British magazines such as *Nova*, so had as strong a grasp of identity and presentation as Bubbles.

'Ian loved Barney,' says Riviera. 'He could be a prickly bastard, but when it came to Barney he knew he was in the presence of ferocious talent.'

The cover of the singer's breakthrough single, Sex & Drugs & Rock & Roll, presented him as a mascara'd debauch. Bubbles maximised the impact by using the black border speed notches, as though the image was printed directly from the negative. Speed notches were also included in the back-cover side-profile shot which was 'torn' across the bottom to make way for the credits.

'Barney was easily the most incredible designer I've ever come across,' Dury told Will Birch in 1999. 'He didn't have the faults or the ego, and that made me feel second-class. I wanted his approval in a strange kind of way.'

Chris Gabrin's cover shot for Dury's debut album New Boots And Panties!! and the inner sleeve compilation of images from his recent past communicated the bohemian diversity of his personality, while the back cover utilised fluorescent orange and green washes in accordance with punk's day-glo aesthetic.

Bubbles opted for a suitably rough but legible script for the credits, title and track information. 'Barney always said he liked my handwriting,' says Cynthia Lole, Stiff receptionist and Riviera's assistant. 'He laid out the artwork and set out what I was to write. The magic marker I used was a bit faulty, and I said: "I'd better redo that Barney."

'He protested: "No, leave it as it is."'

The only Stiff release to carry a Barney Bubbles credit

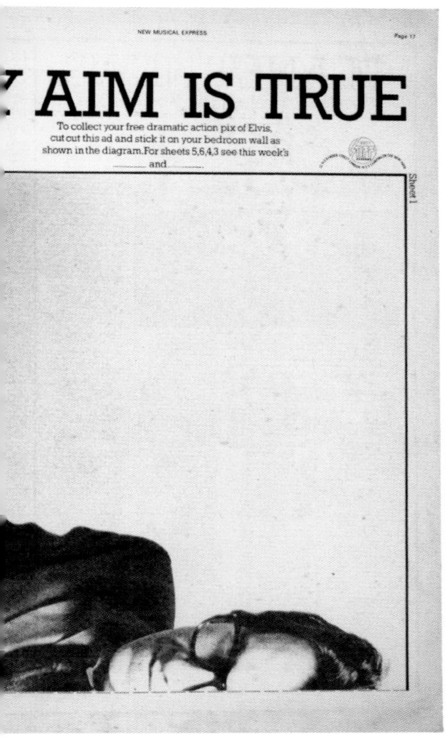

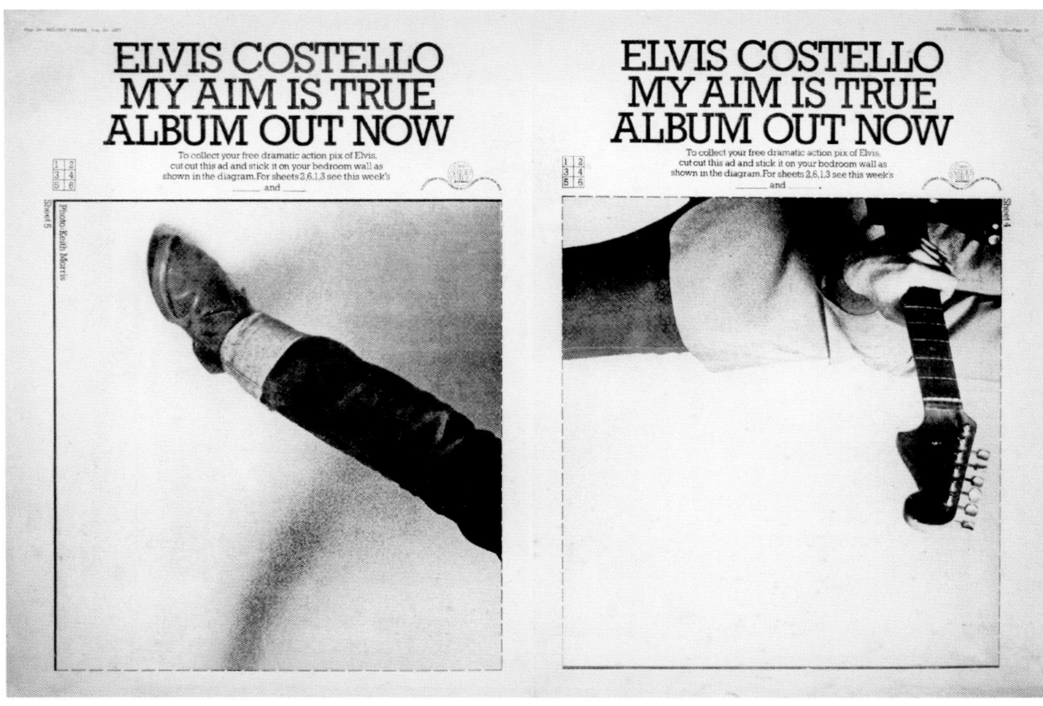

is England's Glory, the one-off single written by Ian Dury for British music hall legend Max Wall. The cover is a 'pen and ink' (Cockney rhyming slang for 'stink') portrait by Humphrey Ocean with Letraset lettering credited to Bubbles. 'That was at Max's insistence,' says Riviera. 'He [Max] was wary at the beginning but Ian charmed him and he ended up being very jazzed about the whole project, probably because we featured his song Dream Tobacco on the B-side.'

As 1977 progressed, so the rest of the British music industry joined the fray started by Stiff and presented their singles in visually captivating sleeves.

Consequently the freelance Bubbles was in demand, though the commission for the cover for Generation X's debut single Your Generation on Chrysalis Records arose by coincidence. That summer, the band's manager and journalist Jonh Ingham (whose byline included the deliberate first-name misspell) was the boyfriend of Suzanne Spiro.

During a phone call to Spiro at Stiff, Ingham mentioned a newly found passion for the work of such early 20th-century avant-garde European artists as Rodchenko, Malevich and El Lissitzky.

'Suzanne repeated the name El Lissitzky,' says Ingham. 'The next thing I heard was Barney's voice shouting from the back room: 'What's going on? Why are you talking about El Lissitzky?'

'Barney grabbed the phone out of Suzanne's hand and demanded to know about my interest in the constructivists. I explained we were looking for a sleeve for Generation X and off we went; we had our art director.'

Bubbles proposed his idea for Your Generation: the numerals 45 in direct reference to the rpm of a 7in single. 'We had a session sitting on the Alexander Street stoop on a sunny midday and out came the spiral-bound notebook with precise 2in sq ideas,' says Ingham. 'One of them was exactly the front and back cover of Your Generation, down to the last detail.'

Both sides of Your Generation featured the same graphic. The black and red arrangement quoted not only a Lissitzky catalogue cover for an exhibition of Russian art in Zurich in 1929 but also Polish op-art pioneer Henryk Berlewi, and in particular the Composition In Red, Black And White, one of 12 accompanying Berlewi's 1924 manifesto Mechano-Faktura (which proposed painting be 'designed' according to the principles of modern technology and mechanical reproduction).

The Your Generation sleeve was a clear indicator of Bubbles' distillation of art history references. Using Berlewi's painting as a springboard, he reassembled the elements into a multi-layered piece connecting with the visual minimalism and energy of the punk period.

'Billy (Idol, Generation X singer) had been making his own T-shirts in a constructivist style,' says the band's bassist and principal songwriter Tony James. 'He used block colour and stencils as part of our development of a brighter, happier look than The Clash referencing Jackson Pollock. Barney looked at our original ideas and took them a very inspired step further.'

For the advert for trade paper *Music Week*, Bubbles urged the band to keep it simple. 'He said that it was a waste of time trying to be clever, that we should just say: "Buy this record",' says Ingham.

In the event, Bubbles placed the message 'Our record in your record shops on Saturday' in the white space left by a trompe l'oeil rip he cut into a photograph of the band by Ray Stevenson; Idol appeared to have torn it himself with his left hand. Signifying the amount of time the band had taken to reach their first release – rivals the Sex Pistols, The Clash and The Damned had each released at least a run of singles by this stage – the ad was flagged with a Bubbles pun: 'Worth its wait'.

On the single's release in September 1977, Generation X played four gigs at London club The Marquee promoted by a series of

TOP: Adverts. My Aim Is True, Elvis Costello. 1977.

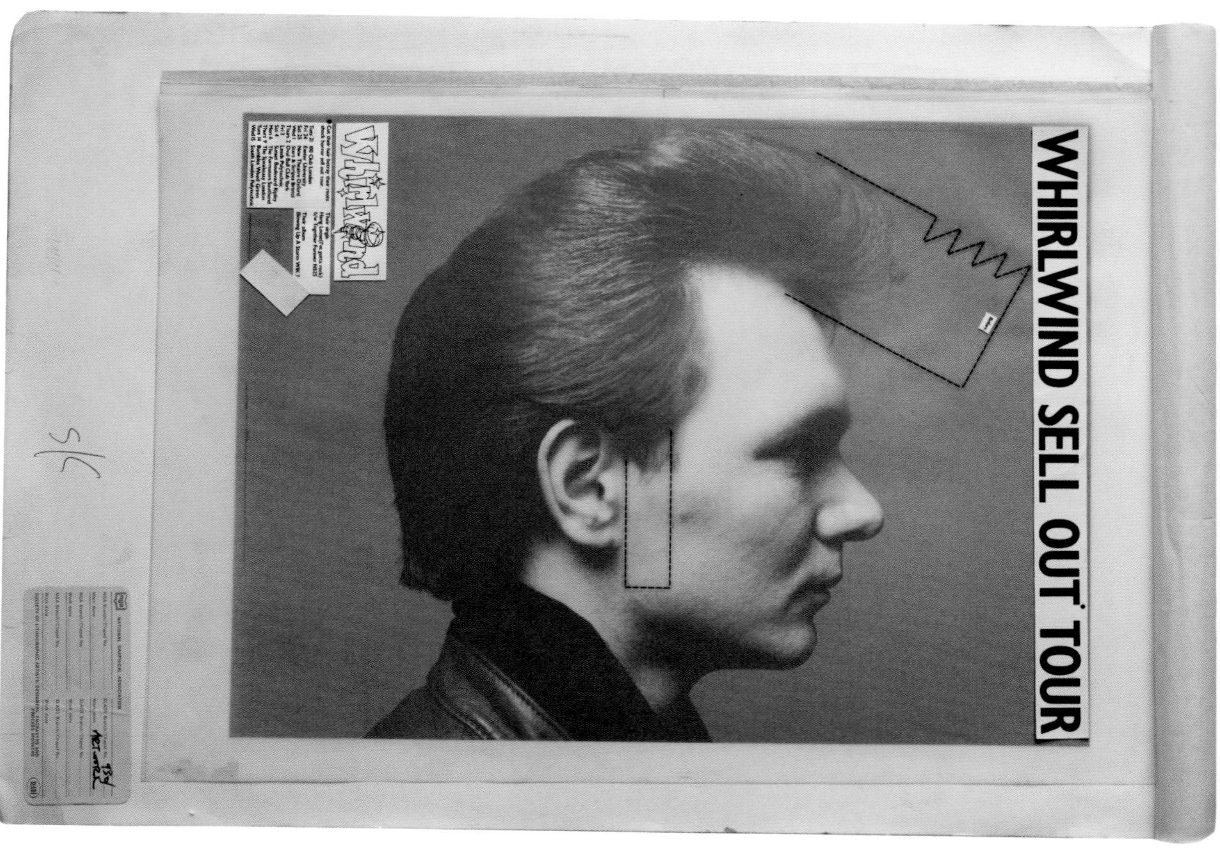

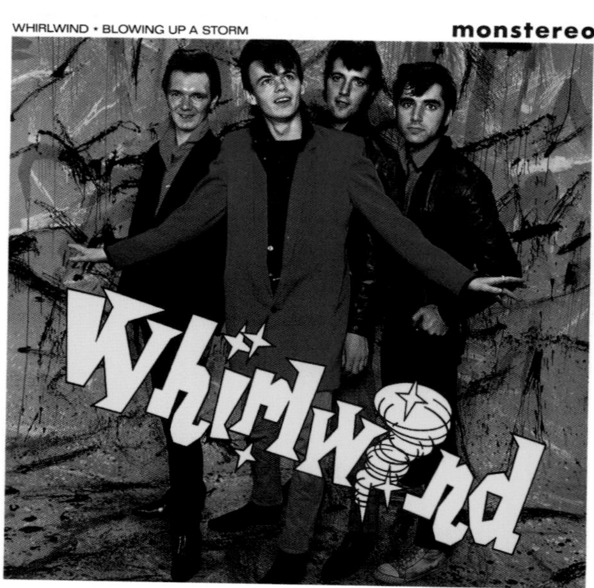

TOP: Artwork. Whirlwind tour, Chiswick Records. 1978.

ABOVE: Blowing Up A Storm, Whirlwind, Chiswick Records. 10in album. 1978.

OPPOSITE RIGHT: Logotype. What A Waste label, Ian Dury & The Blockheads, Stiff Records. 1978.

OPPOSITE FAR RIGHT: Blockhead watch, Stiff Records. 1978.

monochrome Bubbles-designed posters. These were taken from stills from a performance clip made for a pilot music TV show incorporating an archetypal Bubbles intervention. Rather than use the stills, he took photographs of each to up the intensity.

'Barney and I spent a morning in an edit suite running the video,' says Ingham. 'Every so often he would freeze the frame and take a photograph of the image. What delighted me about the final designs was that he incorporated the lines of static as graphics. When all four were posted on a wall in sequence, the lines matched.'

Bubbles also designed the sleeve of the band's 1978 single King Rocker, which was printed in five versions to indicate the colour of the vinyl of the record inside. Each positioned a band-member portrait by Peter Gravelle with decorations in the appropriate spot colour.

But it is the purity of the Your Generation graphic which had the greatest impact. 'I'd lost track of Barney as my interest in Hawkwind had waned,' says Malcolm Garrett. 'To find out he was responsible for Your Generation was mind-blowing. The use of typography and the way the two numerals work together is just so damn clever.'

At the same time as Bubbles was immersing himself in the new wave, he contributed a design for country-rockers Clover, an American act Robinson and Riviera had signed to Phonogram. For Clover's only album release, Unavailable, Bubbles' sleeve depicted a green/orange four-leaf clover in the form of an axonometric projection (a drawing used by architects and interior designers to convey spatial information).

Combined with a high-voltage font, the sleeve for Unavailable failed to lift interest in the outmoded music it packaged, and the band split up, returning to America to reconvene and find success a few years later as Huey Lewis And The News.

In the autumn of 1977, with Costello and Dury hitting the charts and Stiff's profile rising, two general managers were hired. Paul Conroy, the former live agent who had worked with Bubbles on the Naughty Rhythms tour, and Alan Cowderoy, who had started his career as a member of Gracious! (for whom Bubbles had designed the 'exclamation mark' cover in 1970), were brought in to oversee the workload as international interest in the label grew.

'Barney had the oddest work routines,' says Conroy. 'He'd start about four or five in the afternoon and then work through the night, sometimes sleeping in the office.'

Conroy and Cowderoy had barely got their feet under the table when the differences between Riviera and Robinson came to a head. After a serious disagreement over future direction and finances, the partnership was dissolved.

Robinson retained Dury and the rest of the Stiff roster apart from Costello and Lowe, who moved with Riviera to new label Radar, recently set up by former United Artists executives Andrew Lauder and Martin Davies with backing from Warner Music.

They had already commissioned a radar-signal logo in white on a green dial background from Bubbles, confirming his place in the new venture.

'I was running around the world with (Lowe and Dave Edmunds' band) Rockpile and Elvis, so didn't really want to do the day-to-day stuff beyond having a fix on the design aspects with Barney,' says Riviera, whose deal included a 'key-man' clause. If either Lauder or Davies left the set-up, Riviera and his artists' contracts would be terminated.

Bubbles, Riviera and their team – including press officer Glen Colson – were settled in above Radar's offices at 60 Parker Street on the fringes of London's Covent Garden.

As the Radar deal was being finalised, the key Stiff artists – including Costello and Lowe – embarked on the sell-out nationwide Live Stiffs tour which would make household names of Costello and Dury and boost the profiles of the others who shared the bill: Lowe, Wreckless Eric and former Pink Fairies member Larry Wallis.

Chris Gabrin photographed the artists for publicity purposes (a group shot was to appear on the cover of the resultant live album) and Bubbles designed five posters so that he and the photographer could earn pin money. At 60in x 40in, Gabrin's images of each performer were treated with deliberately crude overlaps of lurid-coloured screens.

Roadies were instructed to sell them on the Stiff tour dates. 'They didn't sell because they were so huge none of the punters could be bothered to carry them home,' laughs Gabrin.

It's indicative of Bubbles' talent and nature that even after the Riviera/Robinson split, he worked both sides of the acrimonious divide, continuing to freelance for Stiff and further develop his collaborative relationship with Ian Dury.

To handle the workload, he was joined at Radar's offices at Parker Street in the spring of 1978 by new assistant Diana Fawcett, who details the regimen: 'We worked seven days a week, cleanly and precisely. There was never any mess. It was a collaborative effort, but it was clear he was the master and I was the apprentice. It was my job to clean all equipment daily – especially the Rotring pens, because the ink would clog overnight – and sweep the floor at the end of every paste-up session.'

Fawcett says that time would be made for a snack in the late afternoon. 'Then it was back to the creative work. By then it would be early evening and the phone stopped ringing as London quietened down, so we would listen to the music for the jobs we were working on and thrash out concepts.

'When I came in the next day, Barney would have made the thumbnails (tiny boxed sketches of one or two design options for each commission) ready to show clients.

'I was often pasting up in the morning when he was out showing a client for approval, and then the day started again, drawing up boards for every piece, him taking care of the designs and illustrations and me letter-setting copy.

'Everything was done with absolute discipline and order. It suited our personalities, which is why I think I lasted longer with him than most. We were similar in that we had absolute order in our work whereas our personal lives were chaotic.'

Fawcett's first task was to paste-up a commission from Dury: the Blockhead logo. Dury had named his new band The Blockheads after a song title and decided that the musicians needed a collective ident.

'I phoned him and said, "I want a logo. It's got to be black and white and square",' Dury told Will Birch. 'Then I heard somebody in his office say, "Wow" and he said, "I've done it!"'

In this, another signature work adorning T-shirts and badges more than four decades after creation, Bubbles created a face out of the letters. In doing so, he was drawing on the square black-on-orange logo of the British 40s socialist publishing imprint the Left Book Club, as pointed out in 2008 by Paul Murphy on John Coulthart's blog Feuilleton.

The Blockhead logo was made public in tour advertising and on the label for Dury's 1978 single What A Waste, framed by the label copy information in a tiny type size which ended with the

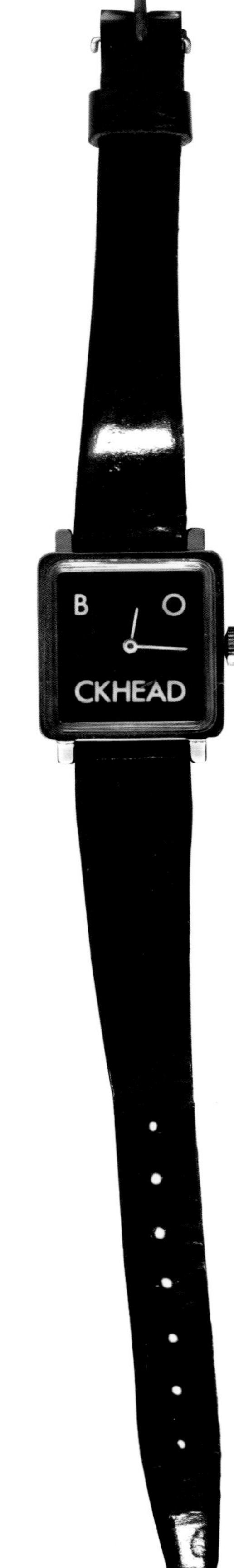

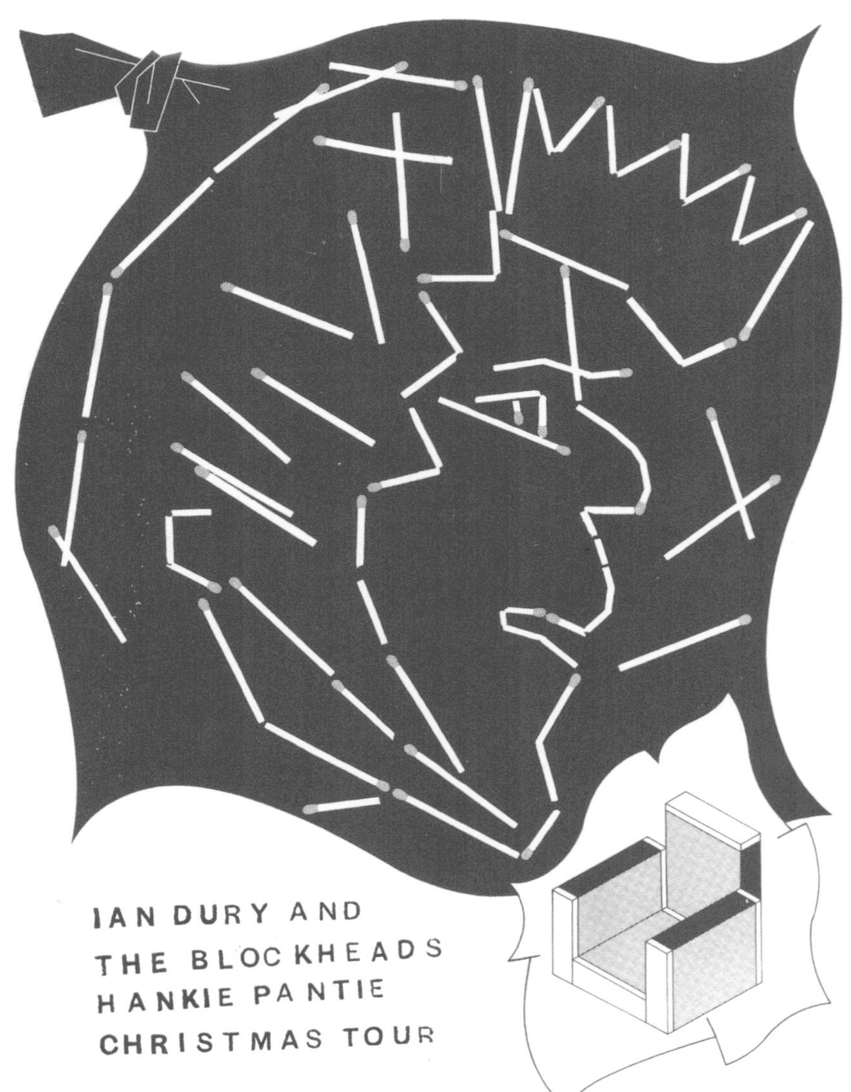

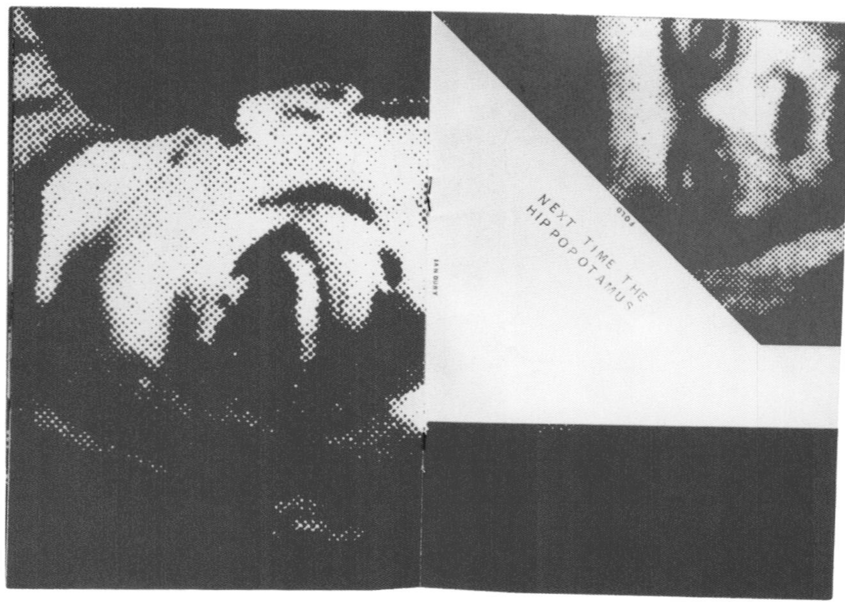

admonitory 'Don't fuck about or else!' The cover contained a photographic abstraction; a black and white image of a heavily piped industrial building, presumably a waste plant, representing yet another face.

Soon the Blockhead logo appeared on buttons, T-shirts and a limited-edition watch. The 'face' becomes apparent when the clock strikes 12.15 and three o'clock.

By this time, Bob Hall had shown Bubbles the technique for creating photograms by placing three-dimensional objects on photographic plates or paper to create 'light drawings'.

Bubbles took as his reference points two distinct modernist advances of the 20s; the Bauhaus artist László Moholy-Nagy's pictograms, which formed part of his investigations into the ways in which photography could serve other media – painting, poster art and textile design – and Lissitzky's photograms, which used everyday objects such as pliers.

'That's something we take for granted now, but in graphics, in the music business at least, Barney was pioneering the use of everyday objects in art,' says Suzanne Spiro. 'He was way ahead of his time because he could see the design and the beauty in the apparently banal.'

For the cover that announced Radar to the pop public – the new label's first release, Nick Lowe's Bowie-inflected single I Love The Sound Of Breaking Glass – Bubbles created a doleful visage from a circular saw, scalpel, paper-clip and ring-pull (for the eye with a teardrop descending).

The arrangement of the song title and information and the central image enabled Bubbles to quote another exemplar of early modernism, Theo van Doesburg, and in particular his Dada cover for the magazine *Mécano*, which also has a circular saw at the centre.

Within a couple of weeks this had been aced by Radar's first album release, This Year's Model by Elvis Costello And The Attractions. 'Elvis had the title, and during Chris Gabrin's photo-shoot, Barney said that Elvis should be behind the camera rather than in front,' says Riviera.

Riviera was keen that there should be no interference from Radar's distributor Warner Music and cooked up several strategies 'to make them wary of us. We didn't want them dictating whether we couldn't use metallic inks or what-have-you, so we were out to show them we meant business.'

Bubbles was more than delighted to fit in with these plans and produced a commercial intervention which simultaneously revealed and commented on the production process underpinning record sleeve design.

His instructions that the album cover be printed off-kilter, revealed the printer's colour code down the right-hand side, pushing the title sideways so the artist became 'Lvis Costello' and the title 'His Years Model'.

In the back cover photograph the band appeared to be involved in a mysterious incident in a suburban sitting room (it was in fact shot in a New York hotel by Gabrin), while the inner sleeve was given over to two abstract interpretations of the album title: a robotic rubber hand held the latest in micro-TV technology; and four shop-window torsos were lined up in a launderette wearing string vests in different shades.

'Barney got the tailor's dummies from a junk shop and Cynthia provided the vests, which he sprayed,' says Riviera. 'Everything was done very quickly because we were up against it. Elvis had a whole new bunch of songs and the Attractions were fed up with playing the tracks off My Aim Is True (where the backing had been provided by Clover) so they interrupted an American tour and made the record in ten days.'

A sticker on the cover announced a 'free album with this single', referring to the inclusion of the Stranger In The House 45 housed in the Radar single sleeve (on which Bubbles used typography as design by repeating the white-on-black phonetic 'bzz').

Bubbles produced industrial-style stickers, stating 'Warning: This is not This Year's Model', to be slapped on phone boxes, electricity generators and the like and was responsible for the series of press ads for individual music papers. Each presented six images and was themed with subject matter headings including 'Drugs', 'Fads' and 'Commodities'. The last captioned the Attractions as (budget record label) 'K-Tel' and Chilli Willi And The Red Hot Peppers as 'Saccharine'.

Aside from Costello, Riviera's priority was to break Lowe as an artist in his own right. With the title Jesus Of Cool (called Pure Pop For Now People in the US), Lowe's debut solo album collected his Stiff and Radar tracks and was released in March 1978.

To reflect Lowe's magpie tendencies, Riviera conceived a cover which showed the singer-songwriter in a series of pop music archetypes. Bubbles not only designed the sleeve, but decorated Lowe's guitar with flowered wallpaper and provided a 60s shirt to help him achieve the 'hippy' persona.

The back cover of Jesus Of Cool conveyed both Bubbles' invention and his fascination with the minutiae of suburbia. He placed glass swans from his parents' mantelpiece in an oven tray filled with water and lined with black bin-liner plastic. A single bulb was shone to give the impression of moonlight on a midnight lake.

Radar's licensing deals brought commissions for a number of one-off releases, including single sleeves for The Soft Boys' (I Want To Be An) Anglepoise Lamp, I Can Detect You (For 100,000 Miles) by Andy Arthurs and Iggy Pop & James Williamson's Kill City.

This was the lead track from the album of the same name licensed from the Los Angeles independent label Bomp! Records. For the single sleeve, Bubbles produced a pink fluoro treatment of the 1928 news agency photograph of the execution by electric chair of the murderess Ruth Snyder. In doing so he recalled Andy Warhol's approach to his Electric Chairs series of the 60s.

The pink splashed onto the back cover: a monochrome image of a bizarre crime scene, where the body appeared to have been impaled on a parking meter. The music press ad campaign used this photograph, to which Bubbles added a join-the-dots puzzle fluttering above the chalk-marks. Joined together, these spelt the title: Kill City.

Experimenting with the boundaries of taste and accepted practice in music industry design became a signature quality of Bubbles' work in this period. For the 1978 Radar release of an album by US bar band the Good Rats, Bubbles and Gabrin inverted the traditional roles of laboratory testing. 'He built this giant cage, and we dressed Bob Bromide in a white hooded outfit with a rat mask, as though he was going to conduct an experiment,' laughs Gabrin. 'I thought it looked amazing. Radar rejected the sleeve immediately they clapped eyes on the contacts.'

With Costello and Lowe now firmly established as Top Ten artists and the Radar roster requiring a constant stream of fresh graphics and designs, Andrew Lauder recruited Malcolm Garrett,

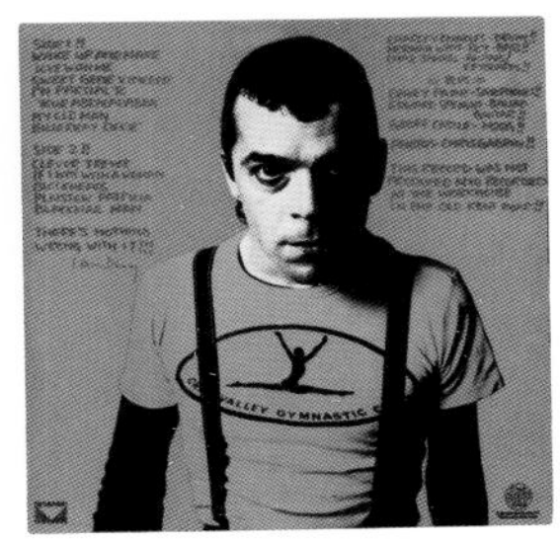

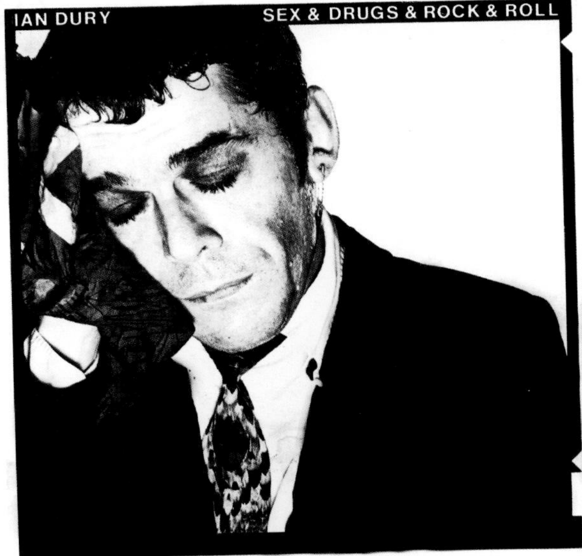

OPPOSITE TOP: Programme. Ian Dury & The Blockheads tour. 210mm x 145mm. 1978.

OPPOSITE BOTTOM: Pages from tour programme. 1978.

TOP LEFT: New Boots And Panties!!, Ian Dury, Stiff Records. 12in album. 1977.

MIDDLE: Sex & Drugs & Rock & Roll, Ian Dury, Stiff Records. 7in single. 1977.

LEFT: What A Waste, Ian Dury & The Blockheads, Stiff Records. 7in single. 1978.

ABOVE TOP: Back cover. New Boots And Panties!!, Ian Dury, Stiff Records. 12in album. 1977.

ABOVE: Back cover. Sex & Drugs & Rock & Roll, Ian Dury, Stiff Records. 1977.

RIGHT: Gatefold cover. The Parkerilla, Graham Parker & The Rumour, Vertigo. 12in album. 1978.

OPPOSITE: Inner gatefold. The Parkerilla, Graham Parker & The Rumour, Vertigo. 1978.

having encountered the Manchester Polytechnic graduate's work with UA-signed punks Buzzcocks.

'Andrew recognised that Barney needed to concentrate on the gems,' says Garrett. 'I wasn't his assistant, but took over the work Barney couldn't or shouldn't have been involved in. He was never less than generous and encouraging.'

Bubbles' talents were also being tapped by Chiswick Records owners Ted Carroll and Roger Armstrong, for whom he delivered sleeve and advertising artwork for acts such as neo-rockabilly band Whirlwind and his particular favourites, the ramshackle Croydon punk band named after frontman Johnny Moped.

'Barney loved Johnny Moped,' says Riviera. 'It was a case of "Bring me your dented and bent out of shape".'

As well as designs for Moped singles No One, Little Queenie and Darling, Let's Have Another Baby, Bubbles contributed a painstakingly detailed sleeve and inner for the 1978 album Cycledelic, including a chronology of the band's musical development, in the style of the Rock Family Trees minted by journalist/author Pete Frame.

'I've been ripped off many times but Barney was the only person to ask for my permission to use the format,' says Frame. 'And he's the only one who improved upon it; it's fabulous.'

Bubbles also directed video clips for Darling, Let's Have Another Baby and the No One B-side Incendiary Device. The deliberately shaky hand-held action and overall lo-fi vibe mitigated against either being broadcast or commercially released, not least because of the content of the latter.

A favoured Bubbles slogan was 'Breaking out of misogyny'; he inserted it into Johnny Moped press advertising showing the back of a naked female with her arms tied to her body. This image derived from the Incendiary Device clip, in which the female's torso is seen from the front with the word 'slut' written on a white T-shirt which is shredded with sharp scissors to reveal another of the band's song titles scrawled on her breasts: VD Boiler.

The sequence is intercut with starkly lit images of the grimacing band dancing around the woman's naked body as if around a maypole, wrapping her in coloured flex. The ritualism, combined with the misogynistic references, makes for as uncomfortable viewing as any of the visuals realised in punk's aftermath.

London's Aura Records, run by photographer/producer Aaron Sixx, also utilised Bubbles for a run of black-and-white single sleeves, including Johnny B. Scott's Rock'n'Roll Legend in 4/4 Time (1977) and K.K. Black's California Sun and Big Star's Kizza Me (both 1978).

The latter came from a clutch of 1974 recordings gathered together as The Third Album in a sleeve also designed by Bubbles. On the front a model was swathed in the red and black Tennessee flag (which has three white stars). To these Bubbles appended fizzing graphic firework fuses. The front cover photograph of Kizza Me progressed the theme with the inflammatory depiction of the flag alight and the stars – without graphic adornment – aflame.

On the back of Kizza Me, ten frames were arranged in the shape of a favourite Bubbles symbol, the pentagram. It is understood the members of the by-now disbanded Memphis group were not impressed at the image of their state flag on fire and the album was withdrawn from sale.

All the while, Bubbles' reputation was rising in music business circles and, in 1978, The Who's management approached him to pitch for the sleeve for the group's latest album, Who Are You.

Fellow designer Richard Evans, who worked extensively with The Who, recalls Bubbles visiting the band when they put on a live show for a private audience at Shepperton Studios. Subsequently, Bubbles proposed an album cover of the title in the thick film cables which threaded the Shepperton soundstages. 'It would have looked fantastic, but they said it was unworkable,' says Bob Hall. In the event, the cables were used on the Who Are You cover image, coiling around the equipment which frames a portrait of the band.

In June 1978, Bubbles was back on the West Coast of America for the first time in a decade, joining Riviera and Lowe on the road and witnessing a number of performances by Elvis Costello And The Attractions, including a breakthrough gig at LA school Hollywood High.

Backstage after a punk show at the Whisky a Go Go on Sunset Strip, Bubbles was introduced to expat British designer David Allen, whose work included the Popeye-style sleeve for the Iggy Pop and James Williamson album Kill City.

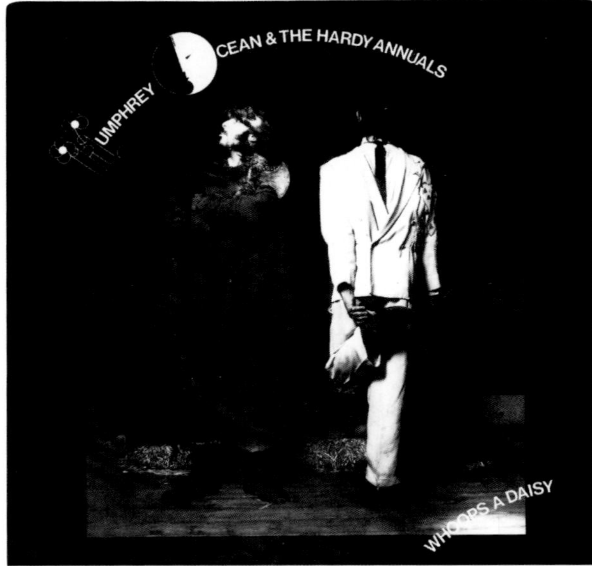

CLOCKWISE FROM TOP LEFT: Back cover. Whoops A Daisy, Humphrey Ocean's Iron Hoof, Stiff Records. 7in single. 1978.

Label. Humphrey Ocean, Stiff Records. 1978.

Poster. Whoops A Daisy, Humphrey Ocean & The Hardy Annuals, Stiff Records. 750mm x 500mm. 1978.

Front cover. Whoops A Daisy, Humphrey Ocean & The Hardy Annuals, Stiff Records. 1978.

'Barney was dressed like an eye test, black-and-white striped shirt and trousers, not quite matching,' recalls Allen. 'We were both sober enough to make sociable conversation and had common ground in that we had both done some work for Devo.'

On his return, Bubbles was summoned to a meeting with the recently appointed *New Musical Express* editor Neil Spencer. On the back of the explosion of new groups and styles ignited by punk, record sales were at an all-time high, and the five weekly UK specialist publications had benefited concomitantly; the *NME* – owned by consumer publishing giant IPC – led the field with weekly sales sometimes surpassing 150,000 copies.

Keen to maintain market dominance, and also to stamp the identity of the new editorial regime on the magazine, Spencer commissioned a redesign from Bubbles, who was charged with creating a supplement to mark the relaunch.

The *NME Book Of Modern Music* (which was compiled by the reader from a series of collect-and-keep free-insert sections over a number of weeks) gave Bubbles free rein. Assisted by Fawcett with input from the *NME*'s design department including the illustrator Andy Martin, Bubbles whipped a multitude of 20th-century art and design references into a mélange suited to the creatively chaotic post-punk period.

Given the A–Z nature of the booklet, Bubbles formulated an alphabet. 'It borrowed from 20s Russia, 60s Britain and beyond,' says Spencer. 'Barney was so wily technically and conjured unexpected colours and effects. To me he was a brilliant, quixotic spirit and, in his self-effacement, utterly English.'

The alphabet was undoubtedly influenced by Bubbles' investigations into the avant-garde art movements of the early 20th century; the following year he visited two important retrospectives staged at the Oxford Museum Of Modern Art for Rodchenko (in February/March) and Kandinsky (September/October).

The scope of the *NME* commission required the daily presence of Bubbles and Fawcett at IPC in the late summer of 1978. They decamped from Parker Street – with Bubbles leaving an encouraging note for Malcolm Garrett – and were installed in the *NME*'s infamous 'bunker', a windowless, sound-proofed construct in the centre of the open-plan space used for record reviewing.

'It was airless and boiling hot,' says Fawcett. 'We had to be there because it also contained the photo archive and was a central point for the *NME* journalists to deliver their copy. But it was a mad-house; (journalists) Danny Baker and Nick Kent would be dropping in and reviewing records loudly while we were trying to concentrate.'

With Fawcett furiously marking up copy and laying out pages, Bubbles outlined the redesign, which was unveiled in the issue of 14 October 1978, though the IPC management were nervous of jettisoning the paper's old-style logo so refused to allow its replacement for another six weeks (until sales confirmed that readers were happy with the new design).

And so, after much wrangling, the 2 December issue introduced the block capital *NME* masthead (which continues to be used in modified digital forms to this day). Bubbles modelled this on the lettering on Rotaflex House at 241 City Road, just around the corner from the site of his new studio in Paul Street, near London's now-trendy Shoreditch.

Rotaflex was a European lighting design company; the name of the premises was presented in lettered boxes back-lit at night. 'Barney thought they looked stunning, and when the *NME* job came up, the Rotaflex letters were perfect for replacing their old squiggly masthead,' says Diana Fawcett. 'It was a case of "that'll do"!'

Working as Ditchwater Designs ('as in dull as ditchwater', chortles Fawcett) the pair settled into the new studio space. This was the entire top floor of the Paul Street building, to which they had been introduced by Bob Hall, who occupied the floor below. 'At times we both lived there, so were definitely ahead of our time,' says Hall. 'Next door was a squat populated by punks, who the local skinheads would come by and bash up. The local pub was a National Front stronghold – it was a totally weird and heavy area.'

One of the first jobs at the new studio was the design for a poster for another 60s survivor, Vivian Stanshall. The former frontman of the Bonzo Dog Doo-Dah Band was presenting his creation Sir Henry Rawlinson in a one-off performance at London's Collegiate Theatre on 18 October, and Bubbles designed a blue and green chequerboard poster overlaid with an image of Stanshall on his bicycle in full Sir Henry mode.

By this time, Bubbles was collaborating with Brian Griffin, who had cut his teeth as a photographer at trade weekly *Management Today* and was looking for a more liberating milieu to express his singular vision. Placed in stylised and absurd situations, Griffin's unsettling monochrome images emphasised the use of shadows.

'I really liked the look of Elvis Costello in his suit and tie, so went to Stiff thinking, "I can do this. Him and his band members look like businessmen",' says Griffin, sipping tea in his apartment beside the Thames in east London.

But Griffin hadn't read up on the latest music biz developments, so discovered on arrival that Costello had long since departed with Lowe and Riviera to Radar. Impressed with his portfolio, Dave Robinson commissioned Griffin to shoot the sleeve for Graham Parker & The Rumour's forthcoming album The Parkerilla.

Photographing outside at London's South Bank Centre, Griffin portrayed Parker as a Victorian freak-show specimen, a figure caught in a Dr Jekyll and Mr Hyde transformation. This image intrigued Bubbles, who had been hired by Robinson to design the sleeve. 'Dave brought Barney over to my flat in Chiswick,' says Griffin. 'Obviously my work had certain sensibilities which appealed to him.'

In turn, Bubbles introduced Griffin to his girlfriend, photographer Frances Newman. A previous partner of Newman's, concrete poet Tom Edmonds, had died in 1971 and concrete poetry – in which arrangements of letters convey the meaning – was by now an abiding interest of Bubbles.

Griffin, who later married Newman, believes Bubbles' design for The Parkerilla symbolises the intersection of these relationships. The outer gatefold presents Griffin's image of Parker horizontally, with the album title picked out in blood-spattered lettering, while the inner is a photograph by Newman of Parker and The Rumour in performance. The credits are overlaid in continuous colour-coded type.

'The outer was all about me and Barney and the inner was him bringing Frances to me, and simultaneously paying tribute to her dead partner via the layout of the typography,' says Griffin. 'Barney always took a fine art approach, one where anything could happen. You knew there would be great invention and a subliminal element. What we're talking about is symbolism.

'That's why Barney's work is so great – it is simultaneously symbolic and magical. What can I say? He brought Barney to

TOP: Music press advert. La Düsseldorf, La Düsseldorf, Radar. 1978.

LEFT: Front cover. Unavailable, Clover, Phonogram. 12in album. 1977.

ABOVE: Back cover. Unavailable, Clover, Phonogram. 12in album. 1977.

CREDIT: Barney Bubbles.

CHS 2165

TONY JAMES
BASS
BILLY IDOL
VOCALS
MARK LAFF
DRUMS
DERWOOD
GUITAR

DAY BY DAY

YOUR GENERATION

Chrysalis

TOP: Front cover. Your Generation, Generation X, Chrysalis. 7in single. 1977.

RIGHT: Back cover. Your Generation, Generation X, Chrysalis. 1977.

everything he did, which is to say he brought genius to everything he worked on with me.'

The Parkerilla marked the onset of one of the richest associations of Bubbles' career. The willingness to experiment he shared with Griffin was soon manifested in such designs as the unflinching sleeve for Peter Hammill's album The Future Now.

Like Bubbles and Griffin, the Van Der Graaf Generator frontman had been enthused by the impact of punk on the British music scene, 'hence the fashioning of a raw, concrete noise' for The Future Now, as he has written on his website.

Sent by record company Charisma to Griffin's apartment in west London, Hammill appeared with his beard half-shaved, a decision apparently taken after an appearance at Liverpool punk club Eric's.

Bubbles' use of Griffin's photographs on the sleeve and fold-out 12in square lyric sheet made for as startling a proposition as Hammill's uncompromising music, spurring the photographer and designer to collaborate on Griffin's first book, the self-published, black-and-white A4 pamphlet *© 1978*.

'I'd noticed these little illustrations in *NME*, thumbnails of Johnny Moped, in simple lines the size of a postage stamp,' says Griffin. 'I didn't know who'd done them, but said to myself, "That's the man I want to work with". And, by sheer happenstance, Dave Robinson delivered me to the man.'

© 1978 presents each of Griffin's photographs (one of which was used by Stiff Records as the Devo album cover B Stiff) complemented by an example of Bubbles' simple/oblique artwork. 'I gave him the brief of using straight lines, circles and curves, and Barney produced these wonderful drawings which transformed the layout and the photographs,' says Griffin.

As if he wasn't already straining under the weight of his workload, that summer Bubbles agreed to realise the visual elements of The Bohemian Love-In, an extravaganza staged by Nik Turner at London's The Roundhouse to promote the release of Xitintoday, an album with his new band Sphynx.

Bubbles also designed the record sleeve and accompanying booklet, riffing on the shared fascination for the symbolism of ancient Egypt with his own investigations into concrete poetry: the front comprised little stars made up of the word 'twinkle', one side of the inner spelt out the word 'day' with arrangements of the word 'night', and so on.

Xitintoday's concept and music was a deeply unfashionable proposition to promote in 1978, and publicist Glen Colson struck upon the idea of a multimedia happening to attract attention. With a number of bands performing (including Tanz Der Youth, the new project from The Damned's guitarist Brian James for whom he also designed a single sleeve), Bubbles conceived a set design, choreography and costumes encasing dancers from Ballet Rambert in bandages and blindfolds.

In the audience were Turner's erstwhile bandmates Robert Calvert and Dave Brock, who had recently changed the name of Hawkwind to Hawklords. Impressed, they invited Bubbles to design the sleeve for their new album 25 Years and develop the Love-In live concept for their forthcoming tour.

Bubbles' 25 Years On sleeve demonstrated the lessons learned at Stiff and Radar. He engaged with post-punk's visually savvy audience by accentuating the sensual on the front cover: a bandaged, oiled, muscular torso of one of the dancers carrying a light-stick with the band's name spray-painted in fluorescent pink (a nod, Griffin has posited, to the logo of Krautrock giants Neu!).

Photographed by Hall, Gabrin and Newman, a tour programme was conceived as a means of presenting the views of the album's fictional Pan Transcendental Industries (apparently engaged in a dystopian future in the industrialisation of religion).

With 'levels' mirroring the content of the album, the programme referenced J.G. Ballard, constructivism, futurism, totalitarianism, S&M and Dada. There were also hints of the influence of the visceral work of 60s group the Vienna Actionists, particularly in a Hawklords slide show compiled by Bubbles.

In this, images were treated and manipulated, photographs were solarised and in some cases the slides themselves scratched. The content ranged from full-colour autopsies to cartoon figures, dance-manual instructions and a tube map of London apparently drawn in blood.

As it was originally conceived, the Hawklords show presented a hyper-real, hysterical vision of life in the 21st century; Bubbles' stage directions had the dancers perform in drab oversized utilitarian apparel, picked out by prison-camp lighting towers while the musicians played.

Yet the concept was abandoned once the band hit the road. Chris Gabrin accompanied Bubbles to the opening night in October 1978. 'It was depressing,' says Gabrin, who had also directed an 8mm film of the show to be projected as part of the live performance. 'They dropped what Barney had created after a few dates and were soon incorporating old Hawkwind tracks.'

Towards the end of 1978, Brian Griffin received a call from Bubbles telling him to ready himself for a photoshoot for the cover of a new Ian Dury single. 'I sat by the phone, but he didn't ring back,' says Griffin. 'The next day I called Barney. He told me, "They needed the artwork so I just did it overnight".'

The new track was Hit Me With Your Rhythm Stick, which sold hundreds of thousands of copies and set Dury on the path from pub-rock also-ran to British national treasure.

On the front of the Hit Me sleeve, articulated black and white quadrants were surrounded by unravelled pink string against a green origami-style plane. The impact of this 'proun' (a method developed by El Lissitzky in the 20s to transform perspective in art and design by presenting the background as three- rather than two-dimensional) was heightened by the printing of the song title and band credit with Diana Fawcett's John Bull set.

On the back, the black-and-white shapes were composed into that of a jaunty puppet dog. In the bottom right-hand corner was another hound, apparently constructed from folded paper.

The success of Hit Me With Your Rhythm Stick sparked a series of sell-out gigs for Ian Dury & The Blockheads' Hanky Pantie tour of the UK in December 1978. For the programme, Bubbles extended the folded-paper theme, featuring band member portraits in seasonal green, red and white with cut-out and fold instructions. On the cover, Bubbles adopted a prison-art technique by picking out Dury's profile in matchsticks. This design was reproduced by Stiff as a promotional item: a handkerchief to be worn knotted upon the head.

Dury's tour and the single capped a year in which Bubbles' reputation had spread throughout the design community attached to Britain's music scene.

Now he was poised to deliver his masterstroke. 'There was a particular reason they got me on board at Radar,' says Malcolm Garrett. 'It meant that Barney could concentrate on the magnificence that is Armed Forces.'

ABOVE: Variations. King Rocker, Generation X, Chrysalis. 7in single. 1978.

OPPOSITE: Front cover. Music For Pleasure, The Damned, Stiff Records. 12in album. 1977.

ABOVE: Back cover. Music For Pleasure, The Damned, Stiff Records. 1977.

RIGHT: Inner Sleeve. Music For Pleasure, The Damned, Stiff Records. 1977.

M U S I C F O R P L E A S U R E

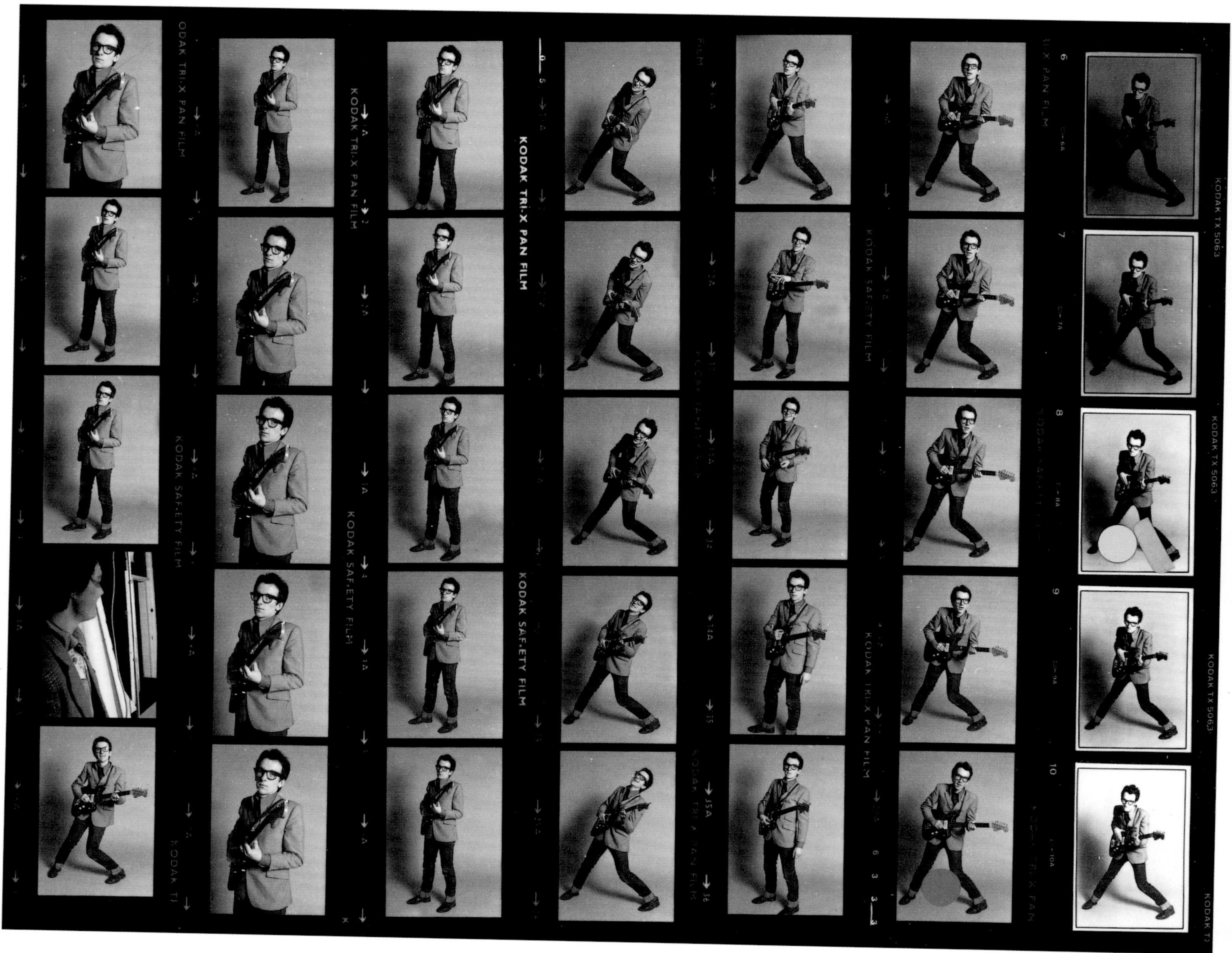

ABOVE: Contact sheet. Photo session for My Aim Is True, Keith Morris. 1977.

TOP: Front cover. My Aim Is True, Elvis Costello, Stiff Records. 12in album. 1977.

ABOVE: Back cover. My Aim Is True, Elvis Costello, Stiff Records. 1977.

LEFT: Front and back cover. Watching The Detectives, Elvis Costello And The Attractions, Stiff Records. 7in single. 1977.

RIGHT AND BELOW: Inner sleeve. This Year's Model, Elvis Costello And The Attractions, Radar. 12in album. 1978.

CENTRE: Back cover. This Year's Model, Elvis Costello and The Attractions, Radar. 1978.

FAR RIGHT: Front cover. (I Don't Want To Go To) Chelsea, Elvis Costello And The Attractions, Radar. 7in single. 1978.

BOTTOM: Promotional sticker. 127mm x 76mm. 1978.

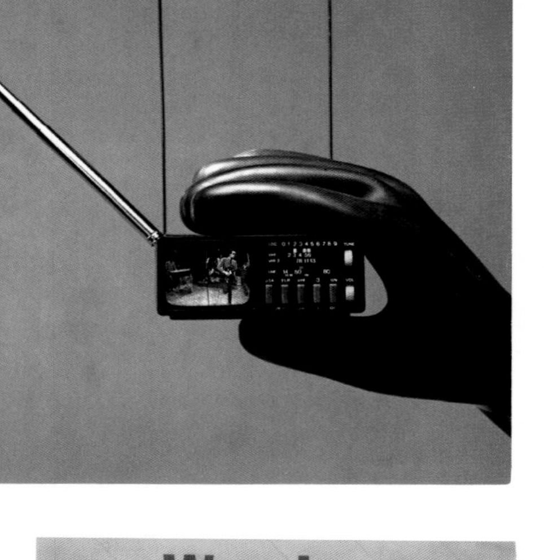

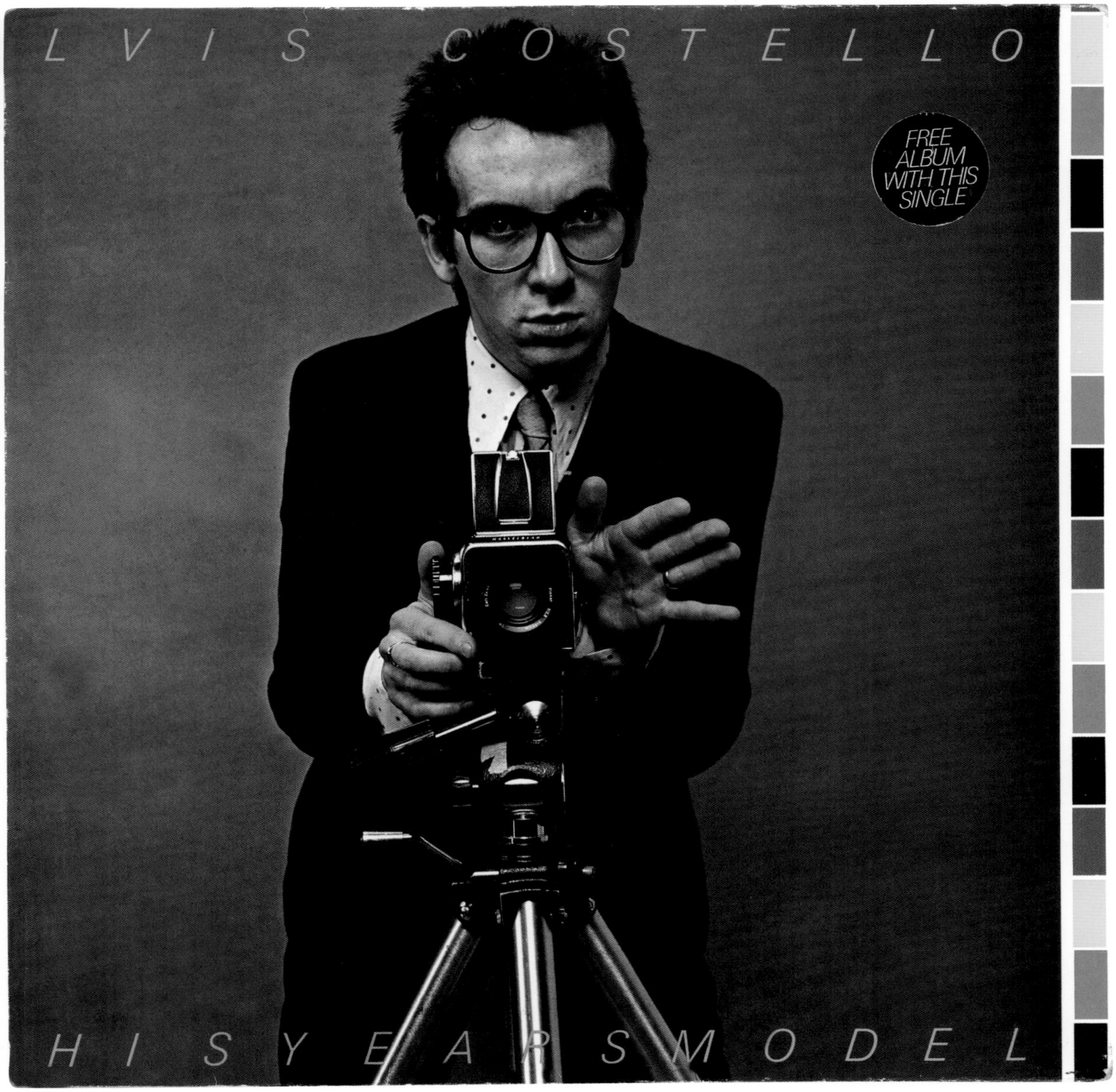

TOP: Front cover. This Year's Model, Elvis Costello And The Attractions, Radar. 12in album. 1978.

LEFT: Advert. This Year's Model, Elvis Costello And The Attractions, Radar. 1978.

LEFT: Poster. Elvis Costello, Stiff tour, with Chris Gabrin. 1500mm x 1000mm. 1977.

ABOVE: Poster. Nick Lowe, Stiff tour, with Chris Gabrin. 1500mm x 1000mm. 1977.

Damned

LEFT: Poster. The Damned. 1500mm x 1000mm. 1977.

ABOVE: Brian Griffin photograph for *NME* relaunch campaign. 1978.

TOP: Artwork. Alphabet for *The NME Book of Modern Music*, IPC. 165mm x 787mm. 1978.

ABOVE AND LEFT: Page layouts and cover. *The NME Book of Modern Music*, IPC. 300mm x 210mm. 1978.

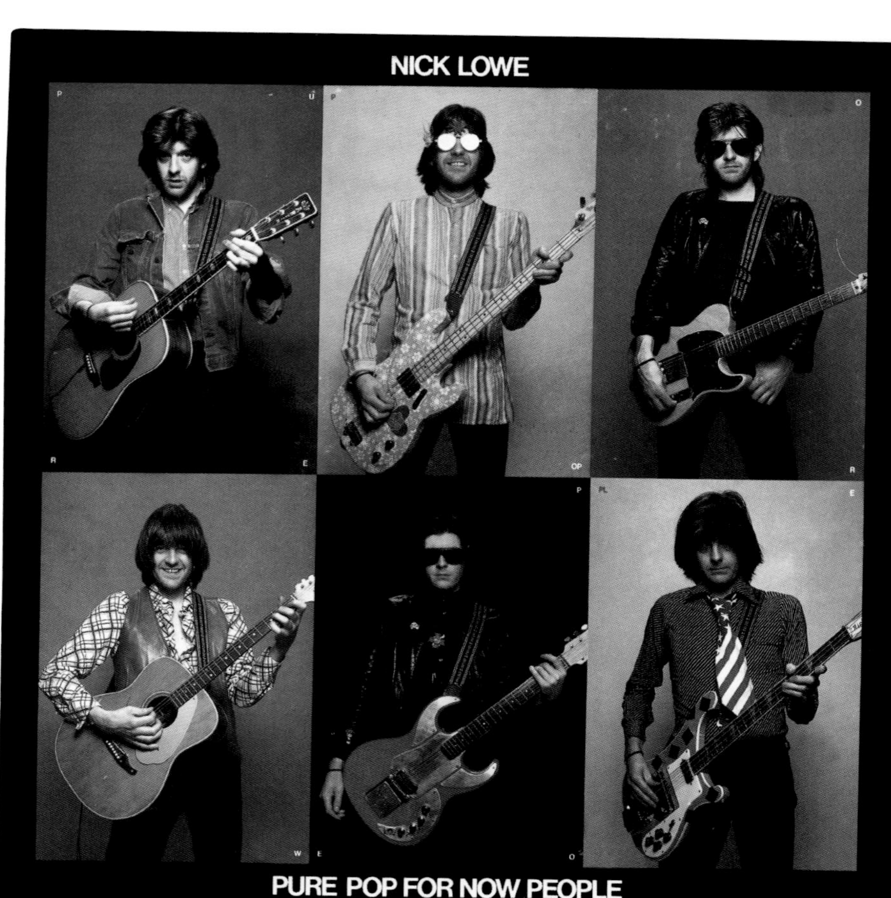

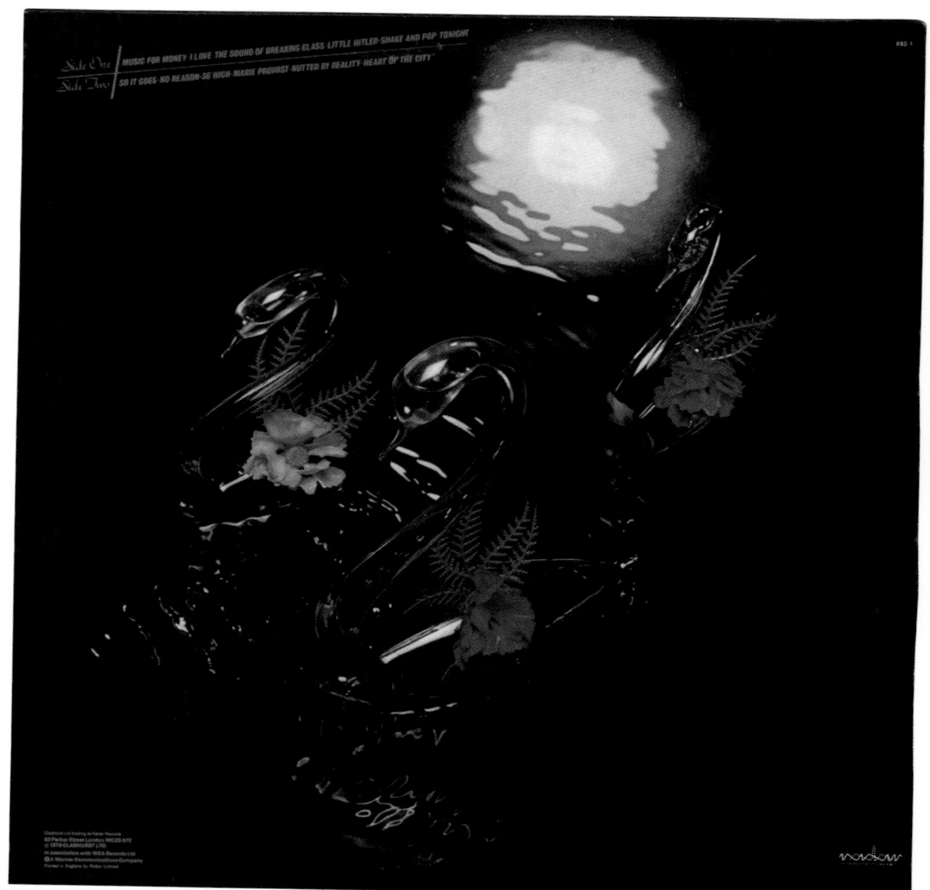

TOP: Little Hitler, Nick Lowe, Radar. 7in single. 1978.

ABOVE: Inner sleeve. Jesus Of Cool, Nick Lowe, Radar. 12in album. 1978.

TOP RIGHT: Front cover. Pure Pop For Now People, Nick Lowe, Columbia Records. 12in album. 1978.

BOTTOM RIGHT: Back cover. Jesus Of Cool, Nick Lowe, Radar. 1978.

ABOVE: Front cover. I Love The Sound Of Breaking Glass, Nick Lowe, Radar. 7in single. 1978.

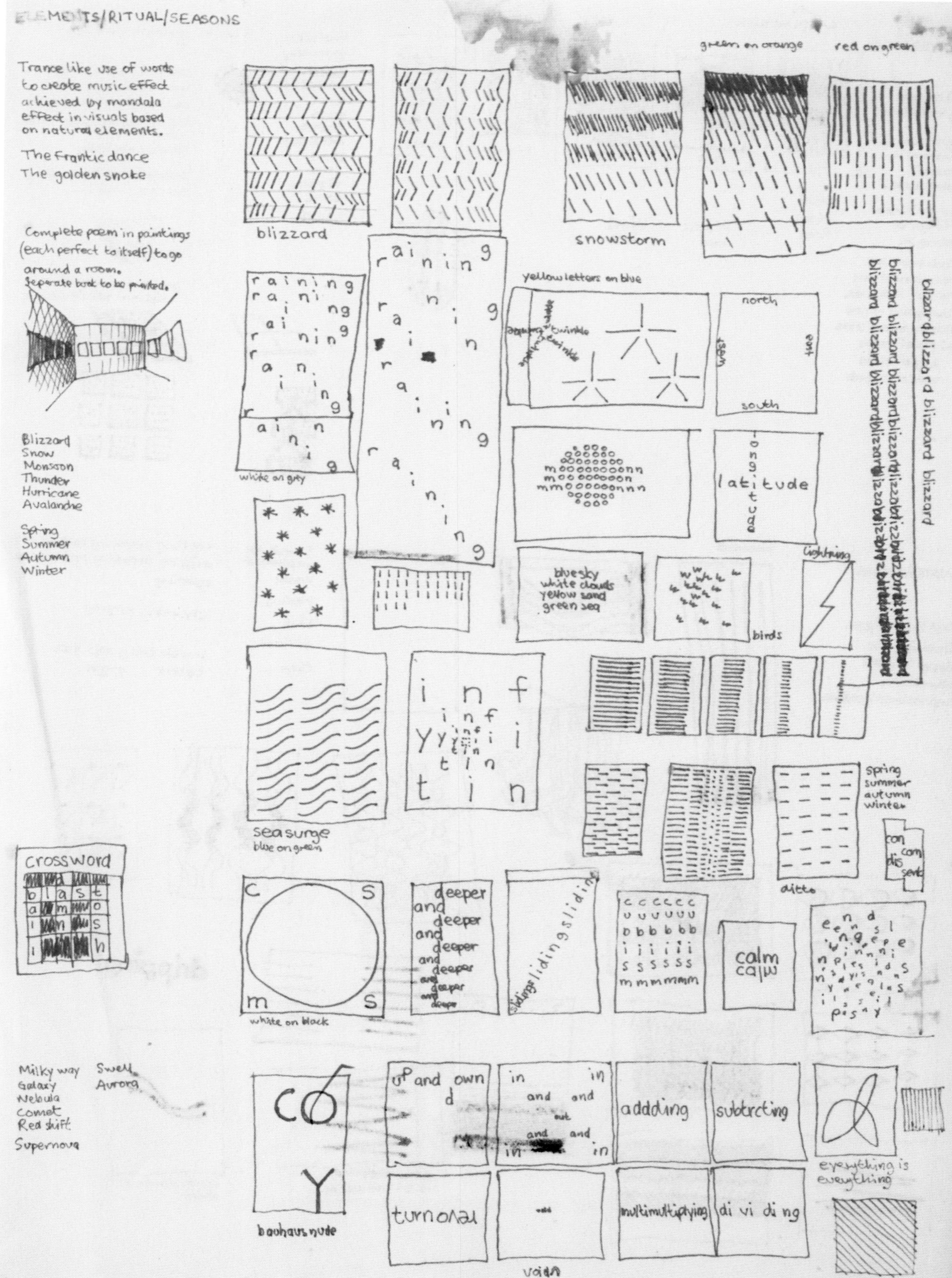
ELEMENTS/RITUAL/SEASONS
Trance like use of words to create music effect achieved by mandala effect in visuals based on natural elements.
The frantic dance
The golden snake
Complete poem in paintings (each perfect to itself) to go around a room.
Separate book to be printed.
Blizzard
Snow
Monsoon
Thunder
Hurricane
Avalanche
Spring
Summer
Autumn
Winter
blizzard
snowstorm
green on orange
red on green
raining
white on grey
yellow letters on blue
twinkle
north
south
latitude
blue sky
white clouds
yellow sand
green sea
birds
lightning
blizzard blizzard blizzard blizzard
sea surge
blue on green
spring
summer
autumn
winter
ditto
Crossword
blast
white on black
and deeper
sliding
calm
Milky way
Galaxy
Nebula
Comet
Red shift
Supernova
Swell
Aurora
bauhaus nude
up and down
in and out
adding
subtracting
everything is everything
turn
multimultiplying
di vi di ng
void

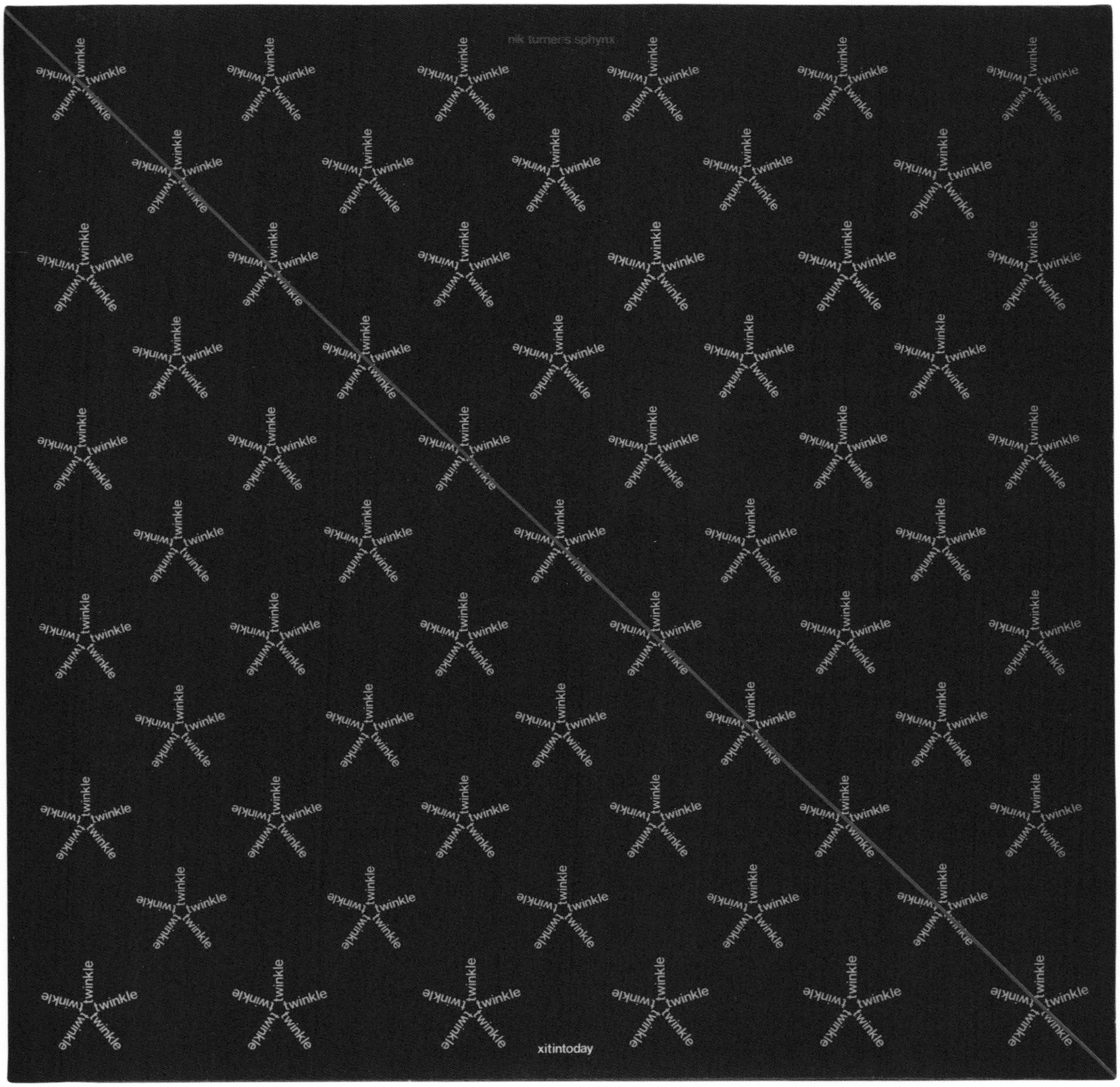

nik turner's sphynx

xitintoday

OPPOSITE PAGE: Working sketches. Concrete poetry exhibition. 1978.

LEFT: Front cover. Xitintoday, Nik Turner's Sphynx, Charisma. 12in album. 1978.

BOTTOM LEFT: Back cover. Xitintoday, Nik Turner's Sphynx, Charisma. 1978.

BOTTOM RIGHT: Xitintoday booklet. 178mm x 178mm. 1978.

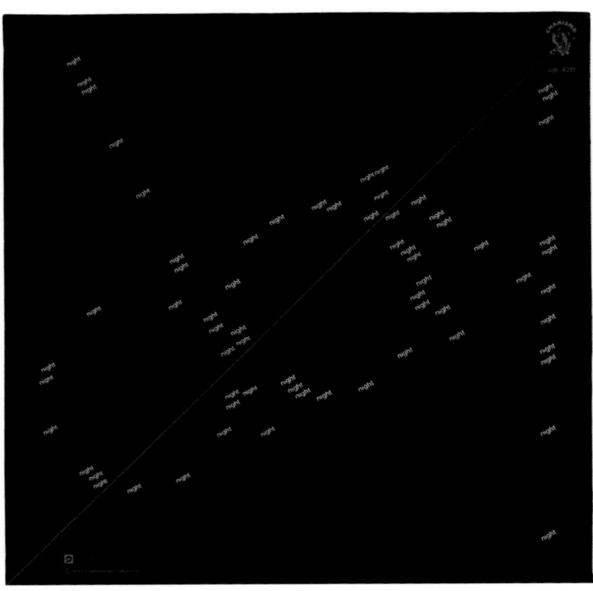

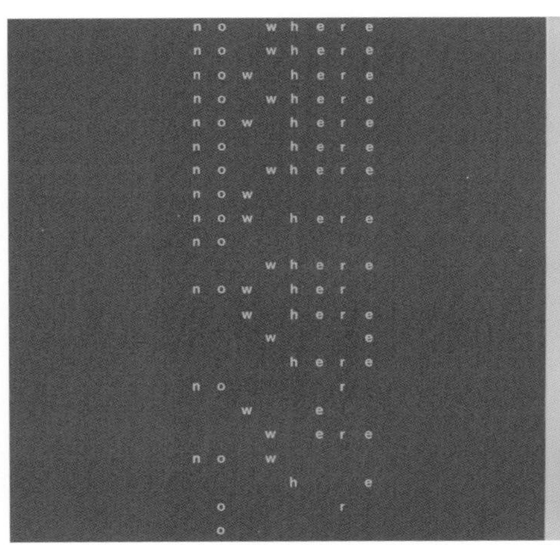

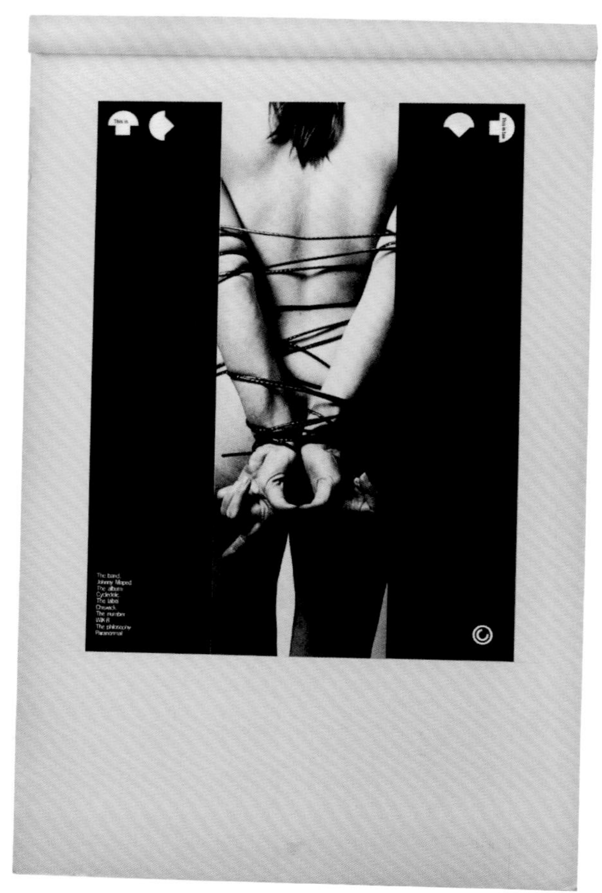

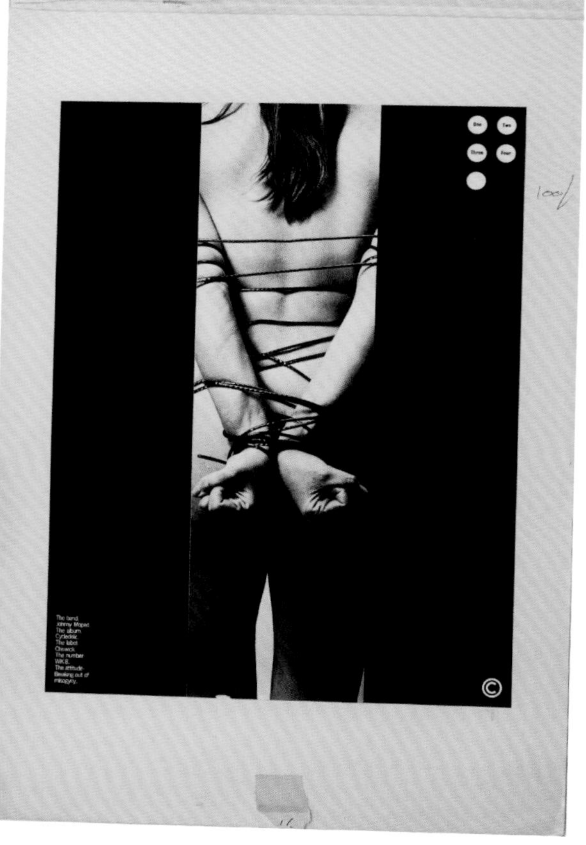

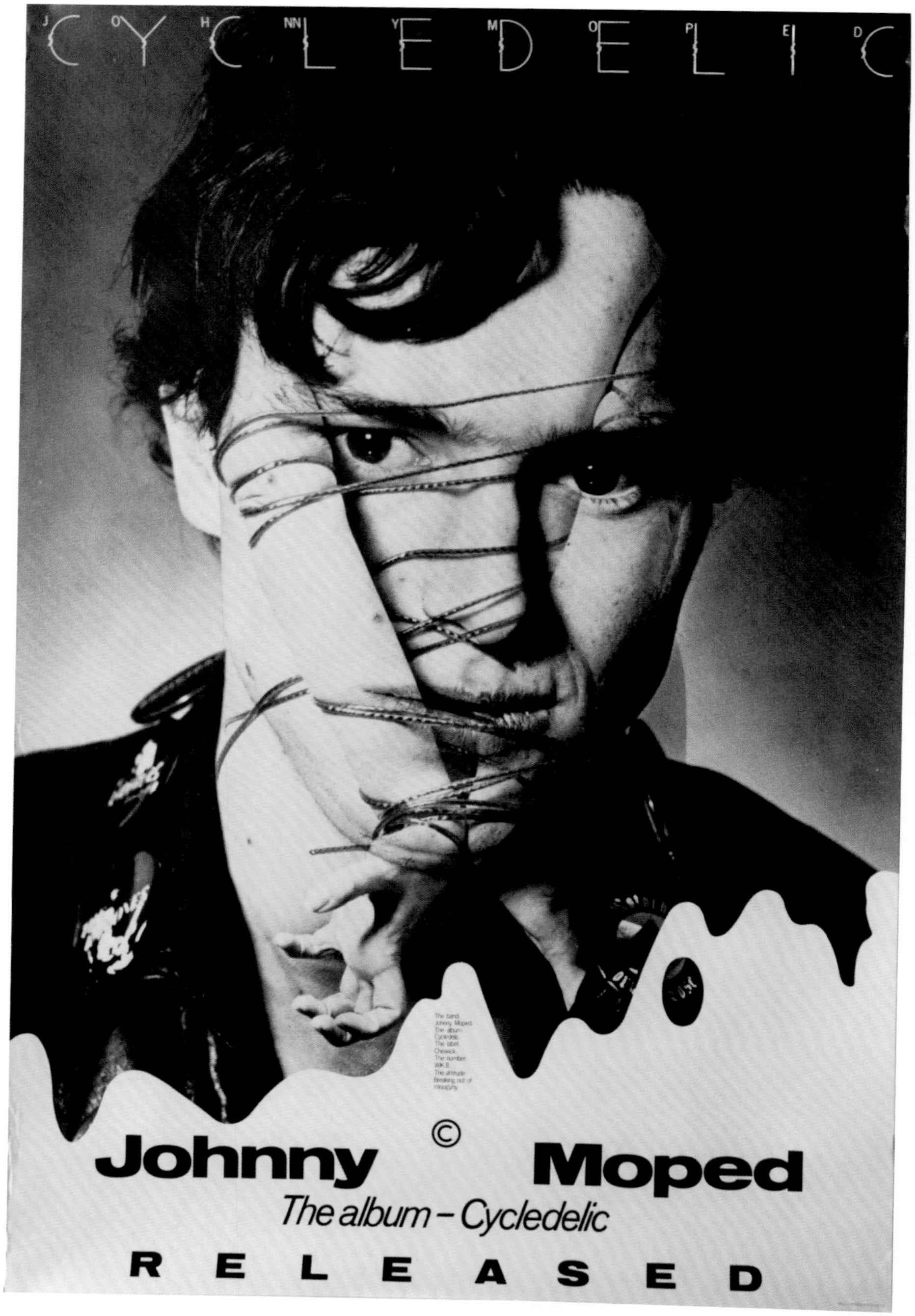

CYCLEDELIC

The band:
Johnny Moped
The album:
Cycledelic
The label:
Chiswick
The number:
WIK 8
The attitude:
Breaking out of
misogyny

©

Johnny Moped

The album – Cycledelic

RELEASED

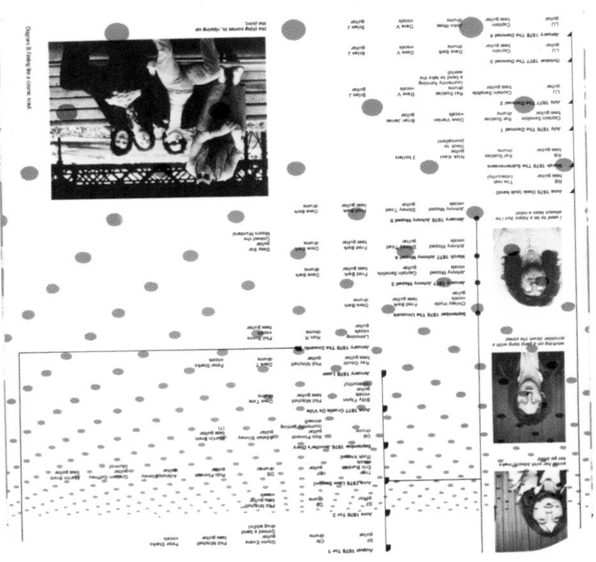

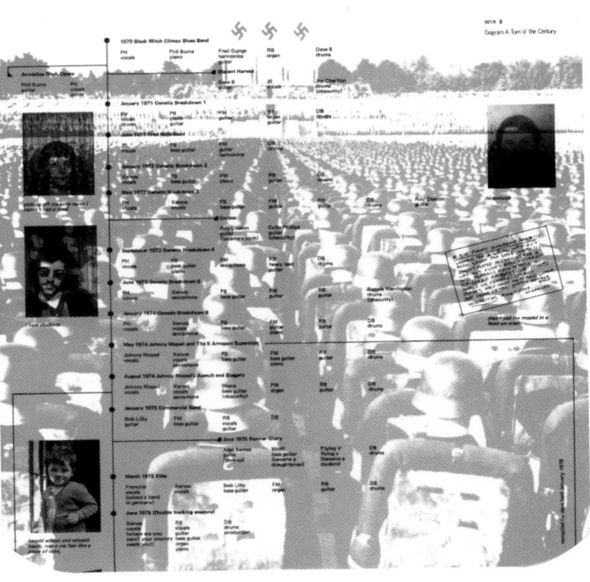

OPPOSITE PAGE
TOP: Artwork. Advert, Cycledelic, Johnny Moped, Chiswick Records. 1978.

BOTTOM: Artwork. Advert, Cycledelic, Johnny Moped, Chiswick Records. 1978.

MIDDLE: Poster. Cycledelic, Johnny Moped, Chiswick Records. 750mm x 500mm. 1978.

THIS PAGE
TOP LEFT: Front cover. Darling, Let's Have Another Baby, Johnny Moped, Chiswick Records. 7in single. 1978.

ABOVE: Back cover. Darling, Let's Have Another Baby, Johnny Moped, Chiswick Records. 1978.

ABOVE LEFT: Front cover. Cycledelic, Johnny Moped, Chiswick Records. 12in single. 1978.

LEFT: Inner sleeve. Cycledelic, Johnny Moped, Chiswick Records. 1978.

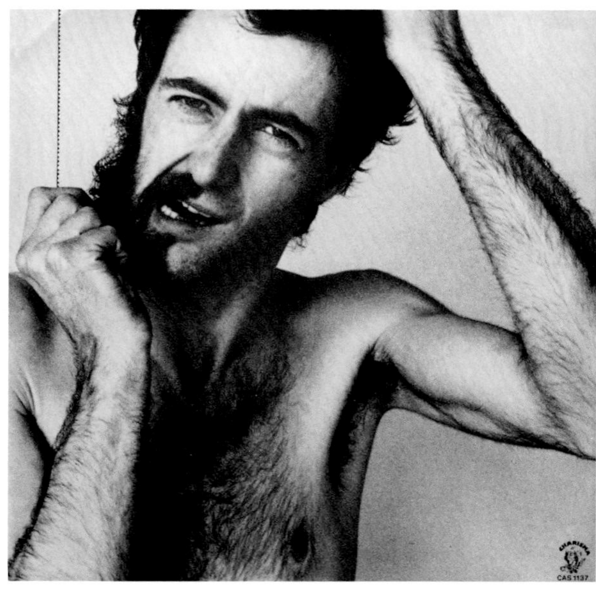

THIS PAGE: Front and back cover. The Future Now, Peter Hammill, Charisma. 12in album. 1978.

OPPOSITE PAGE: Insert. The Future Now, Peter Hammill, Charisma. 1978.

R826 C

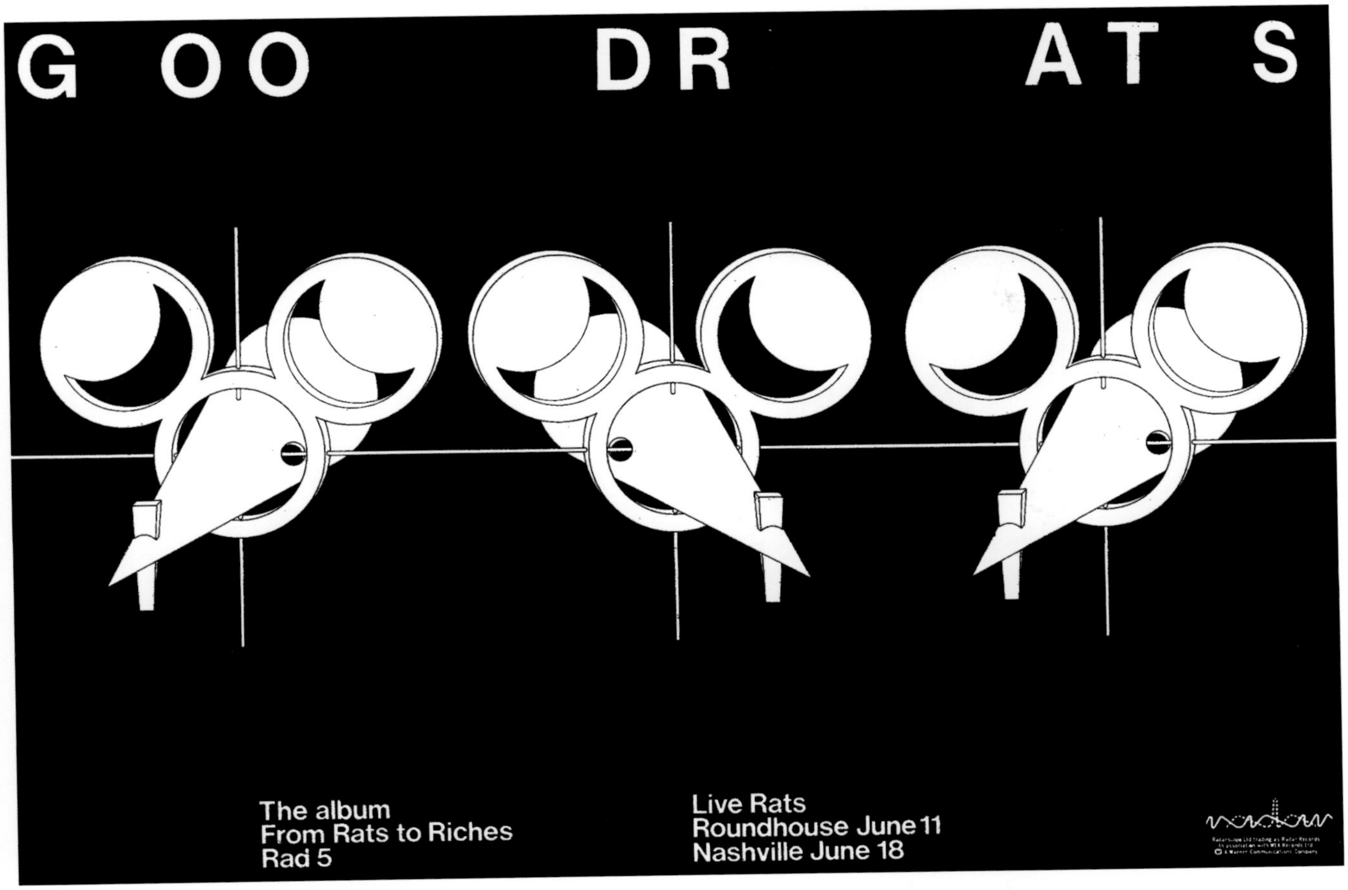

G OO DR AT S

The album
From Rats to Riches
Rad 5

Live Rats
Roundhouse June 11
Nashville June 18

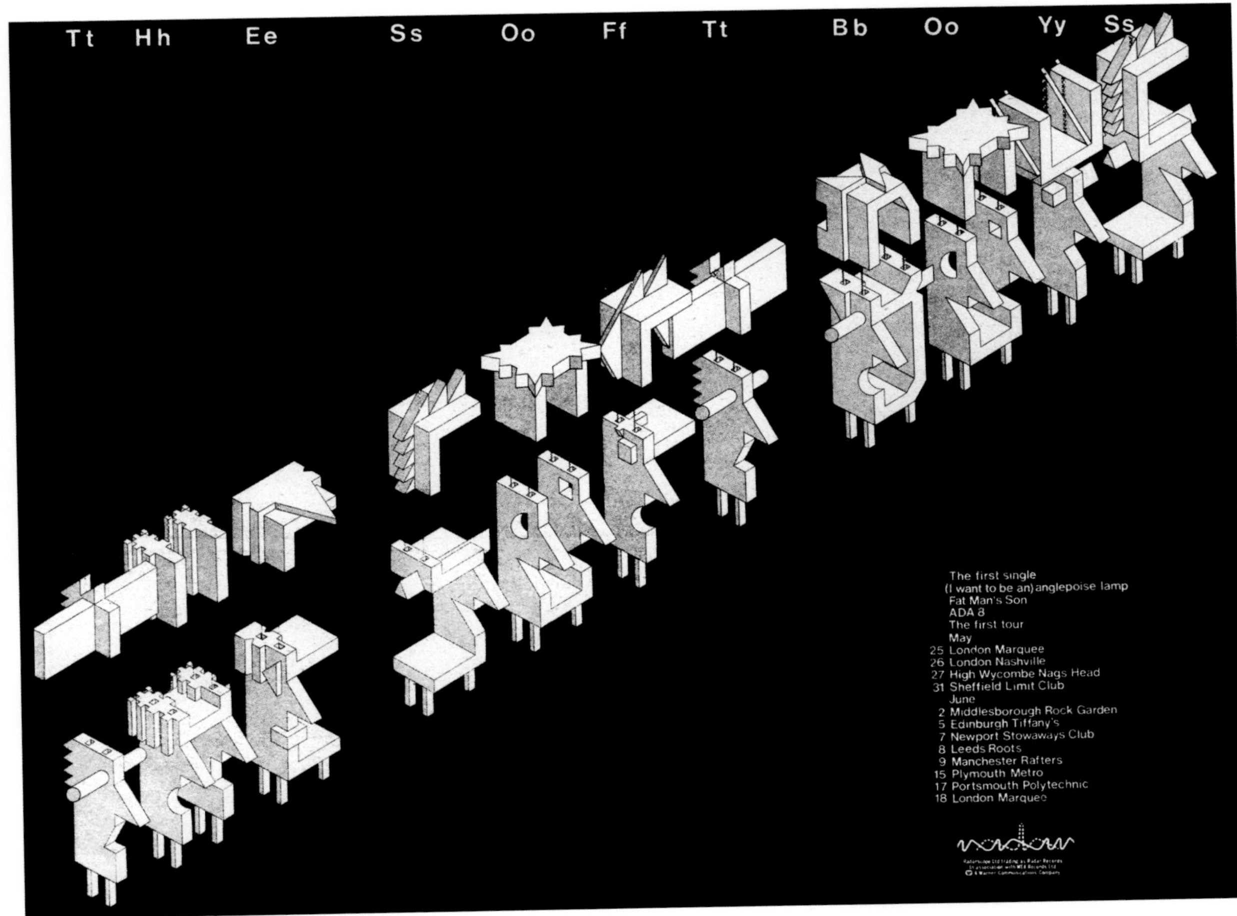

OPPOSITE PAGE: Contact sheet. Chris Gabrin photo shoot, Good Rats. 1978.

TOP: Advert. From Rats to Riches, Good Rats, Radar. 1978.

BOTTOM: Poster. The Soft Boys, Radar. 1978.

D
V
O
E
E
B Stiff

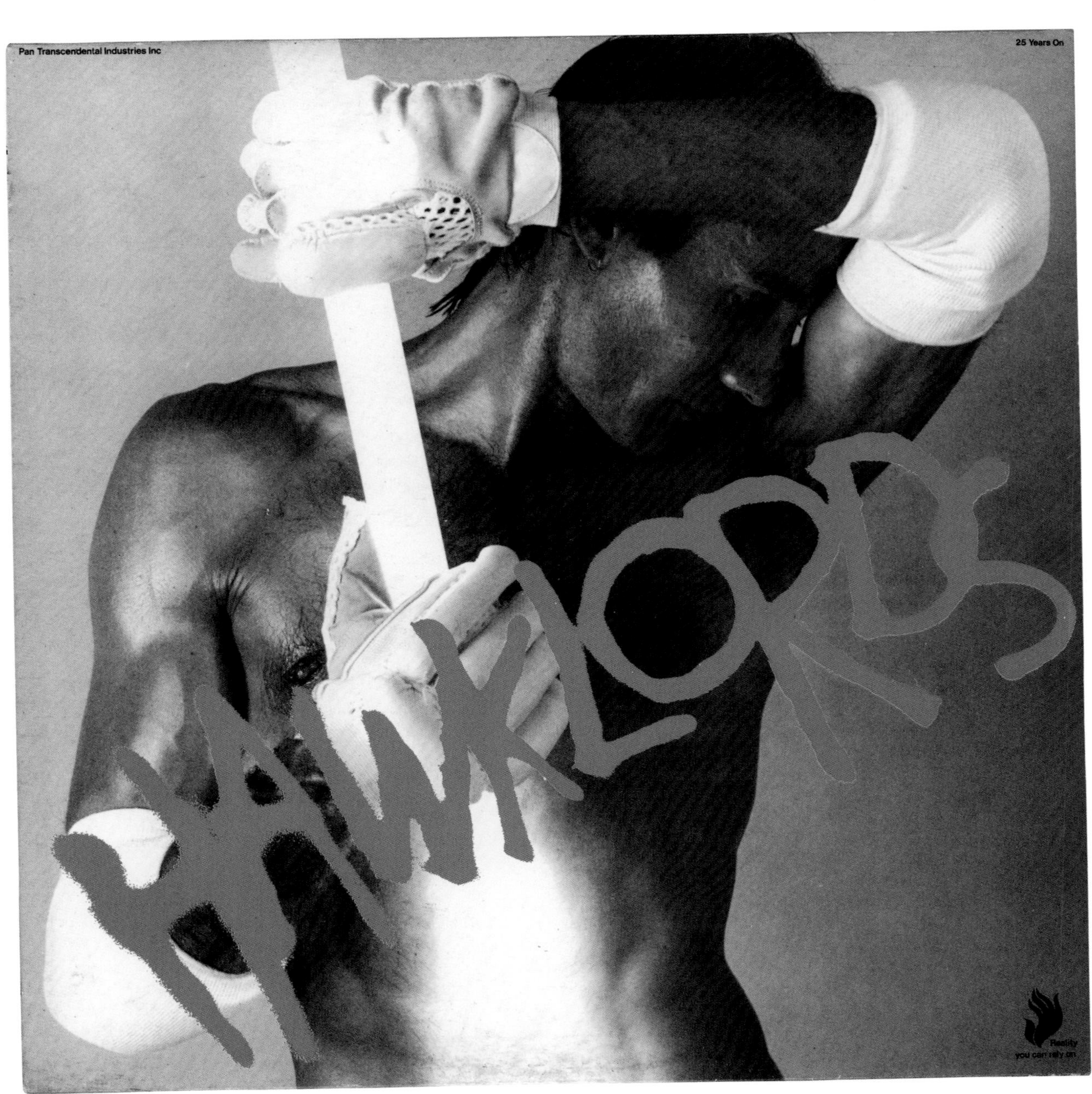

OPPOSITE PAGE: Front cover. B Stiff, Devo, Stiff Records. 12in album. 1978.

THIS PAGE: Front cover. 25 Years On, Hawklords, Charisma. 12in album. 1978.

THIS PAGE AND OPPOSITE: Tour programme. Hawklords. 150mm x 120mm. 1978.

Charisma Records

CDS 4014

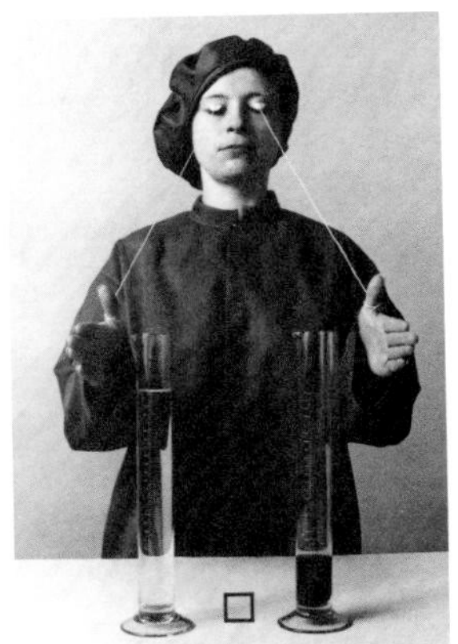

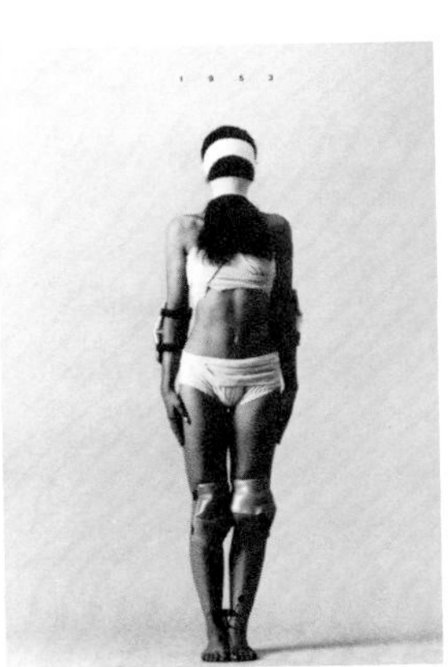

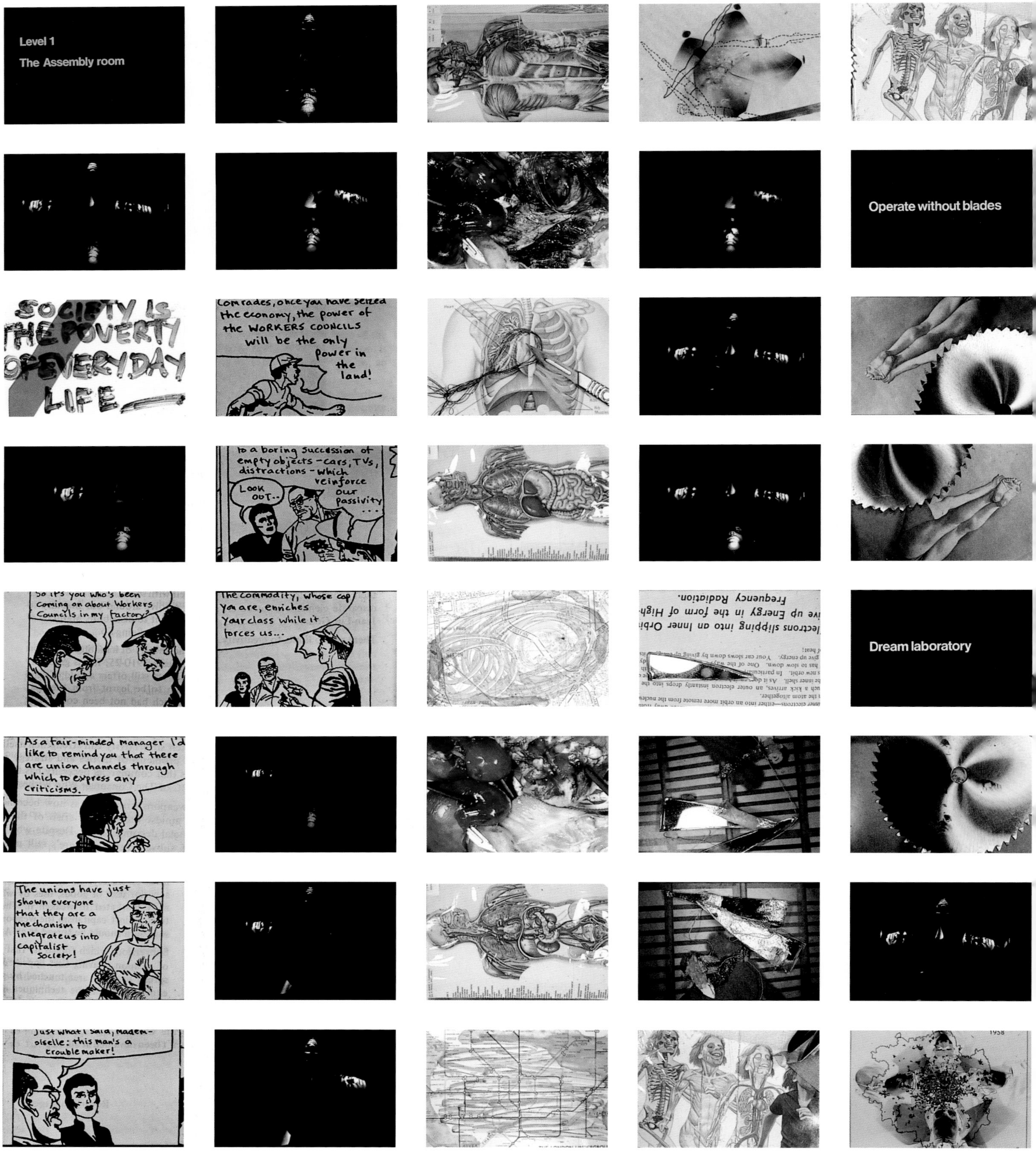

Level 1

The Assembly room

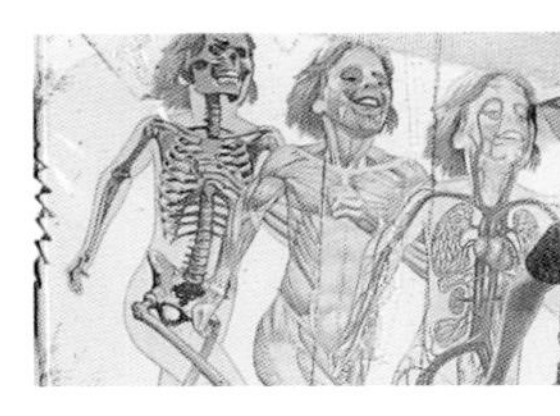

Operate without blades

SOCIETY IS THE POVERTY OF EVERYDAY LIFE

Comrades, once you have seized the economy, the power of the WORKERS COUNCILS will be the only power in the land!

to a boring succession of empty objects – cars, TVs, distractions – which reinforce our passivity...

LOOK OUT..

So it's you who's been coming on about Workers Councils in my factory?

The commodity, whose cap you are, enriches your class while it forces us...

As a fair-minded manager I'd like to remind you that there are union channels through which to express any criticisms.

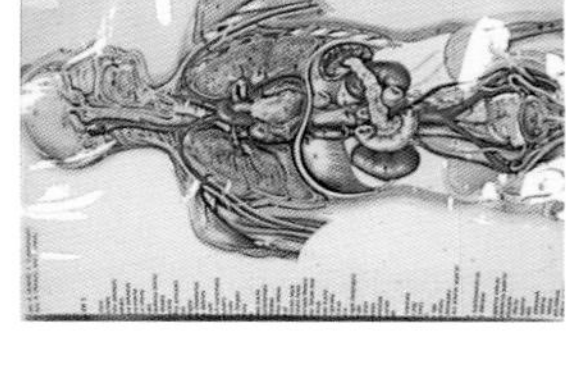

Just what I said, mademoiselle: this man's a trouble maker!

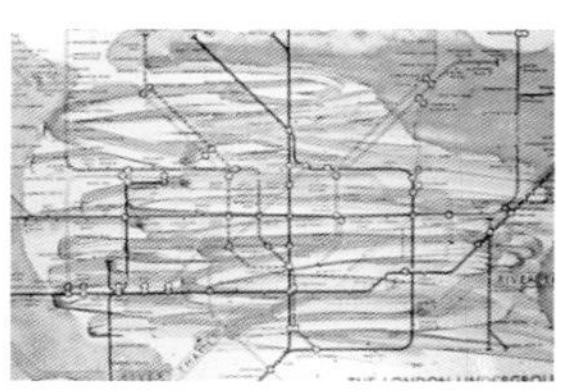

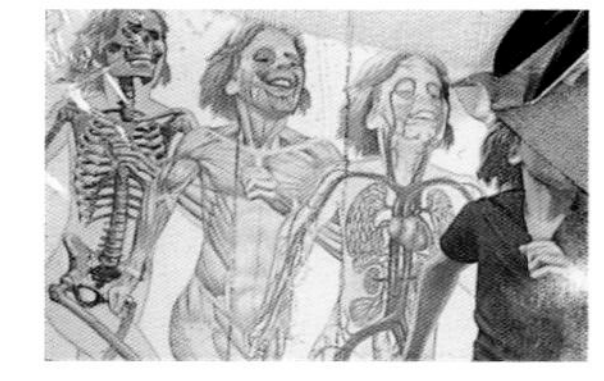

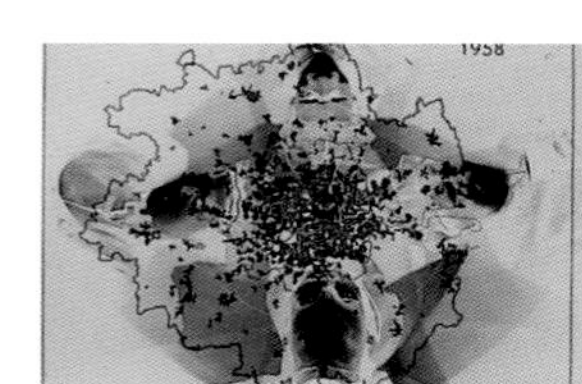

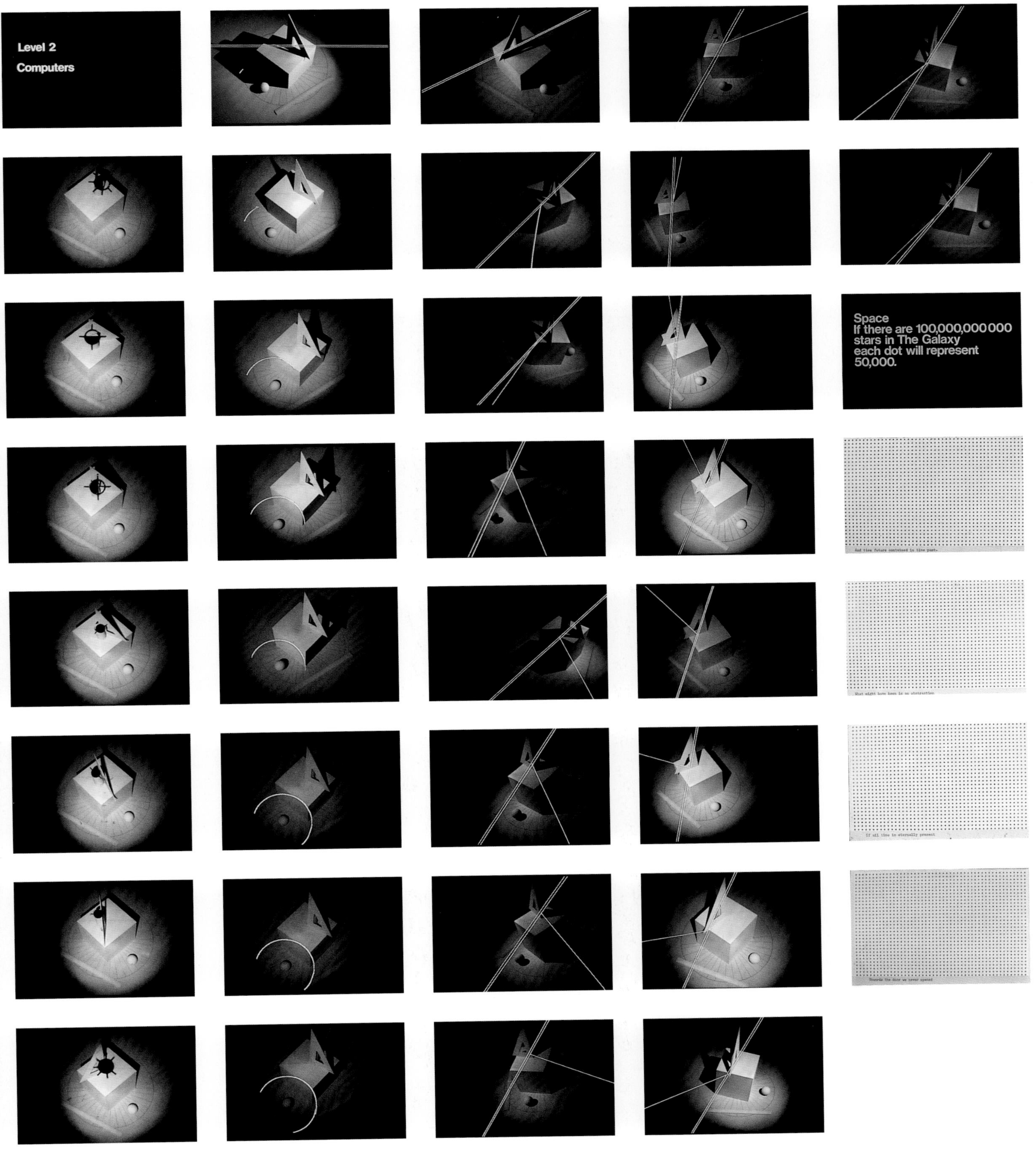

THIS PAGE AND OPPOSITE: Slides 35mm. Hawklords stage show. 1978.

THIS PAGE AND OPPOSITE: Book. © *1978*, Brian Griffin. 297mm x 210mm. 1978.

HAVEN'T THERE!

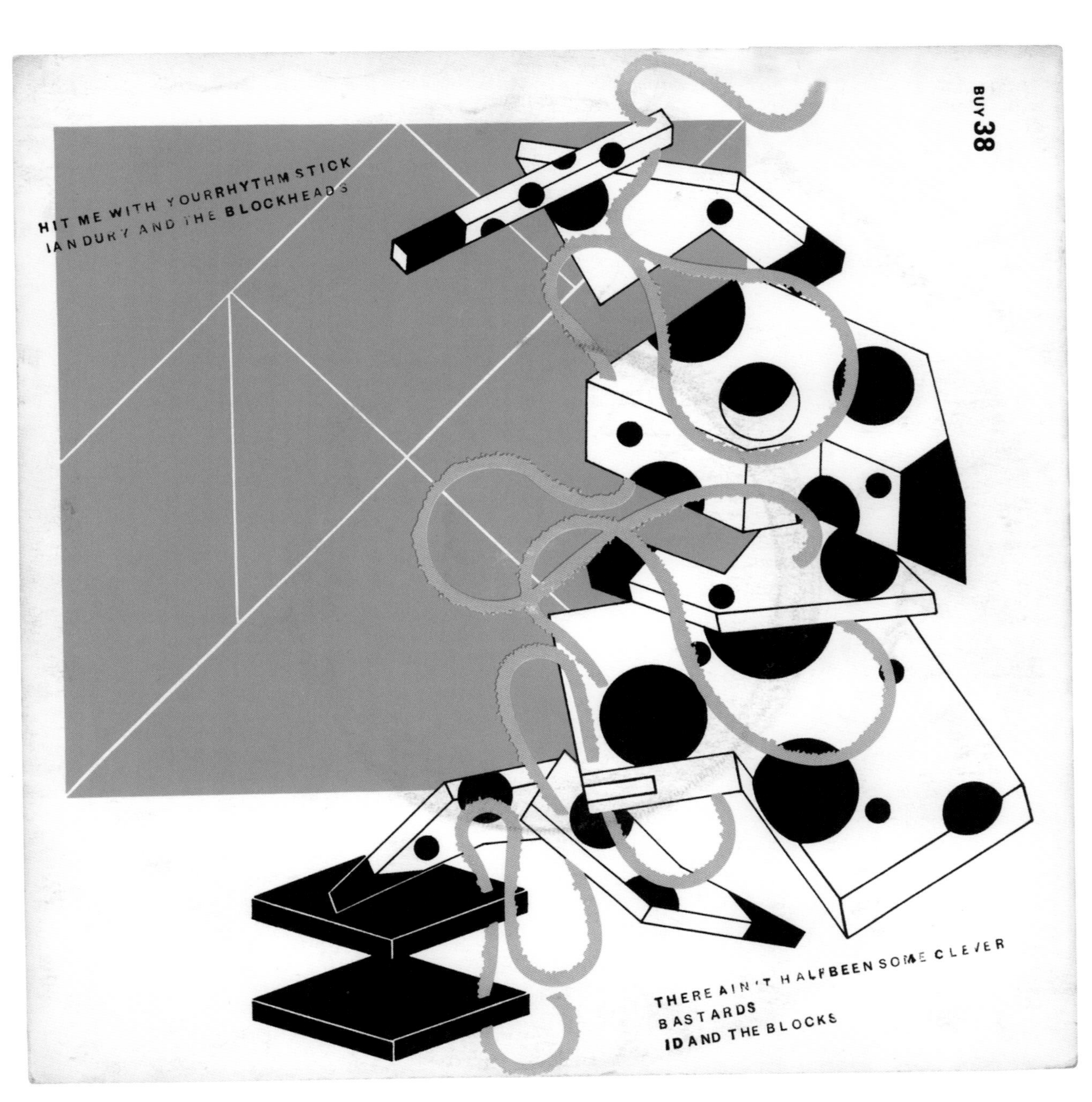

THIS PAGE AND OPPOSITE: Front and back cover. Hit Me With Your Rhythm Stick, Ian Dury & The Blockheads, Stiff Records. 7in single. 1978.

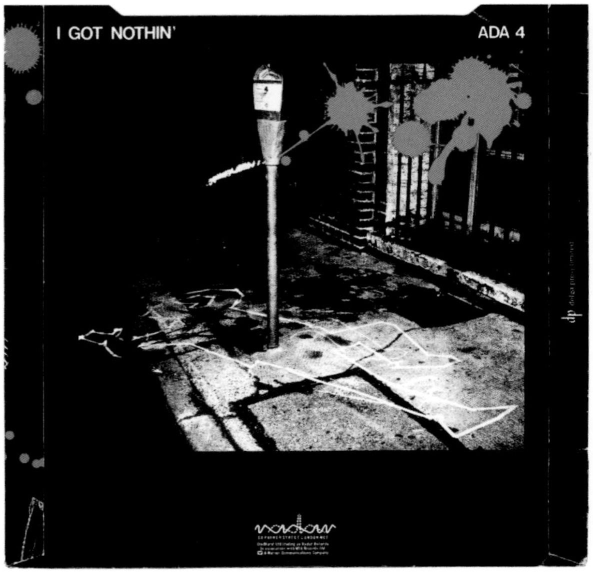

ABOVE: Front cover. Kill City, Iggy Pop & James Williamson, Radar. 7in single. 1978.

RIGHT: Back cover. Kill City, Iggy Pop & James Williamson, Radar. 7in single. 1978.

Labour Of Lust 1979–1981

ABOVE: Barney Bubbles. 1980.

By the late 70s, Barney Bubbles was alive to the creative possibilities exploding out of the art-infused music scene which supplanted punk.

'Post-punk reinvigorated Barney,' affirms Nik Turner. 'He responded to it as an artist just as I did as a musician.'

Although he resolved to investigate areas of creative expression outside the music business routine of record label logo/single sleeve/album cover/music press ad/tour poster, Bubbles was not in a position to abandon this work due to the sketchy financial situation engendered by the tax bill he had avoided since the beginning of the decade.

In February 1979, Bubbles delivered the tour de force campaign for Elvis Costello And The Attractions' Armed Forces, predicated on an album design which communicated Costello's bleak themes of foreboding and global militarism. This was, after all, the year which witnessed the Iran hostage crisis, the sweeping to power of Margaret Thatcher and the Soviet invasion of Afghanistan.

Released by Radar, Armed Forces was also an accomplished work of art direction in which Bubbles harnessed the talents of a team of young creatives.

In a deliberately disorienting move, the front offered a kitsch interpretation of the title: a threatening herd of elephants rendered in the style of David Shepherd, whose comforting wildlife paintings adorned the walls of 70s suburbia.

'Originally Elvis wanted to call it Emotional Fascism, but Barney was totally against that,' explains Jake Riviera. 'So it became Armed Forces. Barney and I often talked about having a symbol of naffness on a really cool record, something like a velvet Elvis Presley painting or The Green Lady (Vladimir Tretchikoff's popular 1950 painting Chinese Girl). When the album title changed I suggested a David Shepherd.'

Bubbles commissioned painter Tom Pogson, for whom he had recently designed a dummy edition of a book of airbrushed depictions of alien life forms and mutant domestic pets. The book – *Smouldering Static* – failed to attract a publisher, though Bubbles was intrigued by Pogson's talents. 'Barney told me exactly what he wanted,' says Pogson in the beer garden of his west London local. 'Although he could have done it himself, he was much more into his intricate graphics at the time. I also painted a pastiche of The Green Lady to appear elsewhere on the sleeve but that wasn't used.'

It was Pogson's understanding that his painting was to appear in 3D. This did not happen, but no matter: the reverse of Armed Forces unleashed a maelstrom of kaleidoscopic images set within the interlocking flaps.

The foundation of this innovation in record packaging was a square of 24.5in x 24.5in card. Set in the centre on the front was Pogson's painting with a sticker in the shape of a grenade advertising the fact that the album included a free EP. In each corner, 6in x 6in panels were cut to enable the flaps to interlock and the back cover to fold in six different ways.

The four off-cuts were used as inserts, featuring on one side a portrait of each band member and on the other a multicoloured chevron and the anti-military statement 'Don't Join'.

Each of the flaps contained at least one individual graphic or design, quoting Mondrian and Jackson Pollock with kinetic and abstract art, geometric patterns and gaudy textile designs (one of the animal prints derived from a pair of Diana Fawcett's knickers).

On the reverse side of the panels were pop illustrations of Maoist militia, tanks, battlefields and US marines, commissioned from French design collective Bazooka.

Led by artists Christian Chapiron and Jean-Louis Dupré (who worked under the pseudonyms Kiki and Loulou Picasso), Bazooka were at the forefront of France's neo-Dada post-punk art movement, producing bandes dessinées inspired by underground and American comics. 'We really admired Barney,' said Kiki Picasso at an east London gallery in 2010. 'He was truly a fabulous artist.'

The feeling was mutual. Bubbles had admired Bazooka's work since obtaining the January 1978 edition of *Libération* which announced their talents to the wider world. 'Barney was so on the money with Bazooka,' says former *NME* editor Neil Spencer, who was close to the designer as the ideas for Armed Forces fell into place. 'I was aware of the bandes dessinées because they were very rock'n'roll and tied into the music press in France. Around the time Armed Forces came out, I started to regularly spotlight Bazooka and the other French artists in the paper.'

The inner sleeve featured band photographs framed by domestic paint colour tabs (part of the home improvement theme which would reach its apotheosis in a few months with Ian Dury & The Blockheads' album Do It Yourself).

One side, headed 'Our place… ', showed a sun-burned Costello slumped face down on a diving board above an aqua blue swimming pool; the reverse ('… Or yours?') lined up the pasty-faced band members outside a charmless British new-build.

The photographers included Gabrin, Chalkie Davies and Brian Griffin, who had been commissioned to shoot a feature on Costello in Los Angeles by Bruce Bernard, features editor of the *Sunday Times Magazine*. 'He was an impossible man,' groans Griffin of the brother of Soho roué Jeffrey Bernard. 'I got over there, holed myself up with the band at The Tropicana, did all the shots, came back and Bruce Bernard rejected the lot, just cancelled the article outright. I never found out what the problem was.'

But Riviera snapped up the images, some of which were used on Armed Forces, while others appeared on single sleeves and the cover of compilation Taking Liberties.

'Armed Forces is when Barney and I really came together,' says Griffin. 'Like him, I was in love with German and Russian art, certainly the expressionist cinema of the 20s in Germany. I don't want to be arrogant but Hawklords had been Barney trying to "do" me, using my approach to stills photography.

'We had an exchange. Barney was very open, and wanted to be educated in things he knew little about. He devoured information constantly and it's still the same with me; we shared an incessant appetite.'

As well as featuring some of Griffin's LA band member portraits on the off-cuts, Bubbles used one on the cover of the free single with Armed Forces. This comprised songs from the performance at Hollywood High School he had attended. Griffin's photographs were placed against a bed of Pollock-esque splashes.

At the centre of the album sleeve, once all was unpacked, was a square on which was spattered in yellow paint the album title and artist credit. To the left, Mondrian-style shapes constructed the profile of a grinning man with a prominent nose – Bubbles himself, secreting away a signature for those dedicated enough to make their way through Armed Forces' visual panoply.

Extraordinarily, this became the front of the US release in a traditional envelope sleeve with Pogson's painting demoted by Columbia Records to the back cover. Some copies of the first US pressing included a DayGlo Bubbles fold-out poster compiling band images with elements from the original design.

In Britain, Armed Forces was trailed by the single Accidents Will Happen, which was packaged in an inside-out cover. The plain white card of the outer betrayed nothing but the title in tiny type on the lip; the interior contained the design – stills from the animated video for the song by computer graphics pioneers Annabel Jankel and Rocky Morton. The sleeve inversion amounted to yet another intervention in the print production process, and was suggested by Bubbles as a visual pun (as if an accident had happened).

His interest in book design fired by involvement in Griffin's *© 1978* and Pogson's *Smouldering Static*, Bubbles designed the 84-page catalogue for Lives, an Arts Council-backed group exhibition staged at the Hayward Gallery in March 1979 and curated by Derek Boshier, who had risen to the fore in the early 60s alongside fellow Royal College Of Art graduates David Hockney, Allen Jones and R.B. Kitaj.

'The premise of Lives was that it would concentrate on artists whose work was based on other people's lives,' says Boshier from his Los Angeles home. 'There was to be no abstract or performance art, nor landscapes and portraiture.'

The show lined up a 22-strong multidisciplinary ensemble, ranging from Boshier contemporaries Hockney, Kitaj and Bruce McLean to illustrators Posy Simmonds, Gerald Scarfe and Fritz Wegner and photographers Brian Duffy, Peter Marlow and Sue Wells.

Bubbles was brought on board by Marco Livingstone, art historian, curator and author of the definitive *Pop Art: A Continuing History*.

'I got the impression that Marco recognised his work from Stiff and elsewhere, but it was the first time I had come across Barney,' says Boshier, who designed a songbook for his former student Joe Strummer's band The Clash the following year. 'I also loved punk graphics, which is why there was a section in the exhibition dedicated to them.'

This was put together by Chris Gabrin as 'Punk'. As 'Ovski' he and Bubbles contributed a 15-minute installation using projections and footage shot for the recent Hawklords project.

'I immediately gathered the extent of his invention and expertise, but what I most remember about Barney was his spirit,' says Boshier. 'He was a very open person. We got on very well together.'

Boshier gave Bubbles a brief with few strictures. 'I took a photograph of each of the artists for the catalogue and told him I wanted those to appear with at least one example of their work. Otherwise I left it totally up to him. I trusted him.'

Bubbles' layout relied on white-out-of-black text boxes for the names of the artists. In the opening end-papers he presented an encircled silhouetted profile turning away from a crass tabloid cutting ('If this is art, I'll have a pint'). The final end-papers revealed the layout and page grids with sections headed 'Your picture', 'Your art piece' and 'Your biography'.

In the place of page numbers, various semaphore signals were positioned in the top right-hand corner of each page; together they communicate no clear message. The cover comprised a section of the full-colour quasi-constructivist exhibition poster and included a tiny representation of a Brian Griffin photograph of a pair of bound hands. Also used on the Johnny Moped single Little Queenie, the hands had been modelled for Griffin the previous year by Simon Callow, then a jobbing actor and now one of Britain's most celebrated thespians.

To this were added photographs from the library of one of the show participants, local paper *Welshpool County Times & Express*.

TOP: Proofs for unused design, East Side Story, Squeeze. 1981.

ABOVE: Promo video. Tempted, Squeeze, A&M. 1981.

OPPOSITE: Barney Bubbles (top, crouching, and bottom, centre). Tempted video shoot. 1981.

Figures were roughly cropped or overlaid with colour panels.

'The Arts Council and I were absolutely delighted,' says Boshier. 'In particular I admired the poster, which we used for the invite to the private view. I didn't receive a credit as curator, but I guess that was in the spirit of his design work.'

Later that year, Boshier worked with Lives participant Brian Duffy on the sleeve for David Bowie's album Lodger, for which he also didn't receive a credit 'simply because I forgot – maybe that was Barney's influence'.

During this period, Bubbles was commissioned by Wise Publications to produce a Bowie songbook. He proposed that the background of each page be a black and white photograph of an individual segment of the Berlin Wall (referencing Heroes, Bowie's 1977 song about lovers meeting at the East/West divide).

Bubbles dispatched photographer Bob Hall to Berlin. 'I spent a week arousing the suspicion of the guards,' says Hall. 'It was hairy at times but I managed it, spending every day moving from one end to the other until the job was done. When I got back to Paul Street, we were really excited and Barney dummied a book consisting of pages of brickwork. Suddenly we got the call that it wasn't going ahead. So that was that.'

Two songbooks designed by Bubbles did make it to publication in 1979. Commissioned by the designer Pearce Marchbank (whom Bubbles had known since the mid-60s and worked alongside at *Friends*) for Omnibus Press, the *John Cooper Clarke Directory* contained the scabrous lyrics of the Mancunian punk poet who had been signed to CBS and toured with Elvis Costello.

Certain techniques in the *Lives* catalogue were utilised; overlapping screens covered the portrait of Cooper Clarke on the back cover, for example, and the notion of using a consistent 'wallpaper' background from the unpublished Bowie project was implemented: the pages in the first half are taken from the 'Cooper' sections of the London telephone directory, and those in the other half from the 'Clarke', with all other details, such as phone numbers and addresses, scratched out.

The influence of the subversive tactics in Bazooka's work for *Libération* and their own magazine *Un Regard Moderne* is also present, particularly in the adverts from a phone directory which appear with amendments, illustrations, portraits and masked-out symbols.

And the shockwave outline of Cooper Clarke's Dylan-esque bouffant hairdo is repeated in extract and detail. 'I still have a copy to hand above my desk to this day,' says Marchbank. 'It's an amazing document.'

Another project for Wise, *The Ian Dury Songbook*, appears to have stretched Bubbles and Diana Fawcett to their limits. Tom Pogson visited the Paul Street studio as it neared completion.

'I guess Barney could never say no,' shrugs Pogson. 'Maybe that was part of his problem. I've never known anybody work as hard. When I arrived that day, there wasn't a visible inch of the studio floor – which was absolutely massive – because it was taken up by all the artwork.'

The Ian Dury Songbook – for which Bubbles used his favourite colours, pink and black – was devised to maintain momentum behind Dury's New Boots And Panties!!, still in the UK charts 16 months after release in the autumn of 1977.

In the pages preceding the album lyrics, Bubbles dedicated a double-page spread to Dury and each of the six Blockheads. The photographs are the same as those which had appeared in Dury's Hanky Pantie programme, and the complementary artwork is radical for the medium of a product targeting pop fans. In terms of texture, palette and execution, however, it is in harmony with Bubbles' design for Hit Me With Your Rhythm Stick; Fawcett was once more required to bring out her John Bull set to print the credits.

Titles supplied by Dury – 'Spectacular Robbery', 'Electrified Floor Plate', 'Mental Radio' – vie with pink masturbatory splashes, candy-stripes, prouns and architectural planes, geometric figures and shapes, bold illustrations and even 50s burlesque star Bettie Page, who is captioned, 'Kitty Ferocity going off something alarming'.

Like Dury, many other former pub-rockers took the opportunity of the late 70s musical boom to reinvent themselves musically and visually. Among these were Graham Parker's backing band The Rumour, who recorded an album for Stiff to which they gave the pre-PC name Frogs Sprouts Clogs And Krauts, after the subject matter of their composition Euro.

For the cover of this March 1979 release, Bubbles proposed a collaboration with Brian Griffin, who was delighted. 'At that time I was working with top editorial people such as Roland Schenk on *Management Today* and Tom Reynolds at the *Sunday Times Magazine*. Barney rivalled them as an absolute professional,' enthuses Griffin. 'I'm not just talking about a talented person here, but super, super, super-intelligence.

'On one of the pillars in the studio at Paul Street, there'd always be a single sheet of paper with all his work written out neatly. Barney was as blind as a bat, so you'd see him peering away at it, ticking things off or adding new jobs.

'At Paul Street there was a drawing board, a filing cabinet and maybe a sofa. He seemed to work 24 hours a day. I can't picture him ever sleeping. You didn't know where his work ended and his life began and you don't know with me either. That's why we fell in brotherly love.'

A mark of Bubbles' respect for Griffin was that he did not art-direct the photographer's shoots or crop his photographs without prior consultation. When Griffin suggested his concept for the front cover of Frogs Sprouts Clogs And Krauts, Bubbles left him alone to realise the project at the Paul Street studio.

'I constructed a sculpture using Charles Woods, one of my models,' says Griffin. 'I bought the flags of all the European Community nations from a place in Tower Bridge and placed them around Charlie, who was holding a soil sampler, as though he had plunged it into the earth and – like the coloured grains of sand I saw in glass phials as a kid on holiday on the Isle of Wight – produced a cross-section of each of the countries.'

To the front cover Bubbles added a heraldic graphic of five spear-points bursting forth from the album title, evoking an aerial display at an official occasion and also the tips of the flag banners.

The arrowheads also zipped away from the song titles on the reverse, where Bubbles enlarged a section of Griffin's photograph, showing the soil sampler in detail. A section of this was again enlarged on one side of the inner sleeve, and the reverse carried yet another enlargement (as well as an enigmatic short story), so that the image was driven to abstraction.

'Barney took my photograph and went into it to reveal the basic dot structure, just like the sampler going into the ground,' says Griffin.

Obliterating the musicians' pub-rock roots (as former members of Brinsley Schwarz, some of The Rumour had known Bubbles for several years), the angular band logo was constructed from straight lines and curves, in a similar fashion to the symbols provided for Griffin's *© 1978*.

Bubbles once again extended his design package to the bespoke record label, on which was placed the new Rumour logo with the text information enlivened by ellipses.

Variants of the graphic of the fly-past of arrows appeared on the posters and sleeves of the singles from the album.

The front of the first, Frozen Years, showed the soberly dressed Woods running on the spot on a snow-covered terrain surrounded

TOP RIGHT: Front and back cover. Accidents Will Happen, Elvis Costello And The Attractions, Radar. 7in single. 1979.

TOP LEFT: Inside. Accidents Will Happen, Elvis Costello And The Attractions, Radar. 1979.

CENTRE: Front cover. What A Waste reissue, Ian Dury & The Blockheads, Stiff Records. 7in single. 1981.

ABOVE: Back cover. What A Waste reissue, Ian Dury & The Blockheads, Stiff Records. 1981.

by tiny versions of the European flags. The reverse again featured the spear-pointed fly-past with an illustration of the five flags created from the repeated profile of a face.

These represented not only the five nations central to the functioning of the EEC, but also the number of members in The Rumour.

And the accompanying music press ads presented close-cropped portraits of each band member, complete with oblique lines and arrows and information appropriate to their astrological signs, echoing the area explored by Bubbles for Hawkwind's members in the early 70s.

For example, that of bassist Andrew Bodnar in the full-page ad in *NME* was captioned: 'Aquarius deals with democratic communication with human beings who look on each other as brothers; its ruler Uranus governs electricity.'

For another *NME* ad a couple of weeks later, Bubbles opted for an illustration of The Rumour logo spiked by the tower of a power plant (similar in execution to the 'vinyl factory' on the back cover of *The Book Of Modern Music* published a couple of months earlier). The five rows etched into the front of the building were repeated in another fly-past, while the tour dates were set in an elongated version of the silhouette from the back of Frozen Years.

The sleeve for the second Frogs single, Emotional Traffic, dispensed with photography in favour of basic shapes.

Traffic-light roundels in red, green and amber indicated the three colours of vinyl in which it was made available. In each, one circle was die-cut to reveal the colour of the vinyl contained within.

The campaign for The Rumour's album included five collect-the-set album posters which together spelt out the album title. On these a telecommunications tower was presented from different perspectives and set against the colours of the French and German flags, with the five arrows swooping around it.

Cropped sections of the 'tower' also appeared in the press ads featuring band member faces, completing the cross-fertilisation of the campaign's main elements.

'I think Barney wanted me to give him something that he hadn't been involved in and then take it over,' says Griffin. 'I didn't care. My image was OK but what he did with it was incredible. Everything he did with my stuff improved upon it.'

While working on the designs for The Rumour, Bubbles accepted another Stiff commission, for the album Save The Wail by R&B group Lew Lewis Reformer. Designer Julian Balme was a recently graduated office junior in Stiff's design department at the time, and recalls Bubbles' utilisation of an enlarged crop of Lewis from the cover of his single Boogie On The Street, released by Stiff three years earlier.

'The cover picture was taken to line, exposing the dot screen and backed by a blue wash,' says Balme, who points out that Bubbles threw in a new label option. 'Barney also redesigned the Stiff logo for the sleeve, simply because none of the current ones fitted the retro feel. It was a throwaway detail that we adored, and, of course, applied to other sleeves afterwards.'

Stiff's absolute priority in the spring of 1979 was the new album from Ian Dury & The Blockheads, Do It Yourself. According to the label's boss Dave Robinson, Bubbles' first option for the sleeve was to produce a handful of variants using wallpaper from the books of 12in x 12in samples then freely obtainable from DIY stores.

'Barney said we should do a few, but my idea was we should do the lot and give each of our licensees around the world their own covers. Some ended with four or five,' says Robinson, who eventually sanctioned 28 variations. 'We released ten in the UK alone. It proved incredibly expensive, so I'm not sure that it costed out too well, but it was worth it. As it happened, the album wasn't up to New Boots And Panties!!, so maybe this is one of those cases where Barney's design was far better than the music.'

Robinson negotiated a deal with wallpaper manufacturer Crown to supply the materials free of charge 'as long as we featured the order number of the particular design. We had no problem with that, because in a way it added something.'

Bubbles was delighted at the opportunity to apply his skills to such a workaday item, and designed the album title and credits in a heavy block font in blue, complete with screw-holes in the lettering. To these he added the ideogram 'Tommy The Talking Toolbox' with the tagline: 'It's… for all the family to enjoy!' The existence of artwork quoting a line from the album's lead track Inbetweenies suggests that Bubbles also contemplated producing variants.

'Barney loved the randomness (of the cover variants) and was always eager to see how one compared with another once the title and track-listing had been added,' says Robinson. 'But it was also a source of frustration. We'd get the albums back from overseas and, despite the instructions, they'd printed the sleeve with a gloss finish rather than matt.'

The back cover contained another visual joke. In Chris Gabrin's photograph, the band members were lined outside a wig shop as their bald roadie (and Dury's bodyguard) Fred 'Spider' Rowe laughed into camera.

This scene was interpreted by Bubbles in an abstract artwork on one side of the inner sleeve. Entitled 'Being Mugs Is Better Than Being Smug', the parking meter, an ornamental shop-front bracket and a puddle in moonlight were all discernible, as was a curious umbrella-like creature.

The other side of the inner was composed of self-timed photographs of the group, engineers and management (literally doing it themselves). On the label, Bubbles reworked the Stiff logo as a paintbrush with the credits appearing inside the brush strokes.

When it came to marketing this priority release, Stiff applied the theme across the board. Street posters were strips of wallpaper pasted to exterior walls, and Crown supplied professional staff who visited music press offices in a series of guerilla raids and wallpapered the newsrooms before journalists arrived at work.

The album's promotional items included actual paint pots carrying the spattered Blockhead logo and Bubbles produced a range of ads based on brush strokes, paint splashes, squiggles and stains, which also appeared on badges, T-shirts and posters.

All this effort achieved merely respectable results; Do It Yourself sold around 200,000 copies. 'There was no single,' says Robinson ruefully. 'At that time Dury insisted they didn't appear on albums, which hurt its commercial prospects.' That summer, during a break in Italy, Dury and the Blockheads recorded a new track to be released as a single, Reasons To Be Cheerful Part 3 (the sleeve of which was designed by Dury's former art-school teacher and friend, Peter Blake).

Meantime, Bubbles also delivered the sleeve for Radar's June 1979 release of Nick Lowe's album Labour Of Lust, festooning it with his favoured graphic stylings of the period. On the front cover, the lanky Lowe, in a red Western shirt, was photographed by Keith Morris apparently toppling over the title lettering.

The project's recurring motif – the body and snapped neck of a guitar arranged as a pop-art hammer and sickle – made its

TOP: Speak & Spell, Depeche Mode, Mute Records. 12in album. 1981.

CENTRE: Turn It Up, Dirty Looks, Stiff Records. 12in album. 1981.

BOTTOM: Me And The Boys, The Inmates, WEA. 7in single. 1981.

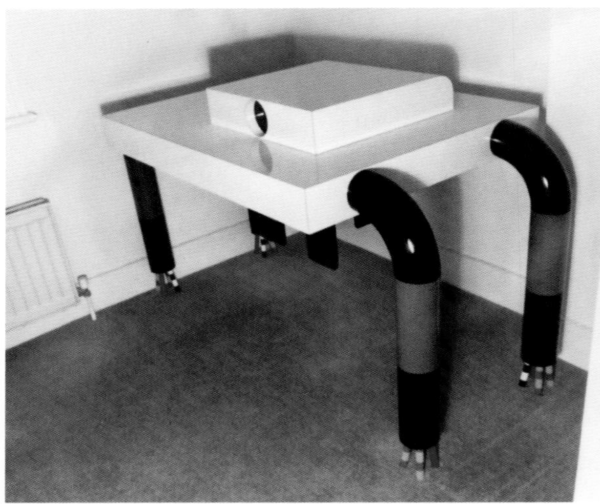

THIS PAGE: The AC/DC Table. Barney Bubbles/Marius Cain. 1981.

first appearance above Lowe's name and was carried through the single sleeves into the advertising campaign.

Although this looks like a graphic, it was in fact a photograph of one of Lowe's smashed bass guitars. On promotional posters this was printed in Soviet yellow on red, with the fly-past arrows from The Rumour designs suggesting both the snapped guitar strings and the blade of the 'sickle'.

On one side of the inner, the spread-legged Lowe mimicked the shape of the broken guitar motif, while the reverse showed the musician's grinning face in close-up, a nod to the cover of Iggy Pop's 1977 album Lust For Life.

'Iggy has some more interestingly etched lines than me, but that was the thinking,' says Lowe. Once again Lowe's face appears on the label, while the other side has the © symbol in pink, a tip of the hat to Griffin's book of the previous year and an ident which Bubbles inserted into artwork elsewhere, notably his designs for Johnny Moped.

'Whatever Barney did was great by me but I particularly loved the sleeves where my face wasn't on them,' says Lowe. 'Cracking Up is fantastic.'

This was the lead single from Labour Of Lust. The cover was a collaged face, consisting of a vivid pink pictogram of one of his assistant Diana Fawcett's surgical gloves on which was placed a black and white smile-shaped crop of a mouth (cut from a photograph of The Rumour's Bob Andrews from one of the recent ads for his group's album).

A reference to the flower-power habit of carrying a smile on a stick, this is both jolly and unsettling, given the song's title. For extra emphasis, Bubbles added a frenzied scrawl over the title in red. On the reverse, the 'Soviet' flag appears, one of its ends curled around a circle.

By the autumn of 1979, cracks appeared in the relationship between Radar and the Riviera/Costello/Lowe camp. Then Andrew Lauder's departure from the label triggered the 'key man' exit clause and, backed by his artists, Riviera prepared to launch his own record company under the provocative banner F-Beat. Bubbles was charged with realising its visual identity.

At the beginning of 1980, F-Beat's first big release was ready to go: Get Happy!!, the new album from Costello And The Attractions, was primed by the singer's involvement in the burgeoning 2 Tone scene. Costello produced The Specials' debut and released the Sam & Dave cover I Can't Stand Up For Falling Down as a single on 2 Tone in the interregnum between Radar and F-Beat.

Taking its title from the 1959 Ella Fitzgerald release, Get Happy!!'s 20 tracks (none lasting more than three-and-a-half minutes) represented Costello's frenzied take on 60s soul and bluebeat. Bubbles' package not only reflected this but also provided another opportunity to play with the printing process.

For the outer sleeve, Bubbles designed deliberate scuff marks, as though Get Happy!! was not a new release but a well-worn favourite from a personal record collection. 'That drove the printers mad,' says a delighted Riviera, who points out that American licensee Columbia removed the marks for fear that US consumers would believe it was second-hand.

Similarly, in the UK the printer initially removed the sleeve wear from the proofs, but Costello's commercial standing won the day and the marks made it to the final design. 'You can only get away with this stuff when you're selling lots of records,' notes Riviera.

For the first edition of this book, the repro house handling the scanning of the sleeves Photoshopped these marks from the back cover, an act which would surely have tickled the designer nearly

three decades after he first caused confusion with this concept.

Stylised to the hilt, Get Happy!! is as loaded a package as the vinyl it contains. Bubbles restricted the palette to overlapping blocks of blue, orange, green and purple, using out-of-register atomic art on the inner and blown-out monochrome band portraits with a repeated oblong shape which appears in outline on the label.

And, in reference to his parlous personal finances, Bubbles mockingly planted his VAT number as the design credit (as did Chalkie Davies for his photography).

Davies' image of Costello on the front achieved a disorienting effect since it was placed vertically, as though the singer were standing up. In fact he had been lying down in a New York street (a reference to the title of the album's lead single and a trick Bubbles had used for the inner sleeve of the Damned's Music For Pleasure, where he directed Chris Gabrin to photograph the band members lying on patterned linoleum and then presented the image horizontally, as if they were standing).

An intriguing graphic appeared in the top right-hand corner of the Get Happy!! front cover (and was inverted on the back): the numeral three placed over three forms and a triangular shape to create a face, possibly Costello or a person wearing 3D glasses to tie in with the overall retro feel.

The Get Happy!! poster insert was a black-and-white illustration of the song titles in silhouetted mid-century modern lampshades. This was sourced from a 1960 advert which appeared in French homewares magazine *Arts Ménagers* for lighting company Rotaflex (the same business whose building logo inspired Bubbles' masthead for *NME*).

For the cassette release, Bubbles produced an entirely different design, with the heads and shoulders from the band portraits centred on two distorted and contrasting orange and purple arrows. The cassette inner presents lavender illustrations of four make-up items captioned 'Made in Korea' (presumably a reference to the cheap production values of the cassette card).

Bubbles ran riot with the Get Happy!! promotional campaign, producing 60in x 40in posters, one in the album's burnt orange which reduced Costello's head to a light-bulb shape (a recurring domestic object in his graphics – the Johnny Moped logo was a line-drawing of a bulb which was also a face).

The sleeve and ads for the hit single High Fidelity created a cybernetic face out of soundwaves, while an ad for another 45 from the album, New Amsterdam, featured graphics of circles and quote marks to render Costello's bespectacled visage peering from behind a beaded curtain.

The beat-style abstract expressionist sleeve for New Amsterdam, meanwhile, carried a credit (of sorts) in tiny type: 'Cover painting "Jazz City Opus 1958" by Sal Forlenza courtesy of The Trustees'.

F-Beat's second 7in release was Splash (A Tear Goes Rolling Down) by former Deaf School member Clive Langer and his band The Boxes. This trailed the album Splash, the orange and black front cover of which featured the musicians in a spiralling scenario in the style of Saul Bass. The photographs were taken by Keith Morris at Putney swimming baths in south-west London, though Langer wasn't happy with Bubbles' first draft. 'I knew of and admired Barney; he had notoriety in punk circles,' says Langer, now best known for his production work for Madness, Dexys Midnight Runners and others. 'But the first idea for the cover just didn't work for me. I got the distinct impression that he wasn't too

ABOVE: The Tree Of Drawers. Barney Bubbles/Marius Cain. 1981.

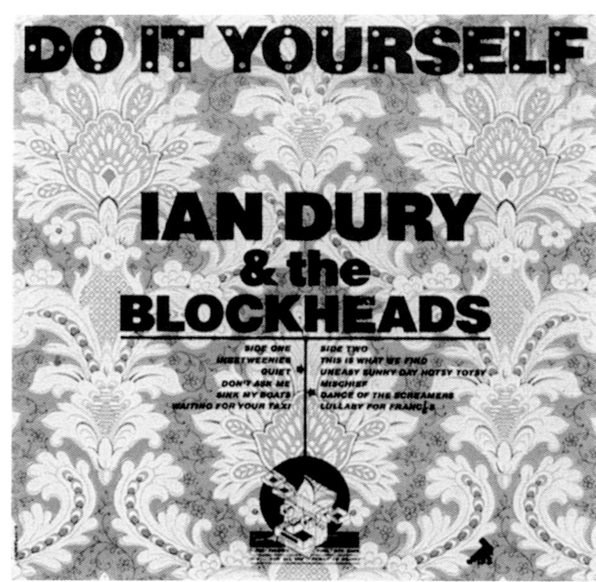

THIS PAGE: Editions (from top: Germany, UK, Germany). Do It Yourself, Ian Dury & The Blockheads, Stiff Records. 12in album. 1979.

pleased, because people rarely rejected what he came up with. On the second go the sleeve looked fantastic – there's a great turquoise variation which came out in Germany.'

Bubbles' advertising campaigns for the single and album played with a variety of visual puns. The music press ads used a close-up of his friend Carol Fawcett's right eye to create a face out of the typographic arrangement, with graphic 'tears' splashing into the shape of a crown.

Double A-side promo copies were sent to retailers wrapped in 12in x 8in posters in which the droplets were stylised as lozenges set against swimming pool blue, and the five-pointed crowns of the album cover were set atop boxes in music press ads for the tour.

Almost simultaneously, Bubbles also applied the Saul Bass treatment to the Bob Hall band photographs which appeared on the monochrome front of the album Passout by Nik Turner's new punk-infused outfit Inner City Unit. 'We thought about calling it UFOnaut or Kunstblitz, but Barney spotted a sign in the Islington Council community offices saying "Inner City Unit", which I thought was perfect,' says Turner.

Meanwhile, the tumultuous activity at F-Beat was to absorb Bubbles for most of 1980, designing many variations of the label logo and singles bags inspired by the decorations on Riviera's jukebox. He also provided letterheads for the record company, its principals Costello, Lowe and Riviera, the music publishing arm and the logo for reissue division Demon.

Bubbles designed bespoke F-Beat variations for the label's releases, including a diamond insignia on purple for Costello's musicians The Attractions, who issued their 'solo' album Mad About The Wrong Boy in the summer of 1980.

The deliberately zany typography, photographic treatment and addition of graphic tics mirrored some aspects of the Get Happy!! design.

And the cover of the album's EP Outline Of A Hairdo appropriated the Keith Morris shot of keyboard player Steve Nieve from the back covers of Get Happy!! and its hit lead single I Can't Stand Up For Falling Down.

On the album's inner Bubbles highlighted letters in the condensed font slogan 'FBEAT WHERE THE ATTRACT!ONS IS' to spell out the record company's west London location – 'FBeat Acton' – and repeated this on the design for the sleeve of the single Single Girl (the cover of which was an illustration of the china dogs on his mother's mantelshelf).

On the back cover Bubbles inserted typograms (where type expresses the meaning of words visually) into the title, with crazed lettering for 'Mad' and 'Wrong' deliberately misspelt. In the accompanying Griffin shot, the musicians gathered around a stepladder turned sideways to represent the first letter of their group's name. The Attractions' album also benefited from the front cover addition of a sticker of a retro profile flagging up the inclusion of Nieve's EP.

At this point, Riviera's wife Antoinette Sales – a fashion illustrator who had created the green 'Riddler suit' worn by Nick Lowe on the back of Pure Pop For Now People – was drafted in to relieve the pressure on Bubbles.

Sales was sent to Paul Street for a crash course in graphics. 'It was an apprenticeship,' she says in a call from her home in Austin, Texas. 'I caught the tube every day for six weeks and as soon as I arrived we'd get going. I loved Barney and we were great friends but, when there was work to be done, you got on with it. He basically instructed me in the mechanics of sleeve design and packaging.'

Sales had previously put together the cover for Costello single Radio Radio and his biggest hit Oliver's Army, and was close to F-Beat's signing Carlene Carter (Nick Lowe's wife and the stepdaughter of Johnny Cash), having designed her stagewear.

'The singles I did for Carlene were very photo-driven,' says Sales, who was also responsible for the cover to the Dave Edmunds album Crawling From The Wreckage. 'I have an aversion to copying anybody else but the choice and arrangement of the typefaces were definitely influenced by Barney.'

She and Bubbles collaborated on the sleeve to Carter's album Musical Shapes, for which he built a wall-mounted sculpture from electrical flex and wire to give the impression of musical notes emanating from the three-legged Dansette he placed on the cover.

'Barney set that up in the dining room of our house in Oxford Road, in Chiswick,' says Sales. 'I designed and set the graphics on the back. Barney taught me how to lay down Letraset and make the placement and spacing impeccable. I had fun with the "N" for Notes, "S" for Selections and "P" for Personnel. In the self-effacing Bubbles tradition, there is no artwork credit.'

On the back of Musical Shapes, Carter lies across a circular rug, which Bubbles had designed to replicate an F-Beat single.

'We'd met this person in the carpet business who could realise anything we came up with,' enthuses Riviera. 'Barney provided the artwork for the F-Beat rug and then started to produce original designs for other people. By that stage he was taking any opportunity he could to create in other media.'

Sales also contributed designs to other F-Beat projects, among them the back cover of Seconds Of Pleasure, the 1980 album by Lowe and Edmunds' band Rockpile. The artwork for the front of this (a painting signed by 'Dag' which made an alarm clock of the second letter of the band's name and has an abstract of a man and woman dancing) was executed while Bubbles took a sabbatical in the latter half of 1980, visiting his partner B. Syme at her home in Melbourne, Australia, where he collaborated with her Melbourne artist friend Laurie Miller on glasswork created by sand-blasting.

During their travels, they visited Singapore and Bali, where Bubbles was inspired to create an artwork of his feet in the shallows on a beach in the style of the *gouaches découpés* (or cut-outs) of Henri Matisse. This became the cover of Desmond Dekker's 1980 album Compass Point, while Australian Aborigine hand-print art inspired the front of the same year's Turn It Up by New York power-pop trio Dirty Looks.

Both designs were for Stiff Records, whose art department was at that stage bolstered by a fresh intake, including Julian Balme's fellow London College of Communications graduate Neville Brody. A lifelong champion of Bubbles, Brody went on to become a graphic design and typographic giant in the 80s following his work at style magazine *The Face* and *The Guardian*. In 2010, he was head of communication art and design at the Royal College Of Art.

A reduction in Bubbles' work at Stiff was in part caused by Ian Dury's departure for Polydor. Bubbles handled the sleeve and advertising campaign for his first album for the major label, Lord Upminster, released in spring 1981. He also produced designs for Dury's erstwhile songwriting partner Chaz Jankel when he launched his own solo career.

At a time when the pop video business was still in its infancy, directing became a new preoccupation for Bubbles as a result of contact with Riviera's friend, the producer Genevieve Terry and her husband, the cameraman John Davey. They had worked on

TOP LEFT: Artwork. Tommy The Talking Toolbox, Do It Yourself, Stiff Records. 1979.

TOP RIGHT: Promotional paint pot. Stiff Records. 1979.

CENTRE: Sticker. Do It Yourself, Stiff Records. 1979.

ABOVE: Label. Do It Yourself, Stiff Records. 1979.

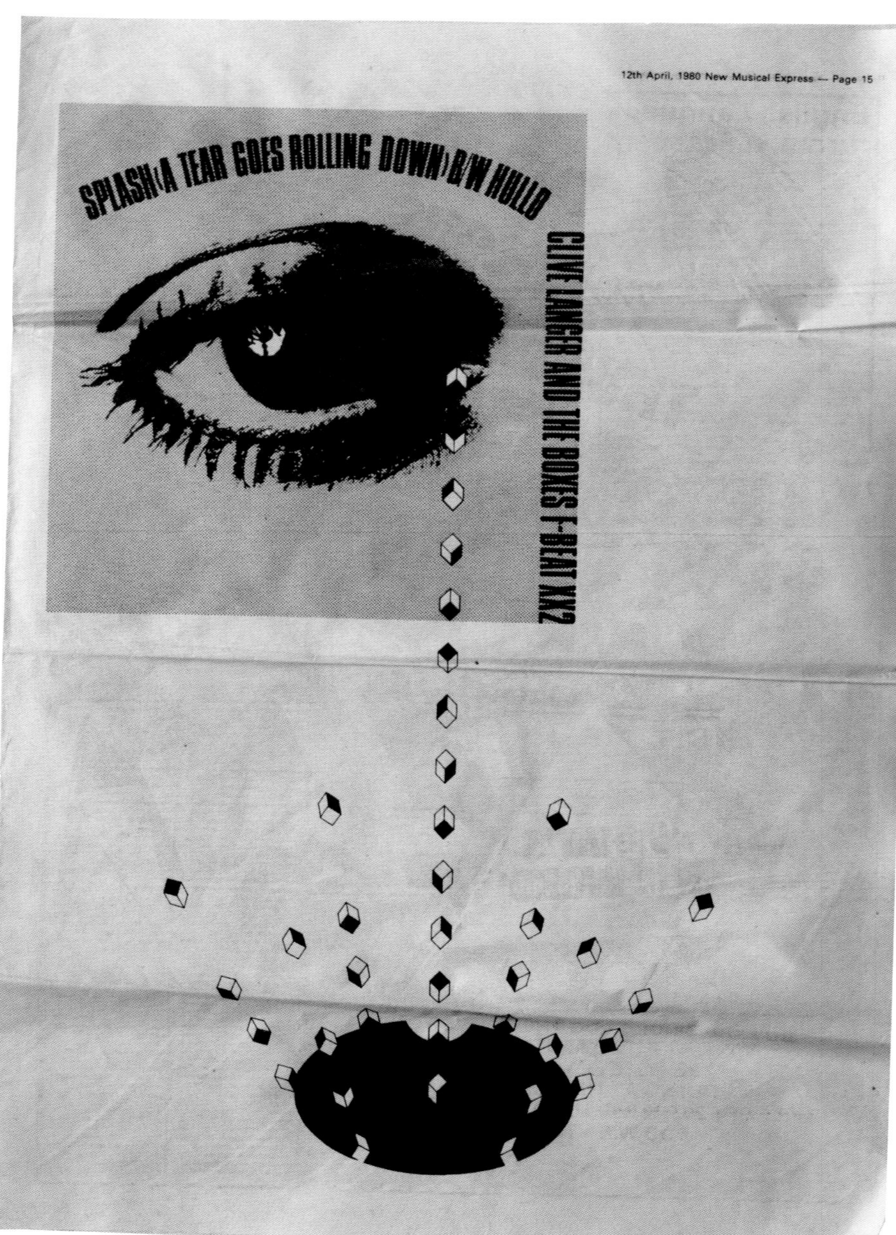

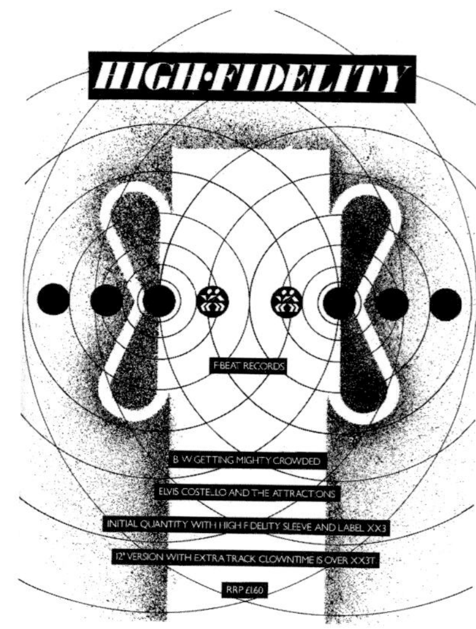

the promo video for Get Happy!! track Possession and on clips by such first-time directors as Bubbles' photographer friends Brian Griffin and Chalkie Davies, so were intrigued by Riviera's suggestion they check out Bubbles.

'I didn't know anything of his work or reputation apart from what he'd done for Jake and Stiff,' says Terry in the lounge of her Exeter home. 'Immediately I found Barney a joy to work with. He was fun, with a unique perspective. In my memory he is forever jumping up and down with glee. I'm not sure whether he ever did this but simple things would make his day complete.'

Their first video with Bubbles at the helm – for Bridge Across The River, a 1981 single by Ensign Records artist Roy Sundholm – set the pattern for future collaboration which would extend to nine more promos, including two each for Costello, Squeeze and former Ace and Squeeze singer Paul Carrack, as well as The Lunatics (Have Taken Over The Asylum) for the Fun Boy Three, Jungle Music by Rico and the epochal Ghost Town for The Specials.

'He fitted in well with musicians because he was so obviously used to being around them,' says Terry. 'When it came to the crew he was most comfortable with the regular team. A couple of times John was unavailable and (cameraman) Dick Pope took over. Then Barney seemed slightly in awe.'

The video for Bridge Across The River was made at AKA studios in London's Farringdon Road, where Bubbles created a 'river', by lining a paddling pool with black bin liners and filling it with water, before directing a single light on to the surface and gently kicking the edge to produce ripples. 'Barney didn't direct in a formal way,' says Davey. 'He sat there and enthused and encouraged, asking about the methods we used and always trying to find a new approach.'

The two Costello promos, for Clubland and New Lace Sleeves (both from new album Trust), were shot over a couple of days on location in a nightclub in Jersey. The intention had only been to make one for Clubland, but Davey produced an amount of unused black and white film in the form of short ends from another project, so Bubbles also directed a noir-ish performance clip of the latter.

'He never wanted too much lighting,' says Davey. 'Barney's thing was: "Why use two lights when one will just about do?"'

It seems that Bubbles was in his element during the editing process. '(Editor) Graham Whitlock was delighted to work with Barney,' says Terry. 'For a start he didn't throw director tantrums, but in many ways this is where the films were made. Here he included reflected lights, interesting cutaways and used shots others might throw away.'

However, his unusual approach for two promos for Squeeze (then managed by Riviera) caused upset with their record company A&M.

'I remember once Barney asked me why the camera assistant was "changing the gate" – making sure there was no grit, dust or fluff which would scratch the film,' says Davey.

'When I explained that to Barney, he said: "But that's great! How can we make it happen so the film is scratched?" He was always interested in degrading the image.'

This became evident during the production of the promos for Squeeze's major hits Is That Love and Tempted. 'They're amazing,' says Davey. 'I looked at them recently and they show he was far ahead of his time.'

At Bubbles' suggestion, Davey used a video – rather than a 16mm – camera for Is That Love. The footage was then played back through a domestic TV which was filmed by Davey on 16mm.

'The camera was locked on to the TV screen and me and my friend David, who did the sound, were crouched behind it randomly playing with the horizontal and vertical holds so that the image would blur or go wild,' explains Davey. 'Barney selected the effects he liked and cut it together with Graham.'

For the final segment, Bubbles directed members of the crew, including Chalkie Davies, to wave mops in front of the band as though they were the heads of excited fans.

The promo was rejected by the record company, which claimed it was not fit for broadcast. 'Initially they refused to pay, but we persuaded them in the end,' says Terry.

A&M was also not happy with the Tempted clip, in which the band was shot against back projections of floating pink elephants. 'He wanted stars and moons, celestial bodies, but I couldn't find them in time,' says Terry. 'When I came up with the elephants Barney was delighted.'

During the shoot, the members of Squeeze toppled over, an accident retained for the end of the promo. Again A&M was dissatisfied and junked the clip, commissioning a straightforward performance from another director.

Bubbles' relationship with A&M was uniformly fraught. The record company also rejected his front cover for Squeeze's East Side Story album, for which he built a set in a stairwell at Paul Street, and squeezed the letters of the band's name against a collage of Bob Hall photographs of neon signs at night. The record company executives insisted on a simple band portrait by Hall.

Terry says Bubbles' promos were his response to the music rather than delivery of mere marketing tools. 'You realise that, as well as looking, Barney was also listening,' she explains. 'There are lots of tight shots and fascinating shapes, all simple but effective, and importantly his videos have beginnings and endings.'

She also believes he was daunted by the rapid progress in video technology at that time. 'Video-editing suites were taking over from cutting rooms, with film footage transferred to tapes,' explains Terry. 'I didn't know much about them and was a bit scared of the cost, but this is how special effects were achieved in other promos so I thought Barney would like to experiment.'

But Bubbles was resistant. 'If anything he was more fearful than me of the cost and the technology,' says Terry. 'He much preferred the hands-on approach of the cutting room and the space it gave for inspiration.'

In May 1981, Bubbles directed the clip for Ghost Town, The Specials' single about Britain's early 80s urban blight. This remains a TV staple depiction of those recessionary times, tracking the low-lit multiracial band driving through the inner city at night.

The band's leader, Jerry Dammers, came up with the central idea, and it was shot on location in the Rotherhithe Tunnel, on the banks of the Thames and in the City Of London.

'Dick Pope's camera was fastened with elastic bungees to the wing mirror and left running,' says Terry. 'At one point the car was driven down the middle of the road to get the centre white lines, but had to swerve and the camera bounced free. Dick nearly fainted with shock but Barney was bouncing up and down. Of course it made for a wonderful sequence.'

With such experiences under his belt, Bubbles investigated longer-form film-making and produced an outline for a film script, Elephant Dollars. According to his handwritten synopsis, this was to be 'a short film featuring rock'n'roll, but incorporating a love of trash movies, pulp sci-fi, bad true romance and the dumbest of humour. Its aesthetic is cheapness, surface flash and hipness'.

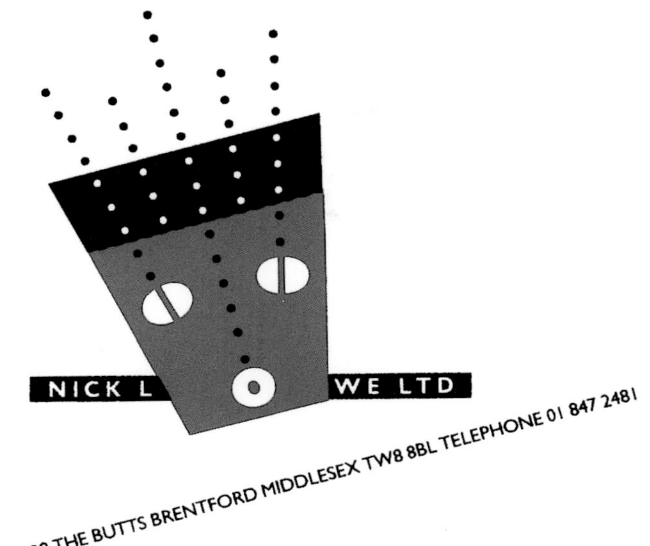

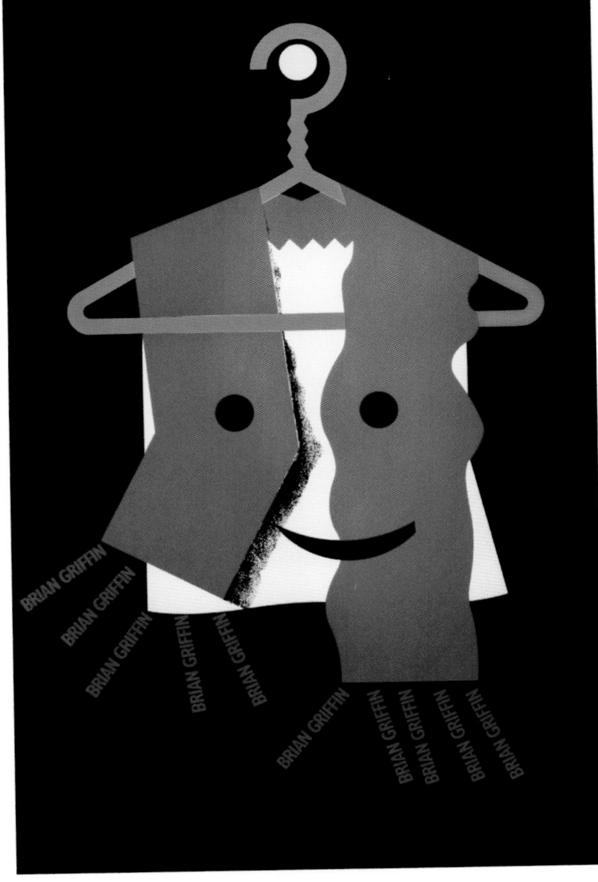

OPPOSITE PAGE
TOP: Advert. Splash (A Tears Goes Rolling Down), Clive Langer & The Boxes. 1980.

BOTTOM LEFT: Advert. Lord Upminster, Ian Dury, Polydor. 1981.

BOTTOM RIGHT: Advert. High Fidelity, Elvis Costello And The Attractions, F-Beat. 1980.

THIS PAGE
TOP: Letterheads. Clockwise from top left: Nick Lowe, Spontaneous Ltd, F-Beat, Elvis Costello.

LEFT: Poster. Photographic exhibition, Brian Griffin. 750mm x 500mm. 1981.

Bubbles' video direction also fed back into his design work; the cover image of Costello's Trust stemmed from a shot of the singer by Chalkie Davies taken during the filming of the promo for New Lace Sleeves.

At one point, the album's name was to be Cats And Dogs, from the lyric to the Costello song Pretty Word: 'Hep cats and dog tags pawing over girly mags…'

Bubbles responded with design sketches which played up the connotations of heavy rainfall; the Attractions as City businessmen with umbrellas and splashes in the form of artwork Bubbles had previously proposed for a private exhibition in 1978. But these ideas were not realised; the replacement title Trust resulted in the new cover.

Within a matter of months, Costello's prodigious work rate necessitated yet another album sleeve design from Bubbles in 1981: Almost Blue.

Recorded in Nashville and consisting largely of versions of country songs, the album demonstrated the artist's growing maturity, which was underlined by a documentary screened as part of ITV's highbrow *South Bank Show* strand and a number of concerts with full orchestra at the Royal Albert Hall.

Bubbles' cover nodded to a similarly mature but contrasting musical genre, paying tribute to the Blue Note label's designs of the late 50s and early 60s, with the 'L' of the second word of the title represented by a torn strip in the artwork.

Australian designer Philip Brophy pointed to the referential invention of the Almost Blue sleeve in a piece for Melbourne magazine *Stuffing* in 1990: 'It is taken almost directly from Frank Burrell's Midnight Blue album on Blue Note,' wrote Brophy.

'Almost Blue was Elvis trying out country & western ballads, so Bubbles' cover makes a point about him attempting another style: the music is "almost" country blues (a second degree version of the real) so the cover is "almost" an original and "almost" the original.'

Such recognition for Bubbles' achievements, from fellow practitioners and in particular the design establishment, was thin on the ground in the early 80s.

'Barney felt that at best he was a commercial artist, which was slightly derogatory,' says Brian Griffin. 'I think he saw me as a much purer artist, not just as a photographer, and didn't feel that his work was valued as highly. Nothing could persuade him that, say, the cover of Cracking Up is on the same level as a great painting.'

This further spurred him into pursuing other avenues. In 1981, Bubbles designed the poster for an exhibition of Brian Griffin's at London's Contrasts Gallery, creating a face from a red scarf, with the photographer's name on the scarf's fringe. 'That was part of my uniform at that time,' says Griffin. 'I always wore that scarf with a beret.'

And his association with Griffin gave rise to another book design. *Power: British Management In Focus* incorporated Griffin's portraits of company directors, politicians, trade union leaders and images of empty business environments with text by Richard Smith and an introduction by British Rail chairman Sir Peter Parker.

Power's frontispiece portrait by Bubbles was intended as the cover, an idea rejected by the publisher (who relented for the paperback issue in 1984). 'Barney made part of my nose and face out of the numerals 71,' says Griffin. 'He thought that was when I started as a professional photographer; in fact it was the following year. The figure next to me, pointing to the future, is supposed to be my boss telling me to get out there and start working.'

In the late summer of 1981, Griffin brought his friend a commission from fledgling independent label Mute for the debut album by electro quartet Depeche Mode. 'I got on with those guys and (Mute's owner) Daniel Miller because I was really into Krautrock,' says Griffin, whose post-nuclear image of a radioactive swan adorned the front cover.

Bubbles took the opportunity to insert potent symbols into his design; the label copy and album logo is represented by a crown, while the credits and song titles are laid out on the back in the form of a royal chess piece.

However, the detectable disengagement in the sleeve was due not just to Bubbles' lack of feel for the music but also his development of a new interest – furniture design.

In the early 80s the post-modern spirit in industrial design became associated with the work of Memphis, the Italian furniture and product design collective whose geometric approach used brightly coloured plastic laminates laden with kitsch 50s references. Yet Memphis held its first exhibition in September 1981, by which time Bubbles had designed and realised a number of pieces in a similarly exuberant style.

An employee of Riviera's – Sebastian Cain – had put Bubbles in touch with his brother, Marius, a trained and highly skilled cabinet-maker. Then in his early 20s, Marius Cain was as undaunted as Bubbles by the professional strictures of traditional furniture-making.

'Barney showed me very neat drawings, on spotless pieces of paper,' says Cain, speaking in his garden in Twickenham. 'We talked it through and he'd check in at my workshop to see how things were going. There was no hassle on delivery. Barney just wanted each piece as nicely made as possible.'

The first commissions came from Riviera, and each had a title: the Flying Trowel desk was suitably sharp-pointed and triangular, held up by a column in the shape of a precarious pile of books; the Turbo Chair tilted backward as if to accommodate acceleration; and the Odeon Cocktail Cabinet (in red and gold flecked 50s Formica) suggested a face with a wavy-lined top trim for hair.

News of Bubbles' designs travelled around Riviera's business contacts. Music publisher Peter Barnes (whose clients included Elvis Costello, Pink Floyd and The Damned) commissioned a white Formica desk which came to be known as The AC/DC Table.

Bubbles designed a matching stool in the shape of a plug which inserted into the top. The table legs resembled electrical flexes, resting on three-pointed feet painted in the colours of neutral, earth and live wires.

This venture – collected under the brand name Editions Riviera – soon attracted the attention of *The Face*, which used the new furniture as the basis for Barney Bubbles' only published interview, in its November 1981 issue.

Declining to be photographed, Bubbles contributed an abstract self-portrait he had created as a gift for B. Syme's mother. The four-page feature, written by Dave Fudger and laid out by Neville Brody, provided a thorough career overview.

Bubbles – who by this time had moved from a residence in Hammersmith, west London, to a large house he had bought in the inner-city area Islington – made clear his feelings of disillusionment. 'I find it's a big racket,' he said of the business of record sleeve design. 'I think everybody should own up, first of all they're doing it for the money and the art definitely comes second.'

Positivity was reserved for young sleeve designers. 'They're so creative – the kids that do the sleeves – it makes me feel staid and boring, and I think: "I've got to get out. It's time for me to go",' he said.

Nowhere is Bubbles' disenchantment with the pop process more clearly expressed than in his designs for Stiff's 1981 Ian Dury releases: the album Jukebox Dury and the companion reissue of the single What A Waste.

Since the publication of Will Birch's 2010 biography, *Ian Dury: The Definitive Biography*, and the simultaneous release Andy Serkis-starring biopic *Sex & Drugs & Rock & Roll*, it is now generally accepted that fame and fortune brought out the ugly side of Dury's damaged personality.

The designer was one of the few who confronted the performer about his often abusive and arrogant behaviour. 'Barney Bubbles told me a few straighteners towards the end of his life,' said Dury in 1999. 'Barney told me: "You were a horrible piece of work in those days Ian." I said: "Barney, I didn't want to be".'

The designer also communicated his views with bleak treatments of the same Chris Gabrin photograph for Dury's compilation and reissued single.

The warmth and affection of the New Boots and Panties!! era was replaced by stark contrasts centring on the bleached-out image of Dury as a Frankenstein's monster of his own creation.

The razor-blade earring which had jauntily swung from Dury's ear was no longer decoration. The negative space became a graphic for Dury's mouth on the back of What A Waste (signalling his increasingly sharp tongue), and on the front was a forthright representation of its use for chopping out lines of cocaine and creatively lobotomising the artist.

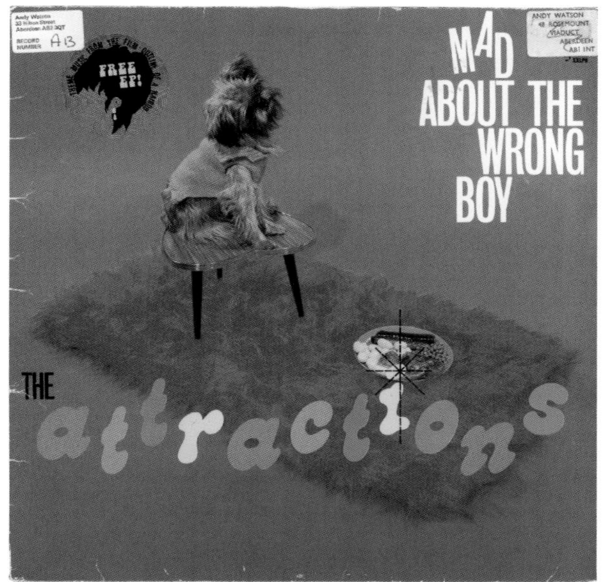

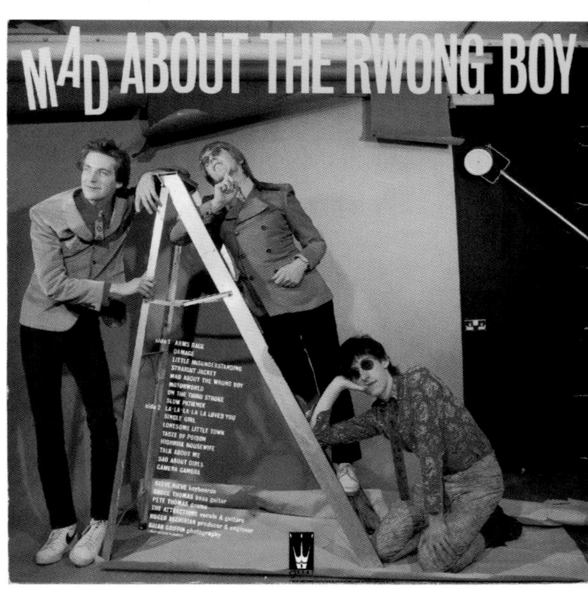

OPPOSITE: Music press advert. Armed Forces, Elvis Costello And The Attractions, Radar. 1979.

TOP: Front cover. Mad About The Wrong Boy, The Attractions, F-Beat. 12in album. 1981.

BOTTOM: Back cover. Mad About The Wrong Boy, The Attractions, F-Beat. 1981.

THIS PAGE: Front cover. Armed Forces, Elvis Costello And The Attractions, Radar. 12in album. 1979.

PAINTING: Tom Pogson.

OPPOSITE: Back cover variations. Armed Forces, Elvis Costello And The Attractions, Radar. 1979.

ARTWORK: Bazooka.

OPPOSITE
TOP: Inner. Armed Forces, Elvis Costello And The Attractions, Radar. 1979.

BOTTOM: Card inserts. Armed Forces, Elvis Costello And The Attractions, Radar. 150mm x 150mm. 1979.

THIS PAGE
LEFT (TOP AND BOTTOM): Inner sleeve. Armed Forces, Elvis Costello And The Attractions, Radar. 1979.

ABOVE (TOP AND BOTTOM): Front and back cover. Live At Hollywood High, Elvis Costello And The Attractions, Radar. 1979.

THIS PAGE AND OPPOSITE: Artwork. Advert, Armed Forces, Elvis Costello And The Attractions, Radar. 1979.

FAR RIGHT: Advert. Armed Forces, Elvis Costello And The Attractions, Radar. 1979.

PAY ATTENTION!

Sounds w/e 6th Jan '79

NB: SEE
INSTS ON
ALL TRACES

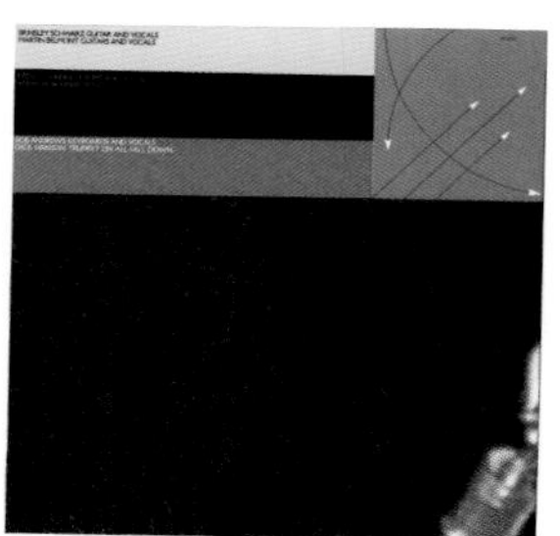

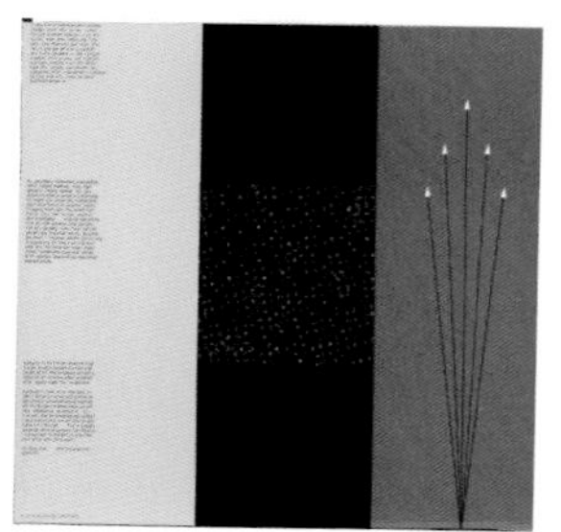

TOP: Front cover. Frogs, Clogs, Krauts And Sprouts, The Rumour, Stiff Records. 12in album. 1979.

ABOVE: Back cover. Frogs, Clogs, Krauts And Sprouts, The Rumour, Stiff Records. 1979.

ABOVE RIGHT AND CENTRE: Inner sleeve. Frogs, Clogs, Krauts And Sprouts, The Rumour, Stiff Records. 1979.

RIGHT: Front cover. Frozen Years, The Rumour, Stiff Records. 7in single. 1979.

ABOVE RIGHT: Back cover. Frozen Years, The Rumour, Stiff Records. 1979.

FAR RIGHT: Emotional Traffic, The Rumour, Stiff Records. 1979.

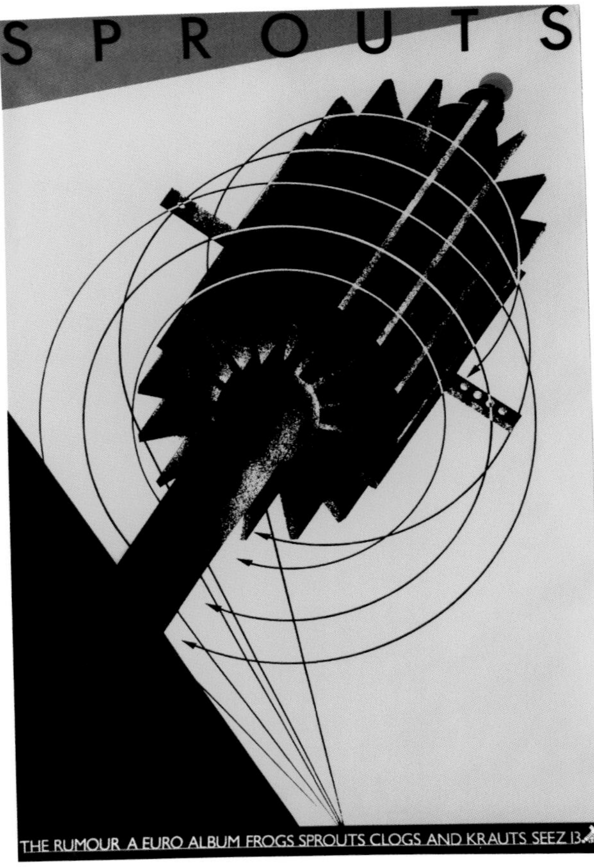

OPPOSITE (TOP RIGHT) AND THIS PAGE: Posters. Frogs, Clogs, Krauts And Sprouts, The Rumour, Stiff Records. 750mm x 500mm. 1979.

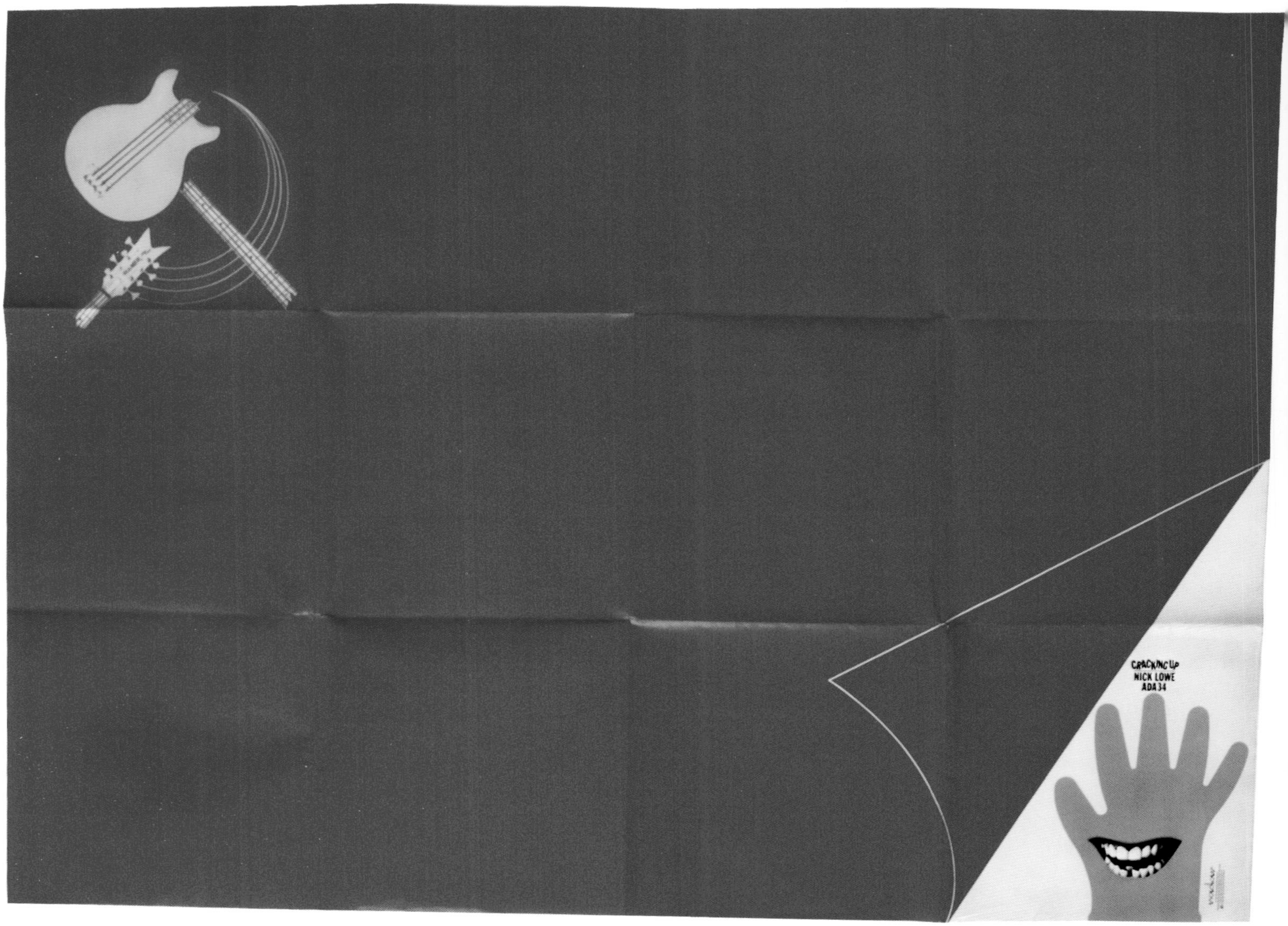

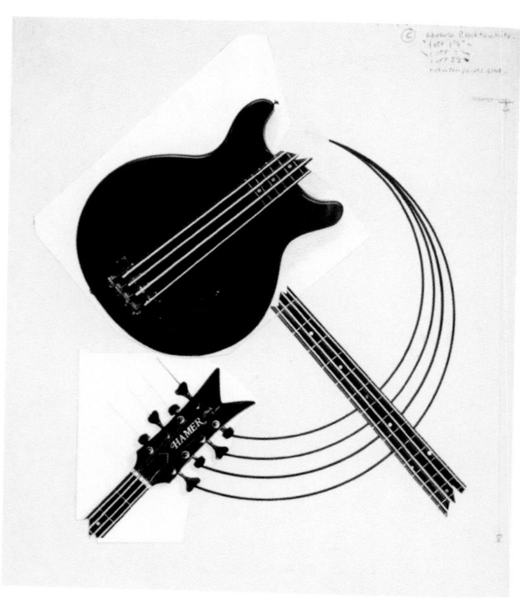

ABOVE: Poster. Cracking Up, Nick Lowe, Radar. 500mm x 750mm. 1979.

RIGHT: Artwork. Cracking Up and Labour Of Lust, Nick Lowe, Radar. 1979.

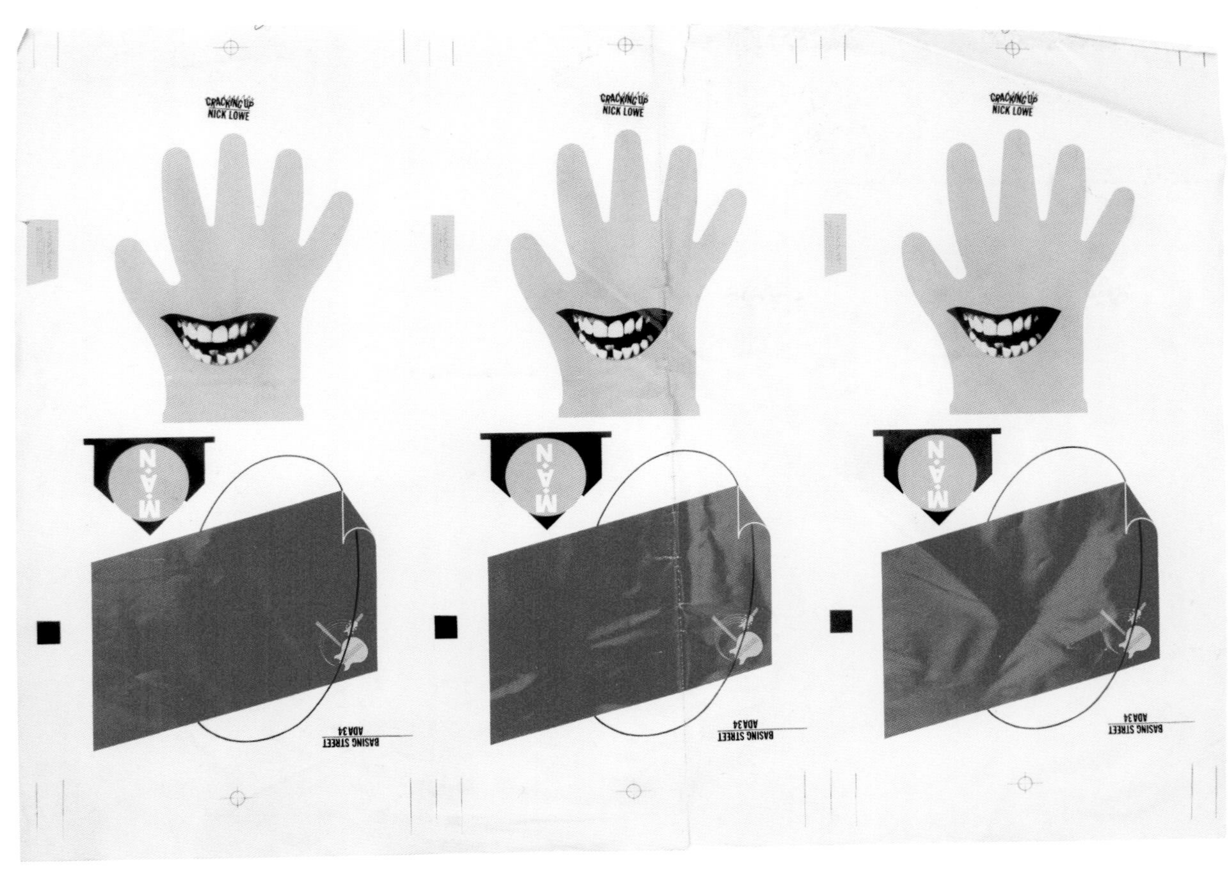

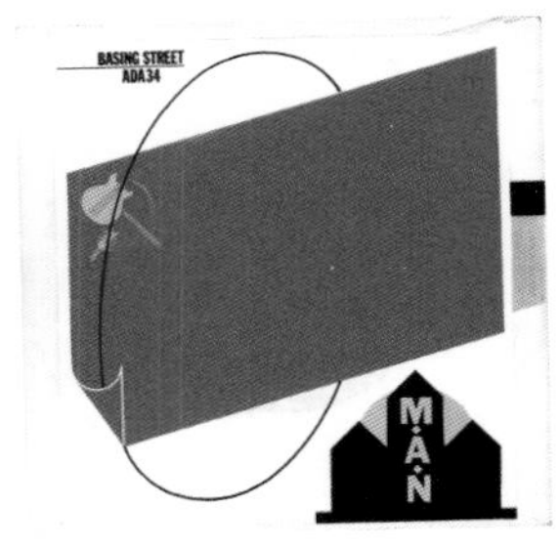

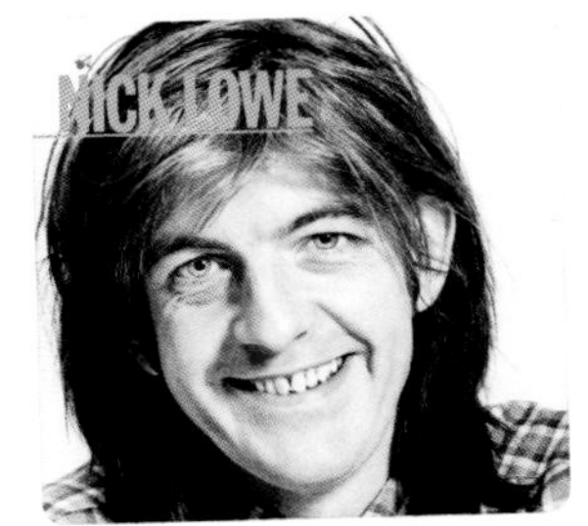

TOP: Proofs. Cracking Up, Nick Lowe, Radar. 7in single. 1979.

ABOVE: Front and back cover. Cracking Up, Nick Lowe, Radar. 1979.

CENTRE LEFT: Inner sleeve. Labour Of Lust, Nick Lowe, Radar. 12in album. 1979.

CENTRE RIGHT: Back cover. Labour Of Lust, Nick Lowe, Radar. 1979.

FAR LEFT: Inner sleeve. Labour Of Lust, Nick Lowe, Radar. 1979.

LEFT: Front cover. Labour Of Lust, Nick Lowe, Radar. 1979.

DO IT YOURSELF

IAN DURY & the BLOCKHEADS

SIDE ONE	SIDE TWO
INBETWEENIES	THIS IS WHAT WE FIND
QUIET	UNEASY SUNNY DAY HOTSY TOTSY
DON'T ASK ME	MISCHIEF
SINK MY BOATS	DANCE OF THE SCREAMERS
WAITING FOR YOUR TAXI	LULLABY FOR FRANCIES

CHAZ JANKEL
IS MUSICALLY
DIRECT.

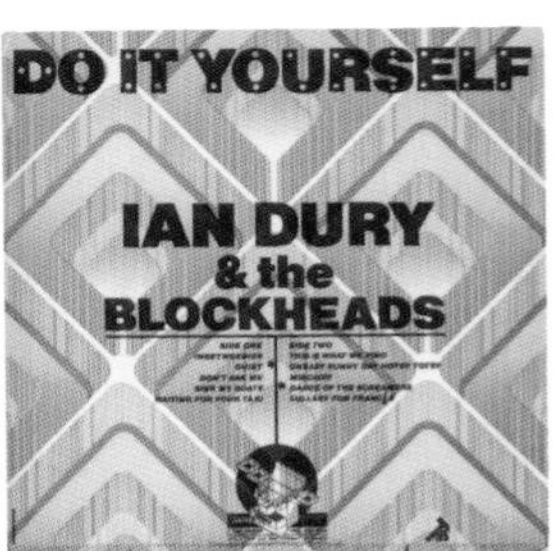

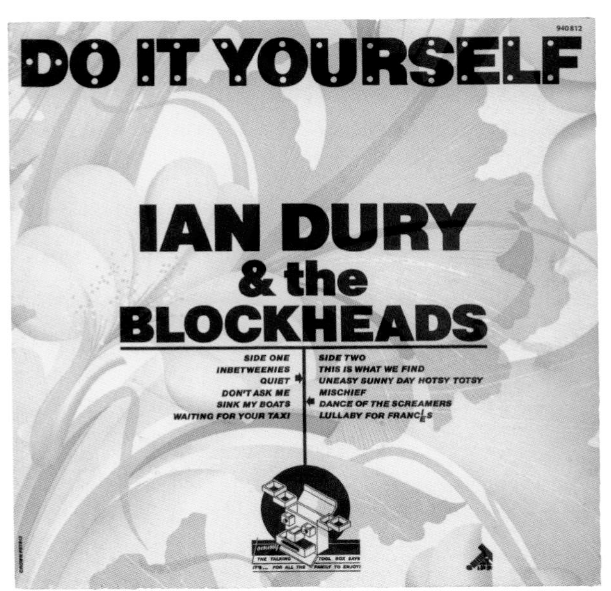

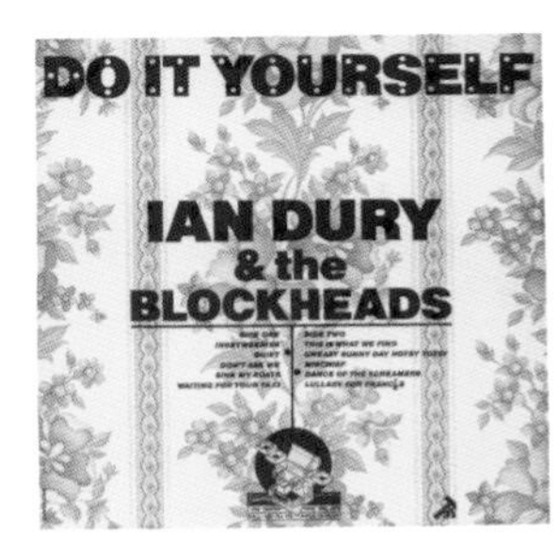

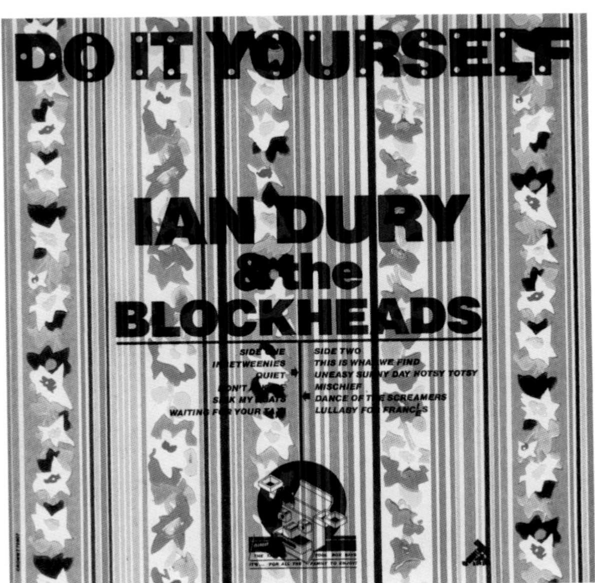

OPPOSITE: Wallpaper poster. Do It Yourself, Ian Dury & The Blockheads, Stiff Records. 750mm x 500mm. 1979.

THIS PAGE: Front cover variations. Do It Yourself, Ian Dury & The Blockheads, Stiff Records. 12in album. 1979.

From top left, clockwise: Netherlands; France; UK; Netherlands; Italy; UK; UK; Canada; Portugal; UK; UK; Spain; US; Germany; UK; UK; UK; Netherlands; US; US; Australia.

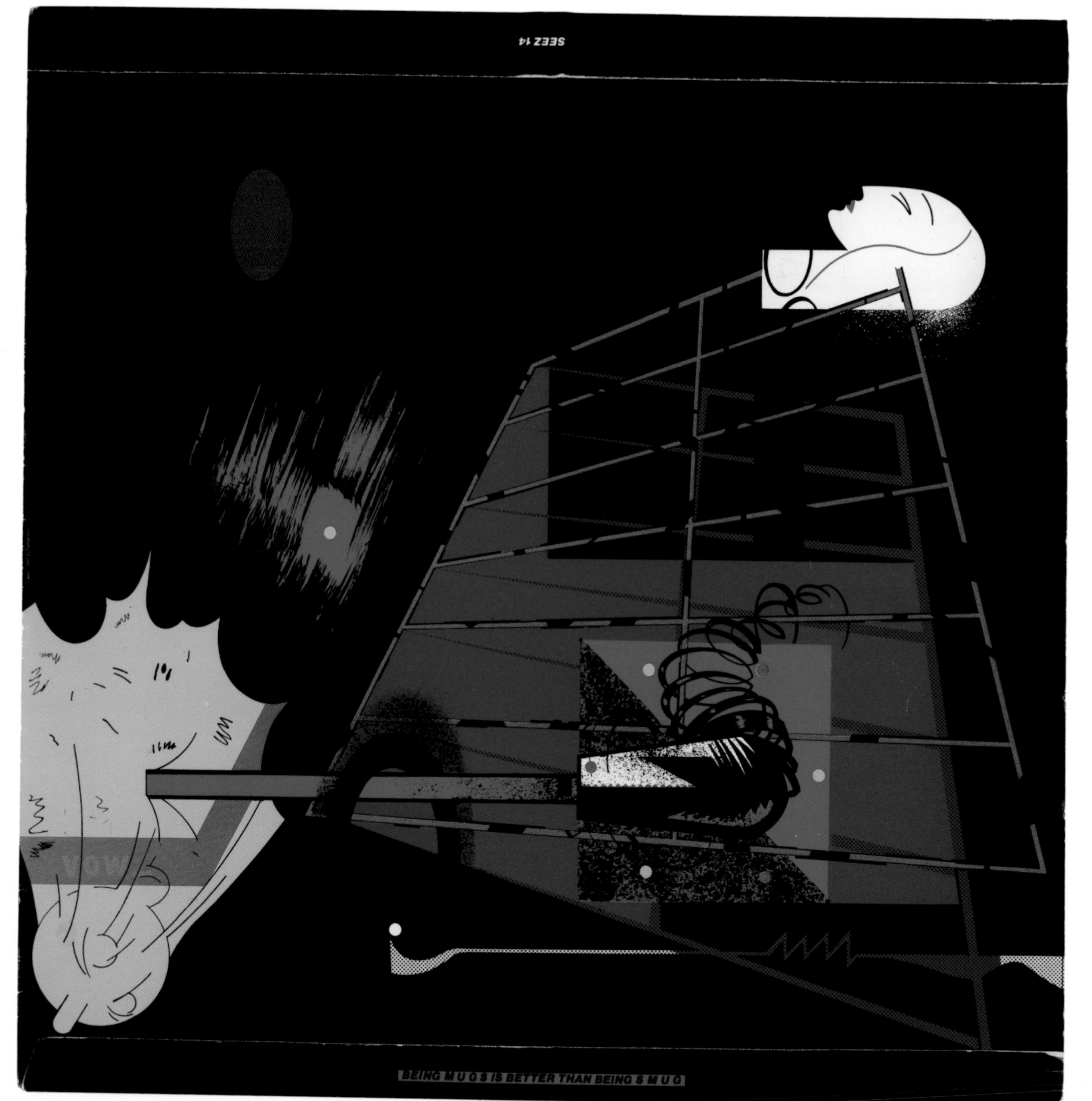
SEEZ 14
BEING M U G S IS BETTER THAN BEING S M U G

OPPOSITE: Inner sleeve. Do It Yourself, Ian Dury & The Blockheads, Stiff Records. 12in album. 1979.

THIS PAGE: Back cover. Do It Yourself, Ian Dury & The Blockheads, Stiff Records. 12in album. 1979.

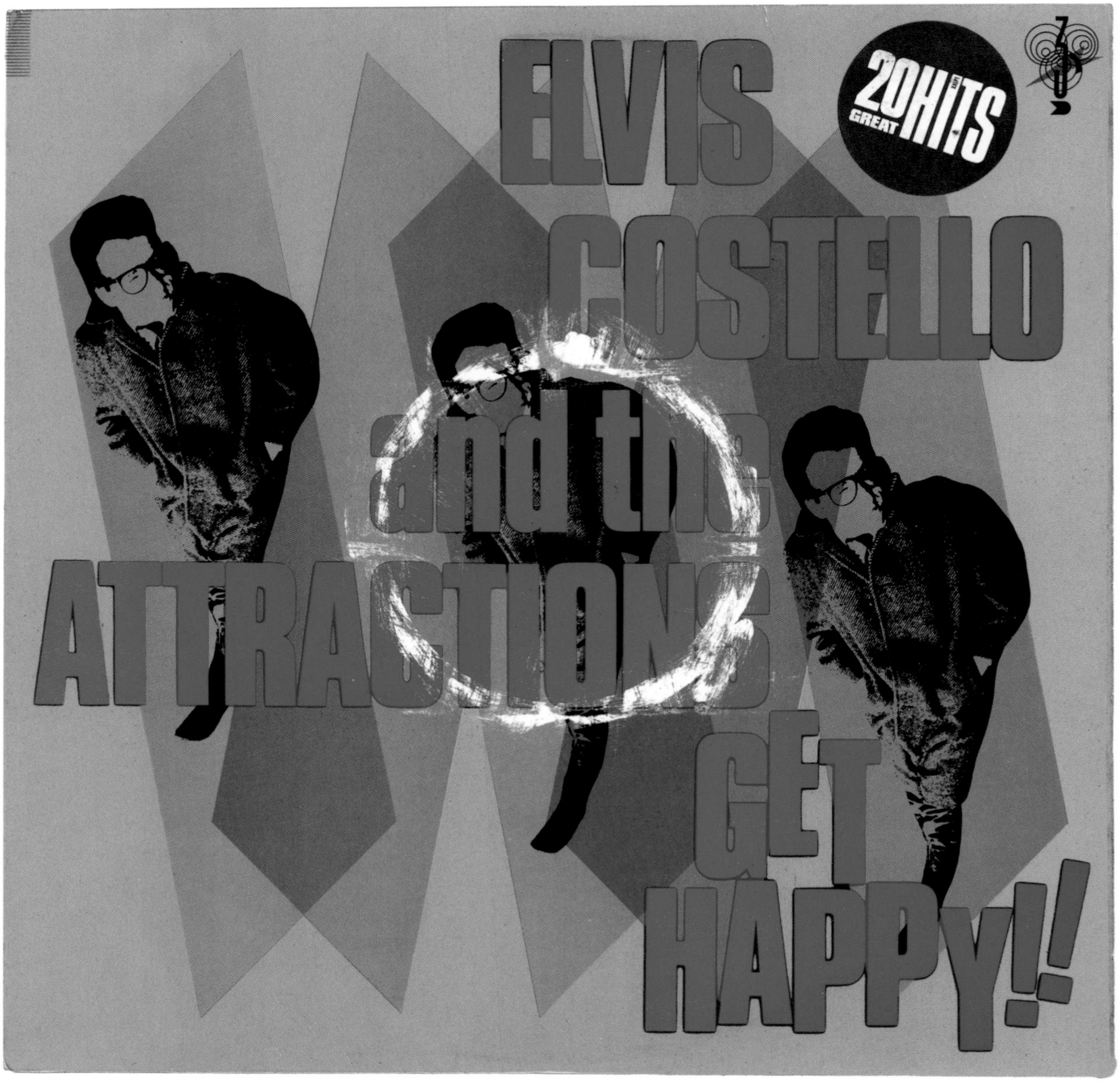

TOP: Artwork. Get Happy!!, Elvis Costello And The Attractions, F-Beat. 1980.

BOTTOM: Front cover. Get Happy!!, Elvis Costello And The Attractions, F-Beat. 12in album. 1980.

CREDIT: VAT 245 4945 42.

TOP LEFT: Back cover. Get Happy!!, Elvis Costello And The Attractions, F-Beat. 12in album. 1980.

ABOVE: Inner sleeve. Get Happy!!, Elvis Costello And The Attractions, F-Beat. 1980.

FAR LEFT: Artwork. Advert, New Amsterdam, Elvis Costello And The Attractions, F-Beat. 1980.

LEFT: Artwork. Advert, I Can't Stand Up For Falling Down, Elvis Costello And The Attractions, F-Beat. 1980.

GET tempted
GET LUCKY
GET LOST
GET ACCUSED
GET PUNCHED
GET between
GO DUTCH
GET possessed
GET OVER
GET dn
GET arrested
GET touched
GET smart
GET YOU
VOTE LABOUR X

GET Happy!
GET LOST!
GET LUCKY!
GET tempted!
GET touched!
GET ACCUSED!
GET PUNCHED!
GET arrested!
GO DUTCH!
GET OVER!
GET up!
GET possessed!
GO between!
GET smart!
GET YOU!
GET IT?

OPPOSITE PAGE
TOP: Artwork. Poster, Get Happy!!, Elvis Costello And The Attractions, F-Beat. 1980.

BOTTOM: Poster. Get Happy!!, Elvis Costello And The Attractions, F-Beat. 750mm x 500mm. 1980.

THIS PAGE: Poster. Get Happy!!, Elvis Costello And The Attractions, F-Beat. 1500mm x 1000mm. 1980.

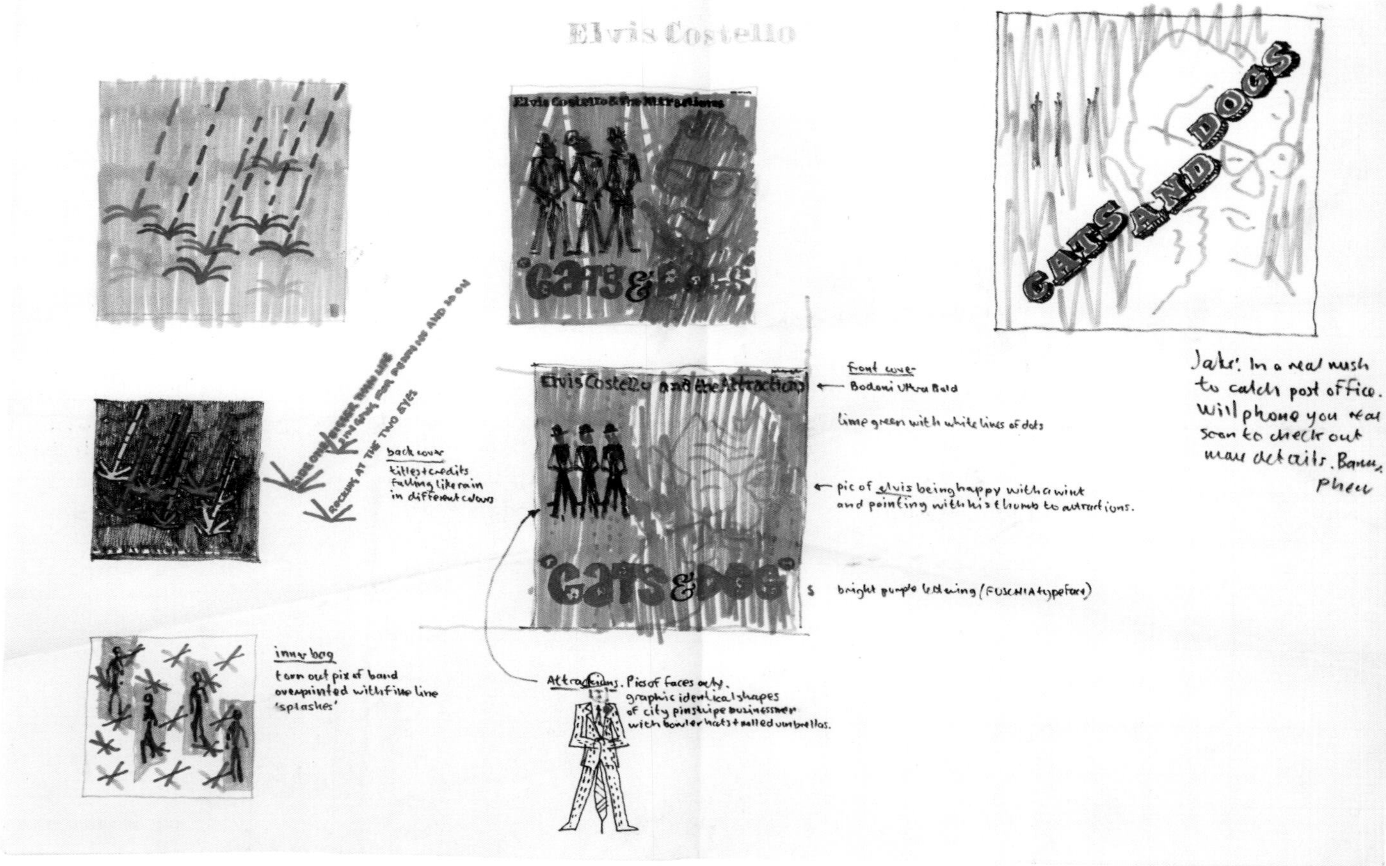

TOP: Sketches. Cats And Dogs (original title of Trust). 1981.

CENTRE: Cassette cover. Trust, Elvis Costello And The Attractions, F-Beat. 1981.

RIGHT: Artwork. Advert, Trust, Elvis Costello And The Attractions, F-Beat. 1981.

TOP: Almost Blue, Elvis Costello And The Attractions, F-Beat. 12in album. 1981.

BOTTOM: Artwork. Advert, Almost Blue, Elvis Costello And The Attractions, F-Beat. 1981.

TOP: Front cover. Musical Shapes, Carlene Carter, F-Beat. 12in album. 1980.

BOTTOM: Inner sleeve. Musical Shapes, Carlene Carter, F-Beat. 12in album. 1980.

F. BEAT SINGLE BAG 4
POS.S/S.LINE.
BASEBOARD TO PRINT PANTONE PROCESS BLUE.
OVERLAY TO PRINT PANTONE 151 (ORANGE.)
COLOURS TO OVERPRINT.
NOTE: ARTWORK IS DELIBERATELY DONE
BADLY, DO NOT ADJUST.
VIEW HOLE TO BE PUNCHED IN FRONT COVER ONLY.

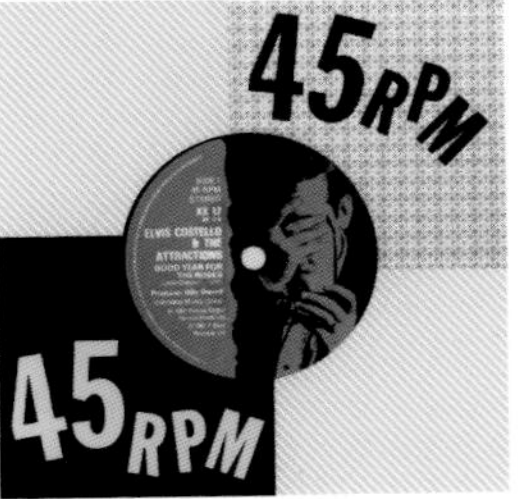

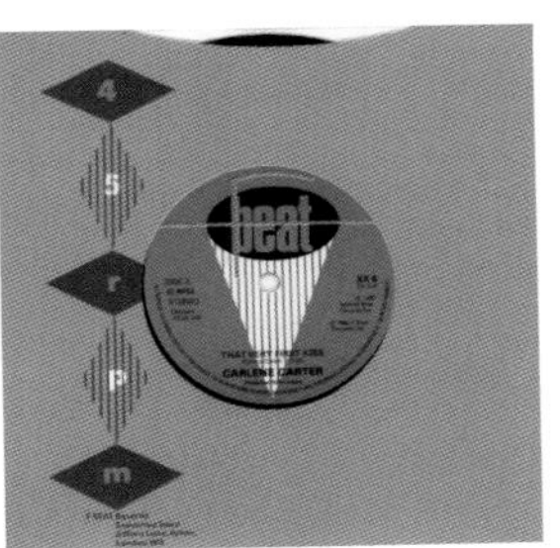

LEFT: Artwork. Singles bag, F-Beat. 1980.

Above: Singles bag variations. F-Beat. 7in. 1980.

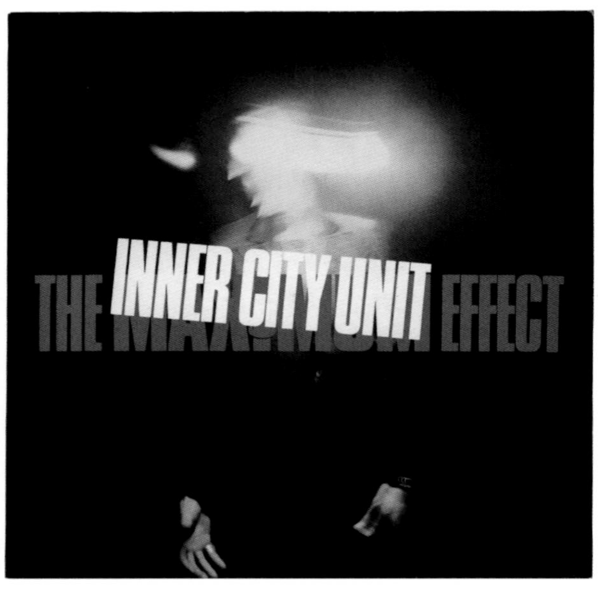

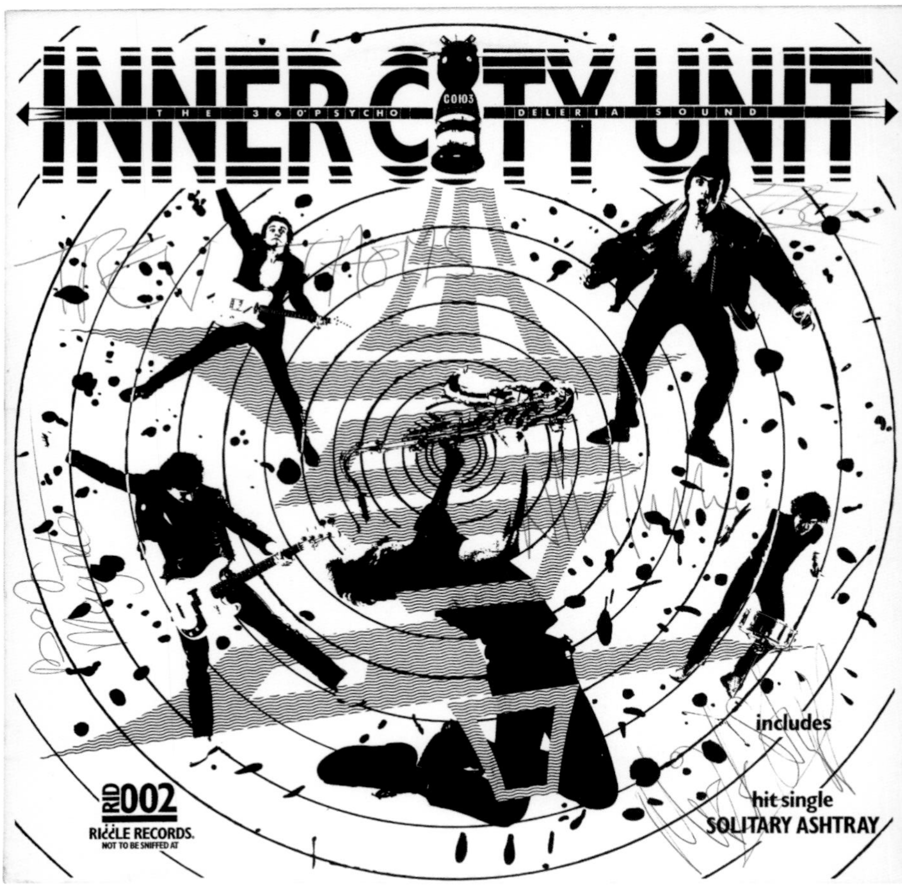

TOP RIGHT: Passout, Inner City Unit, Riddle. 12in album. 1980.

TOP LEFT: The Maximum Effect, Inner City Unit, Avatar. 12in album. 1981.

ABOVE: Stop Wasting Your Time, Ingrid Mansfield-Allman, Polydor. 12in single. 1981.

RIGHT: Spasticus Autisticus, Ian Dury, Polydor. 12in single. 1981.

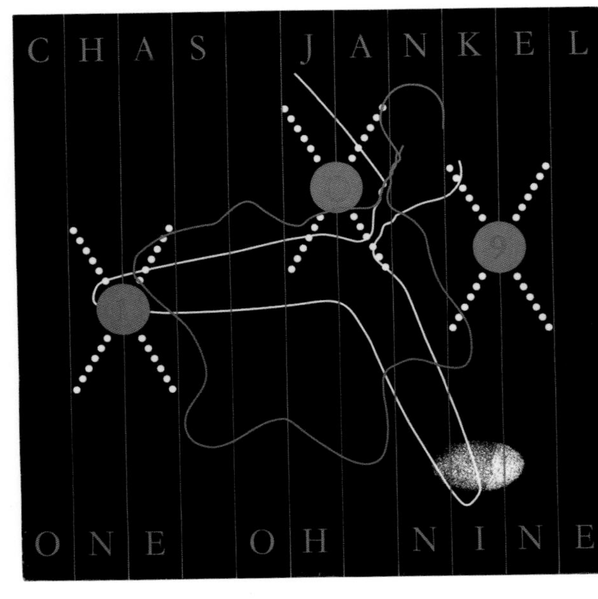

TOP LEFT: A Case Of The Shakes, Dr Feelgood, Stiff Records. 12in album. 1981.

TOP RIGHT: 109, Chaz Jankel, A&M. 12in single. 1981.

ABOVE: Compass Point, Desmond Dekker, Stiff Records. 12in album. 1981

LEFT: Twangin..., Dave Edmunds, Swan Song. 12in album. 1981.

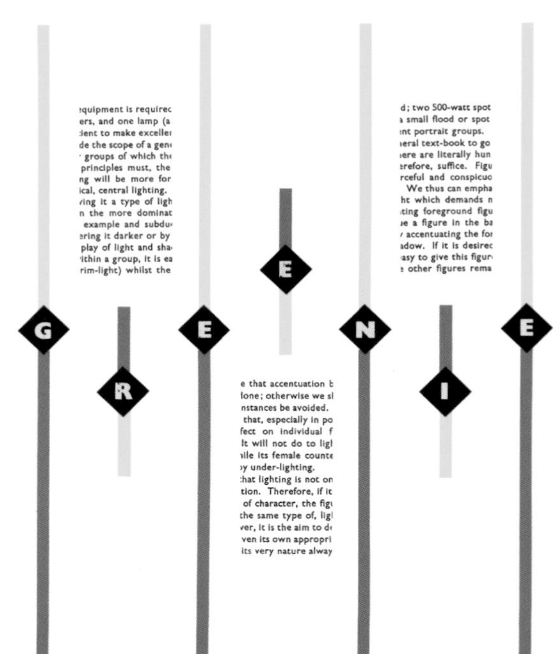

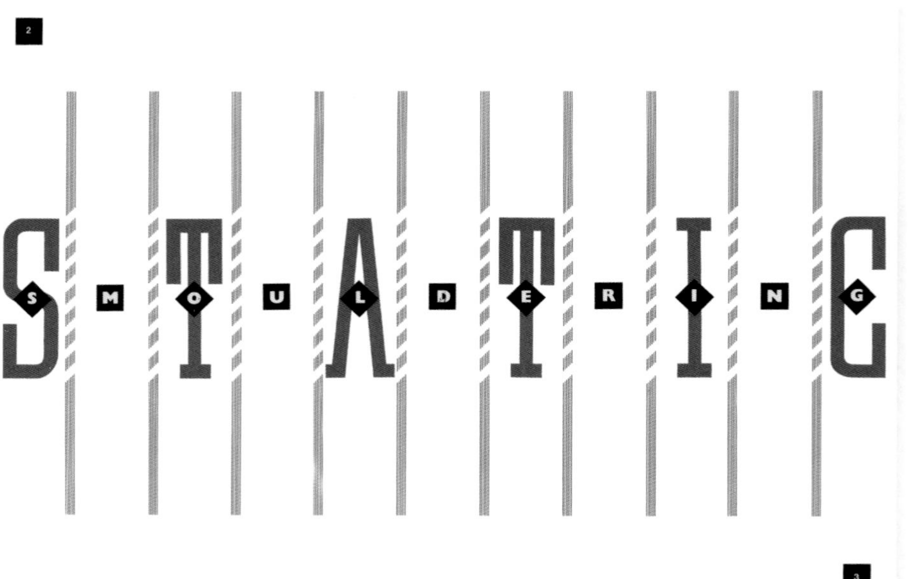

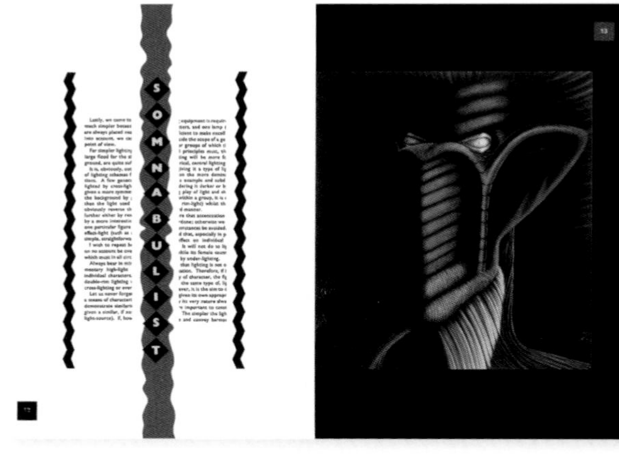

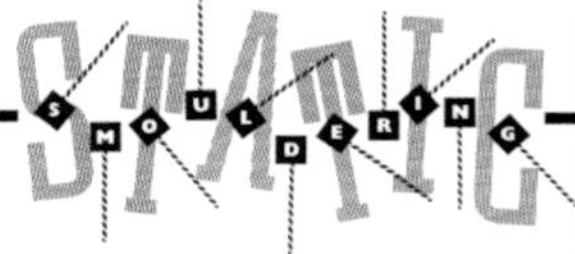

THIS PAGE AND OPPOSITE: Artwork. *Smouldering Static*, Barney Bubbles/ Tom Pogson. 1979.

6

effect-light (such as a
simple, straightforwa
I wish to repeat he
on no account be ove
which must in all circ
Always bear in min
mentary high-light
individual characters.
double-rim lighting v
cross-lighting or even
Let us never forget
a means of characteri
demonstrate similarit
given a similar, if not
light-source). If, how
each figure should be
Group lighting is
therefore, all the mo

light) whilst the oth
nner.
at accentuation by ad
; otherwise we shall
nces be avoided.
, especially in portrai
on individual figure
ill not do to light a
its female counterpa
nder-lighting.
lighting is not only a
. Therefore, if it is a
character, the figures
same type of, lighting
it is the aim to demor
its own appropriate li
ery nature always a r
portant to construct

U L T R A

fill-in lighting must be
and confusing high-lig
Lastly, we come to
much simpler because
are always placed nea
into account, we can
point of view.
Far simpler lighting
large flood for the si
ground, are quite suff
It is, obviously, out
of lighting schemes fo
tions. A few genera
lighted by cross-light
given a more symmet
the background by g
than the light used
obviously reverse th

further either by ren
by a more interesting
one particular figure
effect-light (such as a
simple, straightforwa
I wish to repeat he
on no account be ove
which must in all circ
Always bear in min
mentary high-light
individual characters.
double-rim lighting v
cross-lighting or even
Let us never forget
a means of characteri
demonstrate similarit
given a similar, if not
light-source). If, how

7

10

R U B A D U B B L U B

11

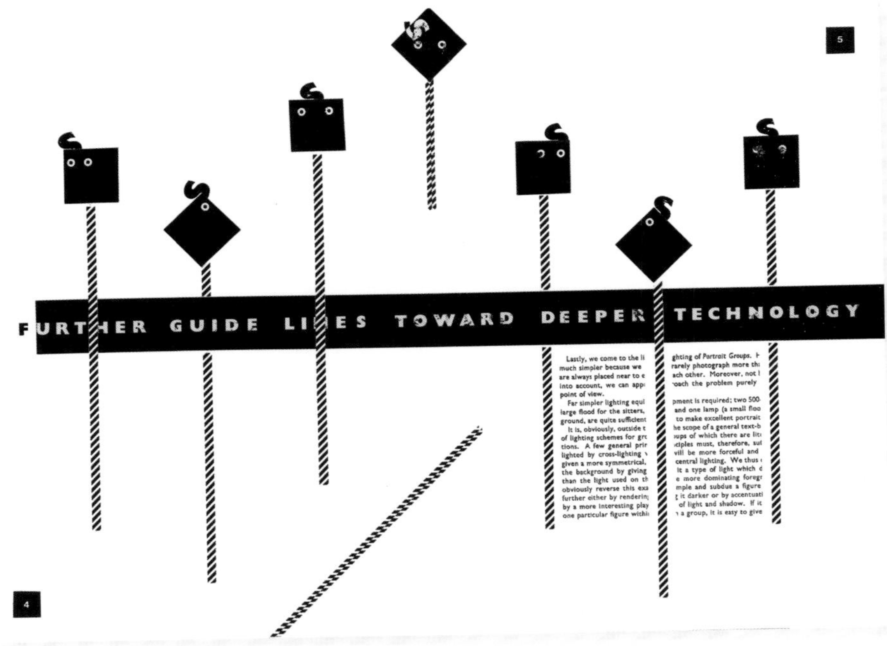

John Cooper Clarke Directory 1979

26 Cooper, S JOHN COOPER CLARKE

I DON'T WANNA BE NICE *(Clarke/Hannett/Hopkins)*

Here he comes now

The fast fingers
The expert eyes
And the same old How d'ya do
Disgust is just his dumb disguise
He wants a word with you
His problems are the end
His mouth needs exercise
The last thing I need is another friend
I Don't Wanna Be Nice
I Don't Wanna Be Nice
I think it's Clever to swear
Better seek some sound advice
Better look elsewhere
Your face is an obvious case
You shouldn't put it about
This is neither the time or place
To sort these matters out
What you see is what you get
You only live twice
A friend in need is a friend in debt
I Don't Wanna Be Nice

No we never met before
I'm very happy to say
Far from perfect strangers
I'd like to keep it that way
I'm not your psycho analyst
I'd rather talk to mice
You're so easy to resist
I Don't Wanna Be Nice
I Don't Wanna Be Nice
I thinks it's clever to swear
Better seek some sound advice
Better look elsewhere
Your face is an obvious case
You shouldn't put it about
This is neither the time nor place
To sort these matters out
What you see is what you get
You only live twice
A friend in need is a friend in debt
I Don't Wanna Be Nice

©1978 April Music Ltd/Spilt Beans/MCPS Ltd.

34 Clarke, F JOHN COOPER CLARKE

JOHN COOPER CLARKE Clarke, G 35

TEN YEARS IN AN OPEN-NECKED SHIRT

Otto Dreckstrasse was the bastard offspring of Count Ludwig Dreckstrasse (the lard mogul) and Tracy. The Count died of self-inflicted stab wounds three weeks before the birth, and Tracy, four months later, perished alone with her sapphires, the victim of a mau-mau-mau hit squad leaving Otto with the one thing that money can't buy-poverty.

At one year old he found himself alone in a post-war landscape of flattened streets patrolled by aimless amputees. He was adopted by Sheba and Rex, a pair of alsations with whom he lived for the next eight years in an art deco cocktail cabinet on a whalley range bomb site. Discarded chips and chewing gum were the day to day diet of the sub-savage dog boy whose reversion to barbarism was prevented only by the spiritual guidance of Sheba and Rex who were devout Catholics.

Four years later it was arranged for him to attend the school of Our Lady of the Seven Robes of Gold by the Garden of Sorrows in the Vale of Tears (school motto 'Behold His Precious Blood'). It was run with Spartan efficiency by the Little Daughters of the Sick under the benevolent tyranny of Sister Scourge. "How do you feel?" she asked, and Otto replied in his native tongue "Ruff".

The world of language proved hyper-accessible to the lad, even then he was no stranger to the written word. There had been days at home when a high wind would festoon him with random information: bus tickets and timetables, bankrupt magazines, yesterday's papers, obsolete menus, the throwaway stuff of the teen market. Caution exposure to heat could cause drowsiness . . . Push the release . . . Details on the reverse . . . Shake the bottle . . . Should we fail to please . . . Do not bend . . . Barmitzvah cards, cartons and cans, cookbooks and comics, comics rich with the gaudy iconography of physical pain, loud with the language of shrapnel. Their pages had burned his eyes, he knew the jagged truth of the broken window and the wordless poetry of the spikes punctured the music of chimes. At the age of six Otto had been educated by accident.

Daily religious instruction furnished his open mind with tales of treachery and slaughter, morbid betrayals in the gardens of the faithful. Episodes of fabulous torture occupied his vision, incense filled his nose with the fatal breath of ghosts while hermaphrodite choirs droned in his ears.

OPPOSITE: Front and back cover. *John Cooper Clarke Directory*, Omnibus Press. 250mm x 180mm. 1979.

THIS PAGE: Double-page spreads. *John Cooper Clarke Directory*, Omnibus Press. 1979.

THIS PAGE AND OPPOSITE: *The Ian Dury Songbook*, Wise Publications. 300mm x 230mm. 1979.

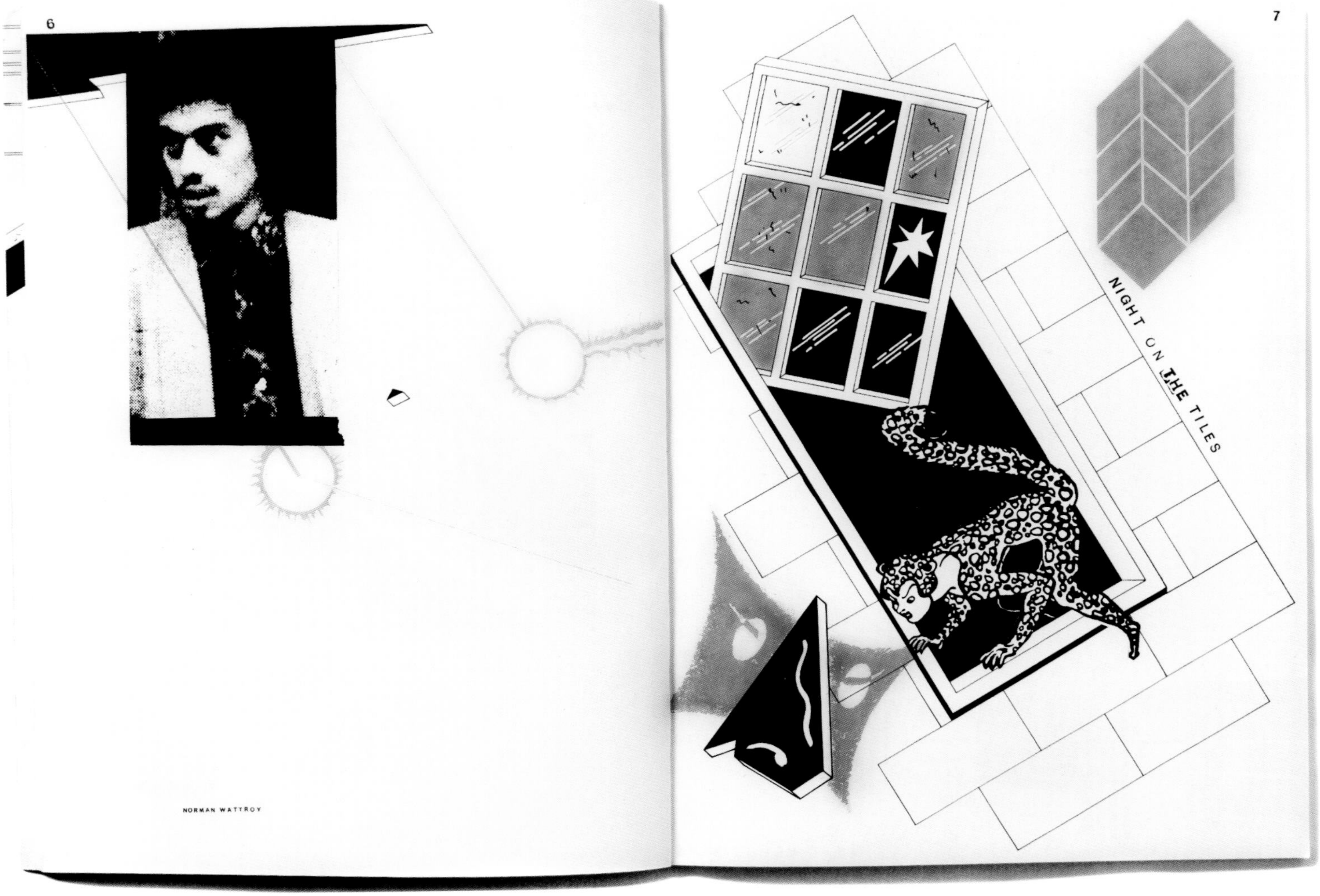

6

NORMAN WATTROY

7

NIGHT ON THE TILES

THIS PAGE: Postcard. Lives, Hayward Gallery. 210mm x 140mm. 1979.

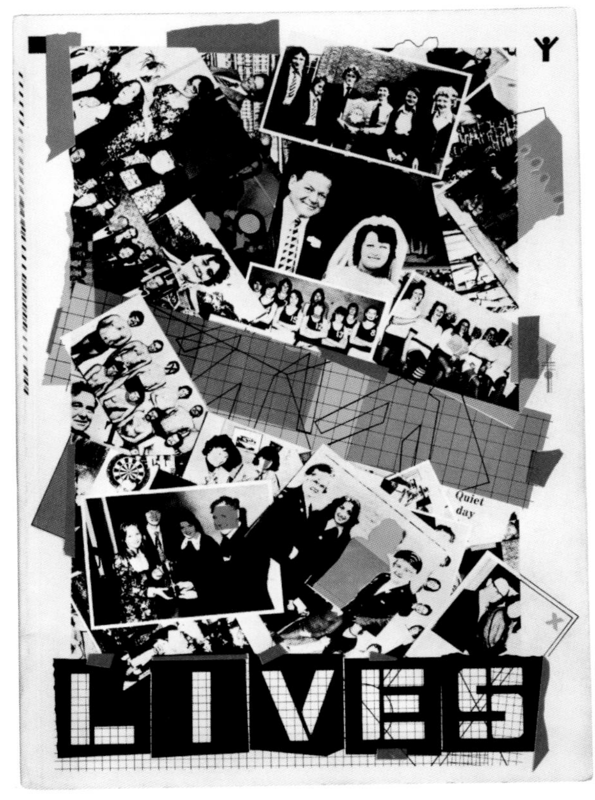

THIS PAGE: Cover and double-page spreads. *Lives* catalogue, Hayward Gallery. 297mm x 210mm. 1979.

FOREWORD

The Romans do it, but alas we do not in Britain, or at least not very much. In Rome you can sit at a cafe table on the street and stare at people strolling by. You can have a real good look. You can study face and figure without it being bad form.

In Britain you can only do as the Romans do by staring at someone asleep, another pleasure of train travel. We are strong on the eye to eye contact, no problem there. But apart from that, we are mostly looking askance. Certainly none of that full-frontal revelling look-see that seems so natural on the Via Veneto. All the more reason, therefore, to welcome this portrait gallery of Power in Britain: we can con uninhibitedly.

A great photographer has a way of focussing a view of things and people that we are familiar with but do not attend to. So look through the lens of a camera when it is handled with the art of Brian Griffin, and the revelation is, as William Blake put it, to see **through** not **with** the eye. Suddenly the subject becomes the object, something you can examine with care and with new imagination.

And what does power look like in black and white? I admire the skill of Richard Smith, the author, particularly because he leaves wise scope to the photographs – and indeed the individual characters who can speak for themselves. He produces almost self-pen-portraits and most revealing they are. Self-pen descriptions are always fascinating, but especially in what they do not explain: naturally we all seem to have a tendency to describe our drives in the most acceptable terms, while probably the strongest, deepest, most mysterious and un-speakable forces matter most, are well out of our insight. Good management is like that too: what you can measure is important, what you cannot can be even more important.

In fact success withholds many of its secrets. Power comes in all shapes and sizes. There is no pattern, no particular jut of the chin, or craginess of the eyebrow (although I suspect the British really believe in eyebrows). The power of personalities is not that predictable.

What shows in this Power album is immense, elegant, and surprising variety: this is not a cosy snapshot album of power at all. Kenneth Keith pats the world on its head. Monty Finniston, glinting with energy, holds in his hand what is presumably a thunderbolt. Leslie Murphy ruggedly re-emerges into the light. Len Murray, alert and amazingly unrumpled, certainly not falling down on his interface. Peter Marsh – who's for tennis? and although he has got a raquet in his hand, he seems to sit in the umpire's chair, or is it that he is simply at the top of the heap?

The book categorises the powers-that-be in sections on Directors, Politicians, Trade Unionists, Educators, Media and so on. This is a brave slash at keeping some coherence over the ungeneralisable theme of power, which remains, thank goodness, intractably individual. It is splendidly tempting to develop sub-categories of captions courageous: the corporate climber-Tarzan of the Decision Tree, the look-no-hands effortlessness of the Boss born in the commercial purple, the outdistancing calm of the sheer Professional; the did-it-my-way, unstoppable Innovator, the wary confidence of the Representative.

But, really for me there is no telling. Only seeing. Have a good stare.

Peter Parker, August, 1981

MANOLO BLAHNIK

Ladies Shoe Designer Manolo Blahnik has shops in Church Street, Chelsea, and Madison Avenue, Manhattan. His Chelsea shop, decorated in pastel shades, is cool and calm. Shoes are placed on plinths as objets d'art; his shoe drawings hang on the wall, a large green vase of fresh white flowers stands on the table.

While working off Broadway with La Mama Company Blahnik approached **Harpers** magazine with his designs.

Harpers liked his shoes and put him in touch with an American manufacturer. He was immediately successful.

He moved to London and had his shoes manufactured by small companies in Leyton and Northampton. 'But,' he says, 'in 1974, many English manufacturers collapsed or were taken over by Americans. They wanted to produce huge plastic wellington boots so I had to go to Italy to get my shoes made.'

Glamourous women and beautiful girls wear his shoes. They are hand-made, feminine, pretty and start at £75 a pair.

'Designing shoes,' he says, 'You have to do it to the millimetre. They have an architectural quality. Each piece has to be stitched in by hand. I relate it a lot to shapes from architecture.

'I have always been interested in art and architecture. When I was three I used to cut little cathedrals out of paper. I like different periods, not just one period. I suppose because I have moved about. I like a fusion of things.'

Blahnik has made London his home, but he perceives a decline. 'London to me is the legend, the mystique rather than the reality. Everything is so dirty now and so grey. London for me used to be this beauty. I love true Englishness: they respect individuals which a lot of people in Europe don't do.

'What we have now is not very inspiring: economics and bad management seem to dominate. This sense of frustration: it gets like a vicious circle. If it wasn't because I love the English character, I wouldn't still be here.

'I love the continuity. English friends, friends who are like cathedrals in their permanence. It is still the best place to be but I wish something happens in England soon. It is as if beauty is sleeping here.'

OPPOSITE AND THIS PAGE: Cover and double-page spreads. *Power: British Management In Focus*, Travelling Light. 275mm x 210mm. 1981.

ABOVE AND RIGHT: The Turbo Chair, Editions Riviera. 1981.

BELOW: The Odeon Cocktail Cabinet, Editions Riviera. 1981.

OPPOSITE: The Flying Trowel Desk, Editions Riviera. 1981.

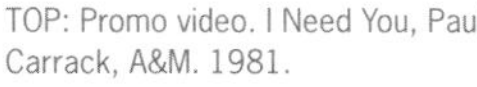

TOP: Promo video. I Need You, Paul Carrack, A&M. 1981.

BOTTOM: Promo video. Always Better With You, Paul Carrack, A&M. 1981.

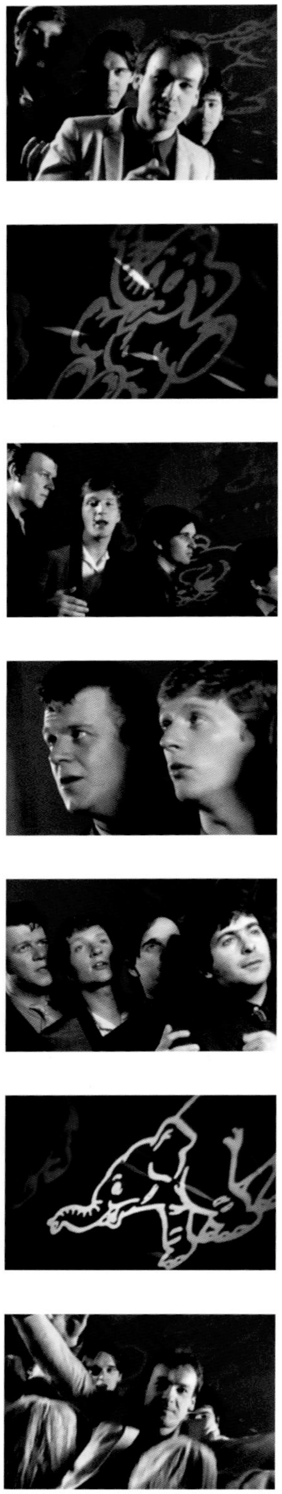

ABOVE: Promo video. Tempted, Squeeze, A&M. 1981.

ABOVE: Promo video. The Lunatics (Have Taken Over The Asylum), Fun Boy Three, Chrysalis. 1981.

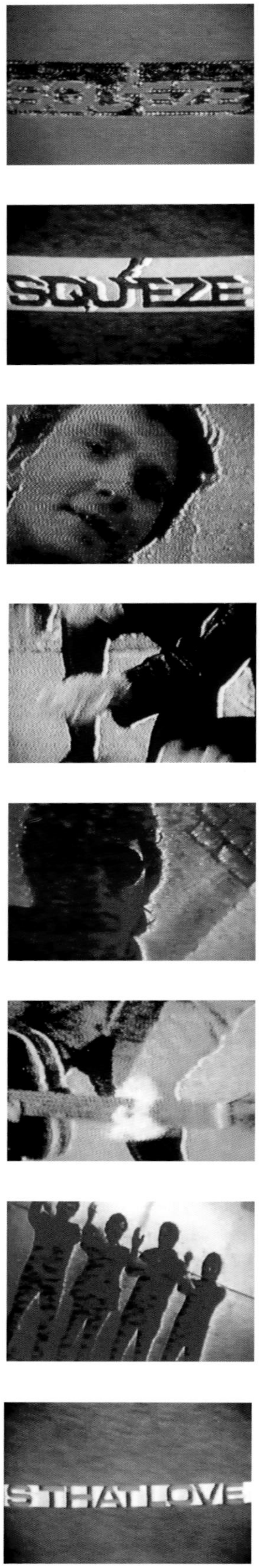

ABOVE: Promo video. Is That Love, Squeeze, A&M. 1981.

ABOVE: Promo video. New Lace Sleeves, Elvis Costello And The Attractions, F-Beat. 1981.

ABOVE: Promo video. Clubland, Elvis Costello And The Attractions, F-Beat. 1981.

ABOVE: Promo video. Ghost Town, The Specials, Chrysalis. 1981.

ABOVE: Front cover. Jukebox Dury, Ian Dury, Stiff Records. 12in album. 1981.

Punch The Clock
1982–1983

As 1982 dawned, Barney Bubbles' professional malaise was compounded by bereavement; his parents had died within a matter of days of each other over the Christmas holiday.

With the new generation of designers snapping at his heels, Bubbles was persuaded by friends to seek out employment opportunities himself, and took a portfolio around some of the bigger music labels, only to hear his unsigned work had already been claimed by others.

In this and other ways, the art departments of the major record companies now pillaged and bowdlerised Bubbles' graphic devices. There were, however, a number of rival designers operating within the music business for whom Bubbles reserved respect. 'He told me he admired Al McDowell at Rockin' Russian, Peter Saville at Factory and Storm Thorgerson at Hipgnosis,' says Brian Griffin.

An area of solace became painting, which Bubbles enthused about in a letter to his son Aten. He mentioned he had embarked on a series of canvases, the first of which he called 'Snakecharmer'.

Titled 'Snakecharmer & Reclining Octopus', this pastiche of Picasso's Three Musicians became the cover of the July 1982 release of Elvis Costello And The Attractions' album Imperial Bedroom (where it was credited to 'Sal Forlenza 1942').

In his sleeve-notes for a CD reissue, Costello confirmed that this was intended to be the first in a series of commissions. 'I'd asked him to paint an impression of the finished record as a change from the usual cover photograph,' wrote Costello. 'You can see that he obviously responded to the more violent and carnal aspects of the songs.

'Recently in Spain somebody asked me about the cover and its obvious pastiche of Three Musicians. I could have said that Barney was tipping a large hat to the masters as we intended to do on the album, but instead I pointed out the lettering on each of the zipper-like creatures. It spells out "Pablo Si".'

For some time the painting was on a wall of Costello's New York apartment, acting as a fond reminder of 'Barney, his wit and panache'.

In the main, Bubbles' paintings were determinedly abstract. Two commissions came from Riviera: a portrait of his friend and patron has a cigar to signify the presence of 'Vinyl Mogul', while that of Riviera's first wife, Antoinette Sales, is apparently the work of 'Jacuzzi Stallion'.

Bubbles gave them more paintings as birthday presents: a masked female face for Sales (this time signed 'Jacuzzi') and an interpretation of an artwork featured in Tony Hancock film *The Rebel* for Riviera.

'We were laughing about the bit where Hancock's in Paris and says about a pretentious painting, "Well it's just a fish skeleton",' says Riviera. 'Then, out of the blue, for my next birthday he gave me his version of it.'

Chris Gabrin was presented with a painting entitled The Echo Enters. This incorporated a concrete poem and depicted a tubular form sitting in a chair. 'He told me it was a portrait of me,' says Gabrin. 'I really like it and still have it hanging on the wall.'

The Rebel may also have been an inspiration; in another scene from the 1961 movie, a character announced that, when he painted a chair, he became a chair.

A 4ft x 6ft mixed-media piece was given to Marius Cain in part-payment for a furniture design. This portrait of Cain's girlfriend Claire used stencils to spell out the first verse to Elvis Presley's

Heartbreak Hotel. Cain's painting was later damaged in a fire at his house. 'Marius was really worried but I think Barney would have said it improves it,' smiles B. Syme.

Abstracts also became gifts for his friend Ricci Ostrov and the sisters Carol and Diana Fawcett. His painting for the latter contained a projection of the Rietveld Schröder House in Utrecht (the only realisation of architecture from the art movement De Stijl). 'He gave me explicit instructions that the painting should hang at 45 degrees,' says Diana Fawcett.

For the music publisher Peter Barnes, Bubbles constructed an 8ft-tall representation of Chuck Berry in painted plywood. 'There was an empty wall space in my house; I talked to Barney about what could go there,' says Barnes. 'He arrived with a number of painted wooden pieces and threaded ropes through them. When pulled, the various parts swivelled and the guitar moved.'

The Face interview had reported that Bubbles hoped 'to remain only doing sleeves for his pals'. For a while his commercial work was focused on album designs for Chaz Jankel (Chasanova) and Dr Feelgood (Fast Women & Slow Horses, in the ampersand of which he drew a profile either of himself or frontman Lee Brilleaux).

For the front covers of 1982's Nick The Knife by Nick Lowe, and its follow up the following year, The Abominable Showman, Bubbles interpreted the singer-songwriter's aquiline features as The Eye Of Horus, the ancient Egyptian symbol of the all-seeing-eye. This had appeared in Bubbles' artwork as far back as the 1972 design for the Glastonbury Fayre triple set (on which Lowe appeared as a member of Brinsley Schwarz).

F-Beat provided a steady flow of work: for a promo album by engineer/producer Roger Béchirian – who worked with Lowe and Costello – Bubbles drew on the smoky 40s/50s work of the founding father of album sleeve design Alex Steinweiss, and the cover of Walls Have Ears by Béchirian's band Blanket Of Secrecy featured a plasticine sculpture produced by Bubbles, again in the style of Picasso.

Released as Ears Have Walls in the US, this release was the first to feature his artwork credit 'Heeps Willard', taken from the hoarding of north London construction company Heeps Willard & Company in his Islington neighbourhood. 'When I visited him around that time Barney dragged me down the road to have a look at the sign,' says Eric Goulden (aka Wreckless Eric). 'He thought the name was hilarious.'

F-Beat signing Paul Carrack was provided with a sleeve for his Suburban Voodoo album, based around a still from a Bubbles-directed promo, and ex-Audience member Howard Werth was granted a delicate graphic repetition of the numeral four for the single 4D Man. Werth was signed to F-Beat offshoot Metabop, for which Bubbles designed the logo. On the sleeve of Werth's album 6ix Of One Half A Dozen Of The Other, the singer-songwriter appeared in front of another Bubbles painting.

A major label commission came from CBS act The Psychedelic Furs; their frontman Richard Butler was an art-school graduate who formed a friendship with Bubbles during his design work on the sleeve and poster for their Todd Rundgren-produced album Forever Now.

Bubbles encoded the Furs' name in a circle of swirling yellow stars set on a luminous pink and green tiled mosaic. In Britain this further established the group's reputation for visual and musical invention but was rejected by their US label on the grounds of illegibility.

Bubbles also produced cover variations for the album's hit single Love My Way. This appeared in two 7in sleeves – one a gatefold – as well as a 12in with head-and-shoulder band portraits on the front. The back cover allusion to the B-side Aeroplane was a photogram of the parts of a model plane kit.

The Love My Way sleeves underline the fact that Bubbles was accessing a larger than usual budget: each was subjected to a printing process which embedded metallic silver in the coating. On the front, silver ellipses appeared as elements of five tangential circle motifs, and were enlarged on the gatefold inner.

These decorations were also arranged in repeat as quasi-chemical structures which not only conveyed the more user-friendly name 'The Furs' but also accommodated smaller size lettering spelling out the full name and the song titles.

The front cover of Forever Now's second single Danger is a Bubbles painting typical of his private work of this period: apparently random squiggles and shapes represented the faces of the four Furs, evoking earlier covers such as Music For Pleasure for The Damned, and referencing other work – the 'paint pot' ring also appeared in promotional material for Ian Dury & The Blockheads' Do it Yourself.

It seemed there was to be no respite from the rock'n'roll workload, though there were sideways steps into other areas, such as a poster for Contemporary Films' 1982 teen documentary *Underage*, which included a cameo by The Specials and was made by Kim Longinotto and Lizzie Lemon.

Another came via Glen Colson, who enlisted Bubbles to design a poster to promote a genuine curio: a spoken word album by cricket commentator John Arlott.

For this, Bubbles combined an image of a cricket ball knocking bails flying with a chart of player positions, in which the words were again set out as typograms: the 'u' in gully is extended, the 'q' in square leg is a square, the 'c' in backward point is reversed, and so on.

'Barney evidently didn't know or care very much about cricket, so it was great to watch him have fun with it,' says Colson, who worked closely with a true British eccentric, Vivian Stanshall. The former Bonzo Dog Doo-Dah Band frontman came up with the title for a project Colson was planning: Neck & Neck & Never Caught was to be another spoken word album combining the Arlott's voice with that of notable racing commentator Peter O'Sullevan. Bubbles produced sketched proposals for the cover but Colson was unable to develop the idea beyond the planning stage.

'I was drumming a bit at the time, and Barney offered to paint me a drumhead,' says Colson. 'I liked this move called a "flam", where you bring both drumsticks in quick succession down hard on the snare. I was delighted when I saw Barney's design said "Flam Flam".'

Drumheads were a Bubbles speciality; in 1982 he painted another for Will Birch, the former Kursaal Flyers drummer whose power-pop group The Records were also delivered a jukebox graphic sleeve for their album Music On Both Sides.

That year Bubbles finally realised a dream and released his own record, the album Ersatz on F-Beat offshoot Pompadour under the guise of The Imperial Pompadours.

This unconventional and abrasive collection of garage-rock tracks and extended sound-collages had been recorded over the previous couple of years with Nik Turner and members of his Inner City Unit as backing musicians.

Contributors also included Robert Calvert. Bubbles described Ersatz accurately in a letter to Carol Fawcett as 'inspired rubbish,

OPPOSITE: Barney Bubbles working on a portrait of Richard Butler of The Psychedelic Furs. 1982.

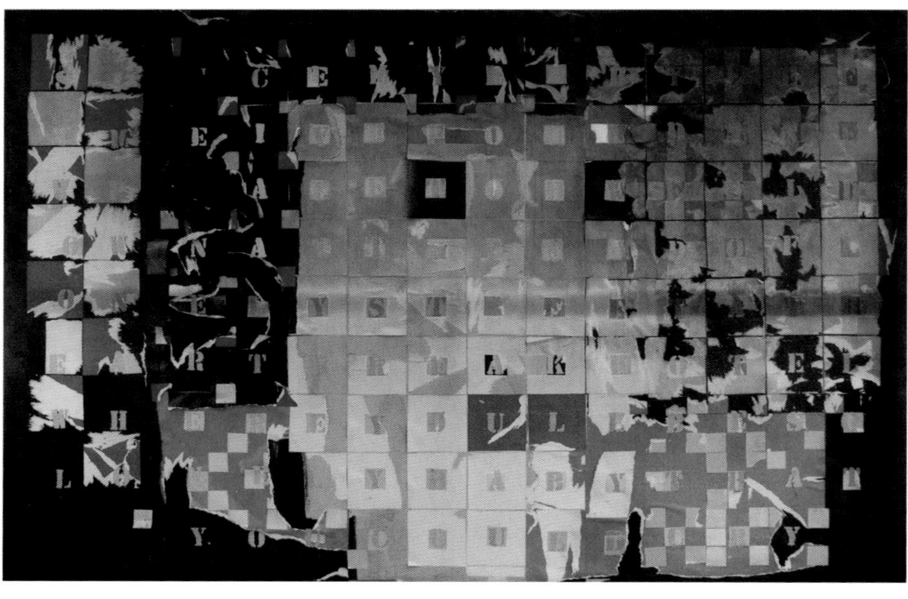

loud and in extremely bad taste', consisting as it does of such trash classics as The Novas' The Crusher (covered by The Cramps the previous year) and Vince Taylor's Brand New Cadillac (better known via the version on London Calling by The Clash). Among the downright obscurities were Black Denim Trousers & Motorcycle Boots by The Cheers and I Want To Come Back (From The World Of LSD) by Fee-Fi-Fo Plus Four.

'Barney wanted one side of the album to be scrappy rock'n'roll,' says Turner. 'Andrew Lauder created for him a tape of songs, he wrote the lyrics down and played them to us once. Then we recorded them using objets trouvés for percussion; I remember banging on an articulated lorry and recording the "boom" it made. We also taped breaking glass. It ended up sounding a bit like concrete music. The solo in The Crusher is an angle grinder.'

Side two of Ersatz consisted of the 25-minute track Insolence Across The Nation, in which Turner mashed up sounds with crazed diatribes. 'Barney said he wanted to do something about the life of Hitler,' says Turner. 'I selected quotations from *Mein Kampf*, Mad King Ludwig and Wagner and also from the women in all their lives, and then recorded random visitors to my flat reciting them.'

The rhythm track of Insolence Across The Nation was recorded in the barn on Turner's farm in Wales over a three-hour period. At intervals all participants changed instruments (Bubbles from guitar to bass). Once this was edited to the requisite length, sections of Wagner recordings by the Berlin Philharmonic were mixed in.

The back cover of Ersatz borrowed a memorable phrase from The Crusher and urged listeners to 'Play LOUD you turkeynecks'. The front was a tortured black and white paper portrait of Elvis Presley in the style of a woodcut by the Flemish expressionist artist Frans Masereel, whose sequential work of the 30s is acknowledged as the precursor of the modern graphic novel. Bubbles returned to Masereel for the front cover of Punkadelic, the 1982 album by Inner City Unit.

Early in 1983, Bubbles provided tuition for F-Beat/Demon art department assistant Jon Carver, who had been deputed to spend a day a week at his Islington studio/house to pick up the finer points of the trade. 'I visited Barney every Thursday over a period of about ten weeks, working under his direction and producing sleeves such as Ragin' Eyes for Nick Lowe,' says Carver.

'Generally I brought my own work along and Barney mentored, then we would break for lunch with a pint and a chat before resuming in the afternoon, finishing up with a review and a crit of the day's work. It was a thoroughly enjoyable and stimulating time.'

By now, Bubbles' friend Brian Griffin was an established rock music photographer, working with such acts as Echo & The Bunnymen, so was in a position to identify design opportunities. Among the major label releases designed by Bubbles on Griffin's recommendation was the Geffen album Points On The Curve by British post-New Romantic act Wang Chung (who later scored a sizeable US hit with the track Dancehall Days).

'I don't think he thought much of the music, but it was important that he was being hired by those guys,' says Griffin, whose photograph of a ship being swamped by a tsunami as a result of a nuclear explosion appeared in the grid on the cover of Points On The Curve.

A series of commissions came from German independent label

Line; Bubbles provided handsome green-on-brown 12in and 7in single sleeves composed from hand-drawn grids. 'He also designed our sub-label logos, including the one for Impact,' says Line's Uwe Tessnow, who was the German licensee for releases bearing Bubbles designs such as the Kursaal Flyers compilation In For A Spin and ex-Family frontman Roger Chapman's Mango Crazy.

Bubbles had designed sleeves for Chapman's part-time band The Riff Burglars. His first proposal for the Mango Crazy front cover was a painting of a psychotic cartoon face. This was rejected in favour of a TV-interference portrait of a man's head.

In the spring of 1983, the rejection of another sleeve was more significant: Elvis Costello's eighth album, Punch The Clock, was to be the first not to feature a Bubbles sleeve.

His pink, grey and white tubular rendering of Costello revisited the 'lightbulb' Johnny Moped logo and the giant Get Happy!! poster, but increased the intensity by presenting an 'electrocuted Elvis' (linking it thematically to the Ersatz sleeve).

On the proposed back cover, the heads of the Attractions were replaced with objects: keyboard player Steve Nieve's was a pharmaceutical capsule, drummer Pete Thomas pink balloons and bassist Bruce Thomas a cog with a broad smile etched upon it.

This did not go down well with the record company or the musicians, and the decision was made not to go with Bubbles at proof stage. Phil Smee, a designer at F-Beat's associate labels Demon and Edsel, was brought in to produce a new, plainer sleeve based around a Nick Knight colour portrait of Costello on the front with a black and white shot by the photographer of the group on the back.

'I was a kind of flavour of the month so they asked me to redo a few of the designs,' says Smee, who also adapted a Bubbles sleeve around this time for an album by the Nick Lowe-produced Western swing group The Moonlighters.

'I retained some of the graphics and went in a new direction,' says Smee. 'But I really liked what Barney was up to. It had a wilful simplicity to it, a bit like Matisse suddenly doing big, simple flower paintings. In a way, Barney seemed to have that bold, bright simplicity and balance.'

Bubbles' inner sleeve design – with horizontally placed crops of musical contributors such as Chet Baker – was retained, and the electrocuted visage surfaced on a badge and a US tour T-shirt.

He also provided artwork for the Punch The Clock singles, including the sleeve for You Little Fool, and drafted a design for the protest song Pills & Soap. This was released by Costello as 'The Imposter' in a plain white paper bag.

There is little doubt that Bubbles took the Punch The Clock rejection hard. Publisher Peter Barnes, for example, recalls the designer spending an entire evening at his house repeatedly looking for reasons why his sleeve was thought too quirky.

Continuing to explore less mainstream forms of expression, Bubbles collaborated with Brian Griffin on one-off art publication Y. 'We decided we'd do an issue each and called the first one Paint Your Windows White,' says Griffin.

The title taken from a government instruction in the event of nuclear war, this was a stark and uncompromising document. In a monochrome newspaper format, the front cover featured a red plastic button attached to a panel captioned: 'If you believe in life insurance why not wear it?'

Throughout Griffin's semi-industrial cityscape photographic abstractions were complemented by oblique graphics and spaced-out typographic arrangements.

By the time of the Punch The Clock epsiode, Bubbles was expanding his music design work away from F-Beat. Ian Dury's producer Laurie Latham had him create not only the sleeve for a single for musical side project the Vampire Bats From Lewisham, but also the logo for the label, Sheet Music, and Bubbles also produced a fluoro sleeve for Cairo, a single by all-female reggae rock band Amazulu.

A new vista opened when Bubbles was called in to Charisma Records by Peter Jenner, who was in the process of launching small independent record company Utility.

'I'd stopped working with Ian (Dury) at this point and was an A&R man,' says Jenner, talking in the offices of his management company in London's Kensal Green. 'I launched Utility but then Virgin bought Charisma. I realised that they didn't understand – or want to understand – where I was coming from, so sat on every decision I made.'

Jenner had already decided the basic element of Utility sleeve design: the 'classic' Penguin paperback format of horizontal, tripartite bands in orange and white or green and white.

Jenner was also clear that Utility's low price – 'Pay no more than £2.99' – should be flagged, just as the relative cheapness of Penguin books had been from the 30s to the 60s.

'I was quite pleased with myself for coming up with that concept, but I needed Barney, because he would lift it to another level and give us an identity,' says Jenner. 'The thing you have to realise about Barney is that he wasn't a tart. He didn't take ages to produce work or over-analyse. And it was always perfectly executed.'

OPPOSITE PAGE

TOP: Chuck Berry. Sculpture. Height: 2500mm. 1982.

BOTTOM: Claire. Mixed media. 1200mm x 1800mm. 1982.

THIS PAGE: The Echo Enters. Painting. 750mm x 750mm. 1982.

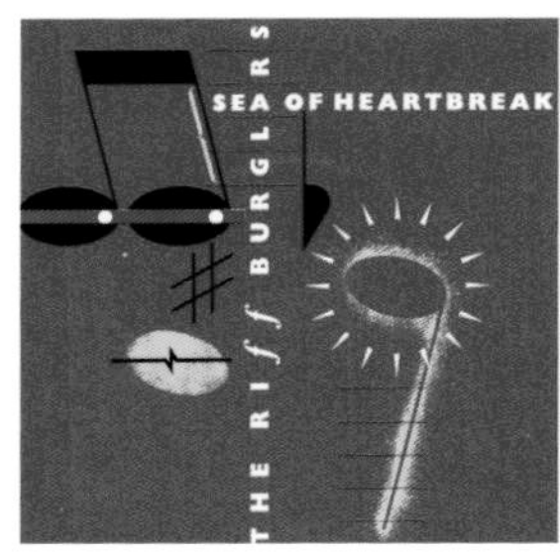

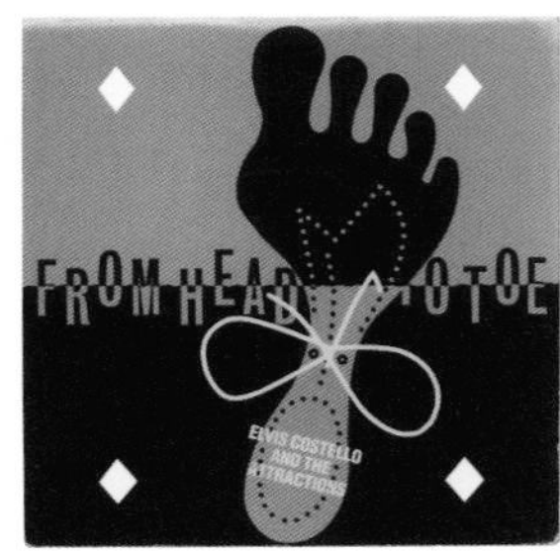

TOP: Front cover. Fast Women & Slow Horses, Dr Feelgood, Chiswick Records. 12in album. 1982.

CENTRE: Front cover. Danger, The Psychedelic Furs, CBS. 12in single. 1982.

BOTTOM LEFT: Front cover, Sea Of Heartbreak, The Riff Burglars, Line Records. 7in single. 1983.

BOTTOM RIGHT: Front cover. From Head To Toe, Elvis Costello And The Attractions, F-Beat. 7in single. 1982.

Glen Colson describes Utility as 'a kind of Stiff idea – there would be releases by diverse acts presented in a harmonised fashion'.

Jenner's priority was the young solo artist Billy Bragg, who had wangled his way into playing his demo tape by pretending to be a television repairman.

During the punk years Bragg served time in the band Riff Raff, who released a series of flop singles, including one on Chiswick, a regular employer of Bubbles' talents. With a set of tough-but-tender politically informed songs, seven of Bragg's demos comprised Utility's first release, Life's A Riot With Spy Vs Spy.

Released in May 1983, the front of this mini-album was a mechanic's light set against the orange Penguin bands.

Bragg had cooked up the sleeve with Bubbles on visits to Islington. 'I suppose Pete thought I would be a prime candidate for a bit of Barney's magic,' says Bragg, talking in the kitchen of his home atop a Dorset cliff.

'I was already a massive fan, had all the Stiff records and loved the work he did for Costello. There's no one like Barney. Armed Forces is one of the greatest sleeves of all time because it's so quizzical. You think: what the fuck is that?'

Bragg says that Bubbles' enthusiasm sparked an immediate exchange of ideas. 'It was a collaboration, rather than waiting on a designer to come up with something. Barney was intuitive. He understood I wanted to go back to basics and establish a clean aesthetic, something that stood out but was for everybody, not the special few who went to (elitist New Romantic venues) Club For Heroes or The Wag.'

Bubbles' preparatory sketches for Life's A Riot developed an idea based around Bragg's prominent proboscis and, again, a light-bulb motif. It was Bragg's purchase of the light which clinched the final design.

'I bought it at a hardware store and gave it to Barney,' says Bragg. 'It's for working on a car at night, with a hook so you can hang it from the bonnet while you're messing around with the engine. He took it from there and came up with this defining image. It's totally Barney – simple and complex. It's all there.'

Bragg says that Bubbles delighted in the use of imagery from 40s Britain, such as 'The Squanderbug'. 'The original was a six-legged spider with a swastika on it,' says Bragg. 'At Utility we were out to use resources sparingly: not spend three years in the studio, no guitar solos, not even a photo of me on the front. Barney picked up on that and created his own Squanderbug (for a detail of the back cover of Life's A Riot), making a face out of a graph.'

Despite the positive music press reception to Life's A Riot, Jenner's working relationship with the Virgin executives now controlling Charisma worsened as spring turned to summer in 1983.

'Peter had practically become an anarchist, doing crazy things to see how much he could get away with,' says Glen Colson.

An example was the proposal for a release by a fresh and provocative performer, Keith Allen. The actor (and father of pop singer Lily Allen) was at that time creating mayhem on the alternative comedy scene with his outrageous act.

Allen signed with Utility and recorded the album Programme 1 Station BPR, on which he assumed various personae at a pirate radio station. Bubbles' cover created a piratical skull-and-crossbones out of a radio signal and incorporated a logo of a 40s telephone captioned, 'Watch Out There's A Telecommunications Van About'. For a utilitarian item, Bubbles

TOP LEFT: Front cover. Walls Have Ears, Blanket Of Secrecy, F-Beat. 12in album. 1982.

TOP RIGHT: Inner sleeve. Walls Have Ears, Blanket Of Secrecy, F-Beat. 1982.

CENTRE LEFT: Front cover. Forever Now, The Psychedelic Furs, CBS. 12in album. 1982.

CENTRE RIGHT: Front cover. 4D Man, Howard Werth, Metabop. 7in single. 1982.

BOTTO LEFT: Proof. Rush Hour, The Moonlighters. 1983.

BOTTOM RIGHT: Front cover. Music On Both Sides, The Records, Virgin International. 12in album. 1982.

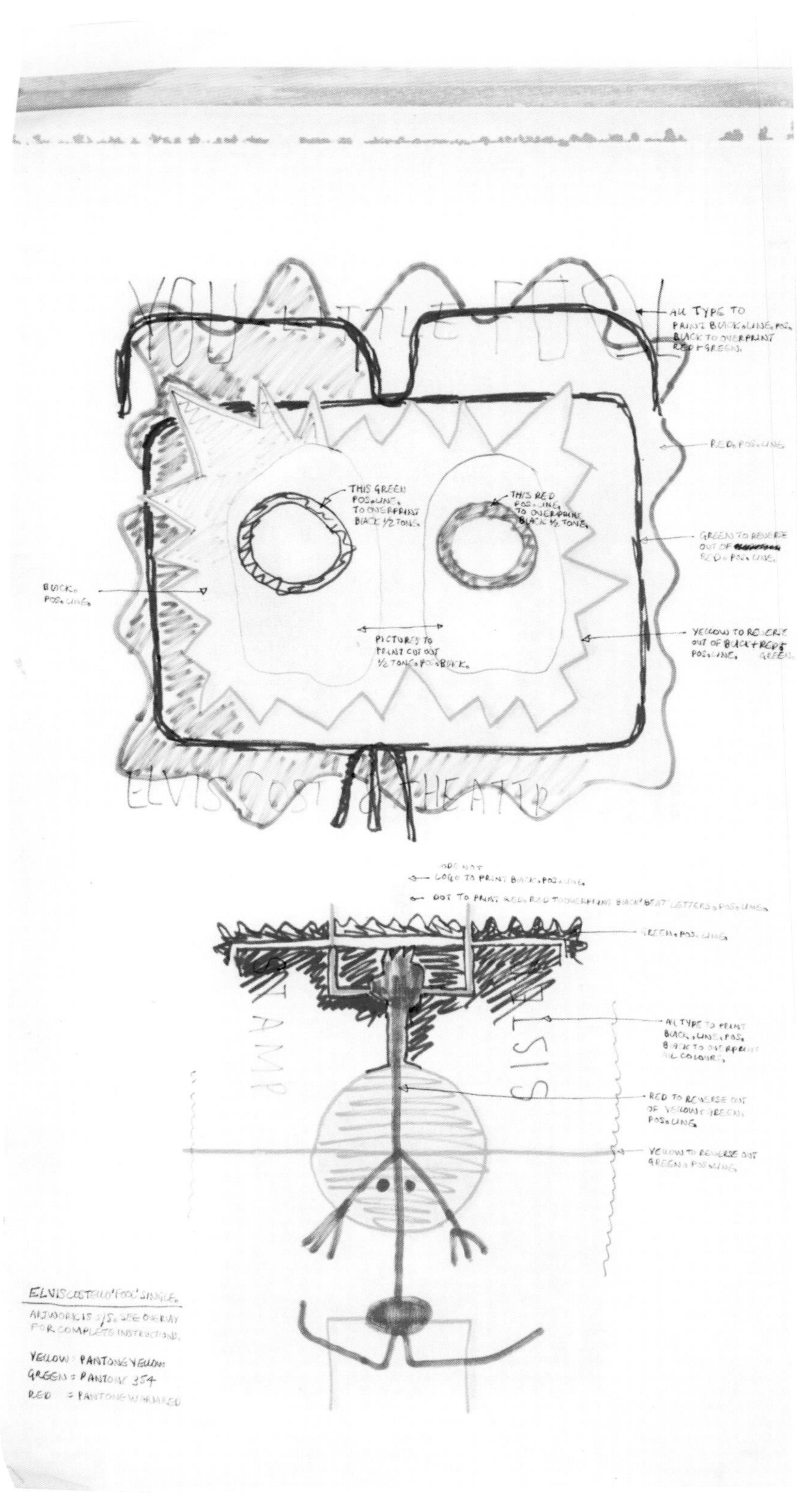

THIS PAGE: Sketches, pen and ink on paper, for single sleeve. You Little Fool, Elvis Costello And The Attractions, 1983.

chose an outmoded stack-heeled shoe. 'The album wasn't released,' says Colson. 'Virgin's sales and marketing team didn't want to know.'

Jenner left Charisma and struck a deal for the Utility artists to be released via former Stiff press officer Andy McDonald's new independent label Go! Discs.

It was via Go! Discs that Bragg's first full-length album, Brewing Up With Billy Bragg, was released (though because of the contractual wrangling with Charisma this wasn't to be until more than a year later, in November 1984).

Bubbles, who designed the Go! Discs logo, drew again on Masereel for the front of Brewing Up.

'I mentioned that I loved Masereel's work and even took one of his books along to show Barney; of course he got it immediately,' says Bragg.

Once more using black paper on white to create the impression of a woodcut, Bubbles delivered a twin image of the same scene: one view showed a light radiating from a house in an industrial cityscape and the other positioned a contemplative figure lit from overhead at a window .

During their discussions about the European art movements of the immediate post-First World War period, Bubbles turned Bragg on to the work of El Lissitzky, and in particular the artist's graphic commentary on the Russian Civil War, the 1919 poster Beat The Whites With The Red Wedge.

Bragg was to use Red Wedge as the name for the collective of British pop stars determined to politicise young voters in the mid-80s. 'That's where I got Red Wedge from!' exclaims Bragg. 'It came from Barney.' Taking its cue from Lissitzky's original poster, the Red Wedge logo was designed by Bubbles' fan Neville Brody.

'Peter had a strong idea, I had a strong idea but Barney had the discipline to bring the whole thing off,' says Bragg. 'It's as though he was another member of the band. In some ways he was a pop star himself, because he connected so closely with us and our aims. He was like the musician you send into the studio to record a solo and they come up with something so brilliant and off-the-wall it changes the track for ever.'

Bubbles also designed sleeves for Jenner clients Resistance, a duo, and the soul singer Mercy Ray. The cover of her Virgin single You Really Got To Me returned him to his enduring interest in the geometric abstraction of early modernism.

By now, Bubbles was assisted by Pauline Kennedy, who had spent a period as art director at the *NME*. A key project was the sleeve for Ian Dury's new album 4000 Weeks Holiday, an important release for the singer, whose career was on the wane.

In dispute with The Blockheads, Dury recorded the album with a set of musicians dubbed The Music Students and posed for the cover for photographer Bob Hall. Bubbles was present at the session; in one frame he and Dury enjoy a moment together.

For the 4000 Weeks Holiday cover, Bubbles cropped the black and white photograph so that Dury was alone in profile, the CND sign shaved into his hairline to denote his status as an ambassador for the organisation and one of the overarching preoccupations of the album (a track released as a single was entitled Ban The Bomb).

Over the photograph Bubbles placed graphic spermatazoa, wriggling from a central point and forming a circle around Dury's head. On the back cover he drew an op-art prism over which were laid the song titles and produced a set of symbols indicating the roles played by each of the participants.

Bubbles also had Dury painstakingly write out the song lyrics to appear on both sides of the inner. The release of 4000 Weeks Holiday was scheduled for late autumn 1983, but delayed by a protracted disagreement between Dury and record company Polydor, ludicrously over inclusion of a track entitled Fuck Off Noddy.

Worried about being drawn into a public debate then raging about paedophilia (since Dury's lyrics concerned the sexual antics of various characters from nursery rhymes and children's books), Polydor was also concerned about the possibility of an injunction from the estate of Noddy's creator, Enid Blyton.

During this period, Bubbles had became increasingly tortured by depression and suffered a number of episodes, the grief he felt at the loss of his parents apparently compounded by an ultra-sensitivity to a variety of issues, from the plight of the Australia's Aboriginal population to the fears he shared with Dury and many others over the arrival of American nuclear weaponry in the UK.

In addition, the volume of design work does not appear to have relieved Bubbles' financial situation, wobbly as it was due to the unpaid tax bill from several years previously.

That autumn, Bubbles contemplated the reawakening of his professional relationship with Robert Calvert, Nik Turner and Dave Brock, who had been united again in Hawkwind and were set to record and tour a new project, The Earth Ritual (intended as a sequel to Space Ritual).

Bubbles sketched out options for the album sleeve and was due to visit the musicians as they rehearsed for the tour in the West Country to discuss presentation and set design ideas.

It seems this was not enough to lift his spirits. Despite the full-time support and care of family and friends, Barney Bubbles took his own life at his Islington home on 14 November 1983.

Aged 41, his death was registered in the names of Colin Fulcher and Barney Bubbles. The music business was stunned and those in his circle naturally devastated at the loss.

In the aftermath, Dury's 4000 Weeks Holiday limped in to British record stores in January 1984 and received a cool critical and commercial reception, housed in an inferior sleeve which drastically modified Bubbles' design (which was used for copies released in Portugal).

Pauline Kennedy took up the design reins at Utility and Go! Discs and created signature artwork for Bragg and others such as The KLF during the rest of the decade.

Her work openly utilised many of Bubbles' tropes and approaches. 'I channelled Barney for two years,' says Kennedy. 'It was my way of grieving for him.'

A few months after his death, The Damned's former drummer Rat Scabies released the single Let There Be Rats on his own label Paradiddle, for which Bubbles had provided one of his last designs: a circular black on silver logo.

'He did it for me for free,' says Scabies, who cherishes the design for a tattoo Bubbles gave him. 'It's a chain with a link missing; he said he always thought of me as the original "missing link". Barney was a great guy.'

Hawkwind dedicated their 1984 EP The Earth Ritual Preview to Bubbles, and The Psychedelic Furs' album of the same year, Mirror Moves, was credited 'After Barney Bubbles' (their second album had featured the line 'After Andy Warhol').

'Barney Bubbles was one of our greatest designers, both of and beyond his age,' says the poet and novelist Michael Moorcock. 'He made lasting images for fleeting times.'

TOP: Front cover, C'Est C Bon. Carlene Carter, Epic. 12in album. 1983.

BOTTOM: Back cover, C'Est C Bon. Carlene Carter. 1983.

TOP: Untitled. Painting. 750mm x 750mm. 1982.

BOTTOM: The Rebel. Painting. 750mm x 750mm. 1981.

TOP: Cross Words. Painting. 750mm x 750mm. 1982.

BOTTOM: Untitled. Painting. 750mm x 750mm. 1982.

THIS PAGE: Vinyl Mogul. Painting.
900mm x 900mm. 1982.

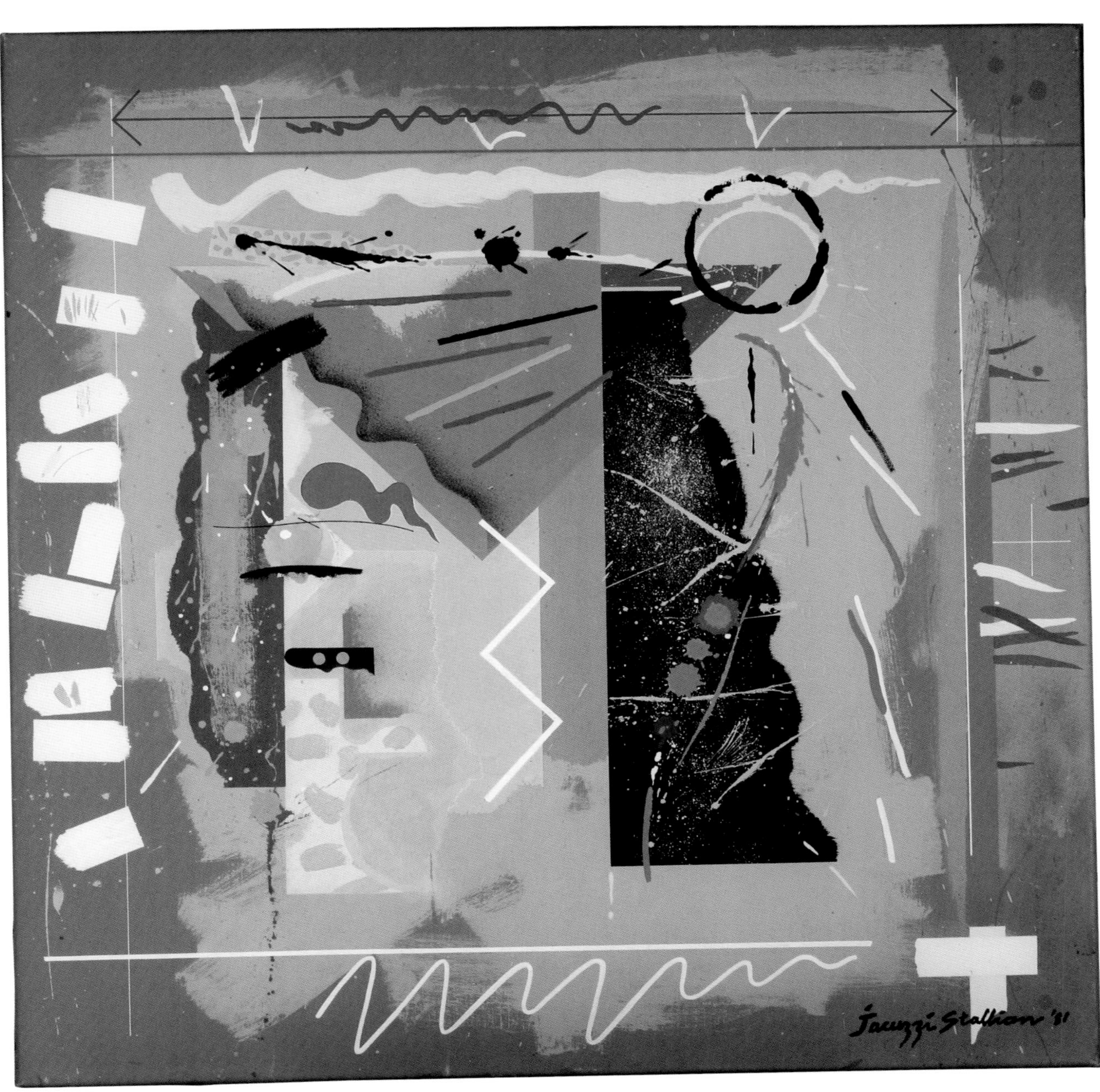

THIS PAGE: Antoinette Sales. Painting.
900mm x 900mm. 1981.

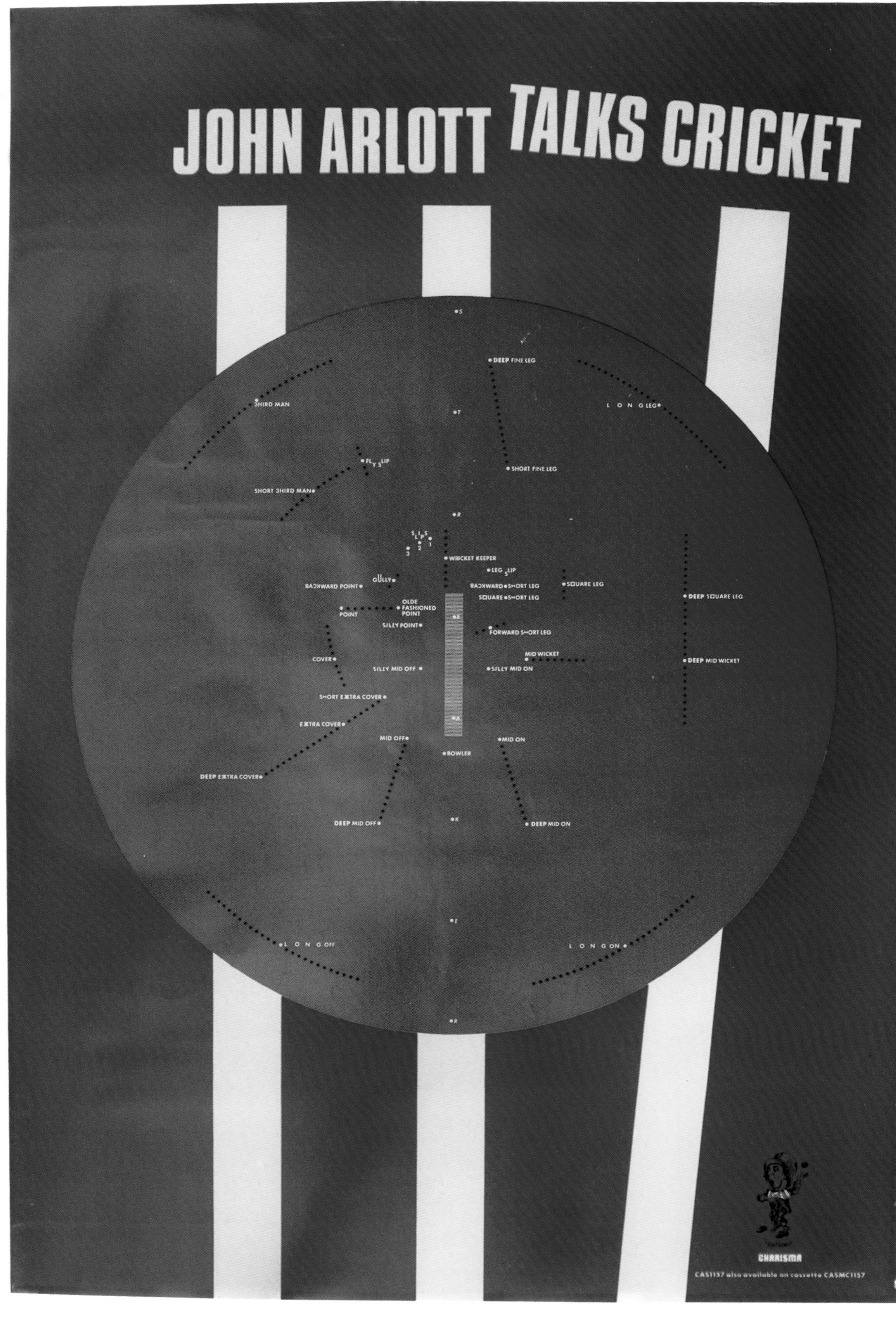

THIS PAGE: John Arlott Talks Cricket.
Poster. 900mm x 750mm. 1982.

PAINT YOUR WINDOWS WHITE

NUMBER 1

I went out of my room at about half past seven and went to the b
ar. I had a few and a drunk started talking to me. He had an ex-ar
my vibe about him. He was tall and fairly muscular. He had shar
p features, a ruddy complexion and a blonde moustache. I didn'
t reply to him. He was telling me about his sword; how it was sh
arpened and how it was tested. I felt embarrassed. My main int
erest, I said, aside from motorsport at which I can no longer acti
vely compete because I've got a glass eye, is Britain's major art

THIS PAGE: Y, *Paint Your Windows White*. Newspaper. 420mm x300mm. 1983.

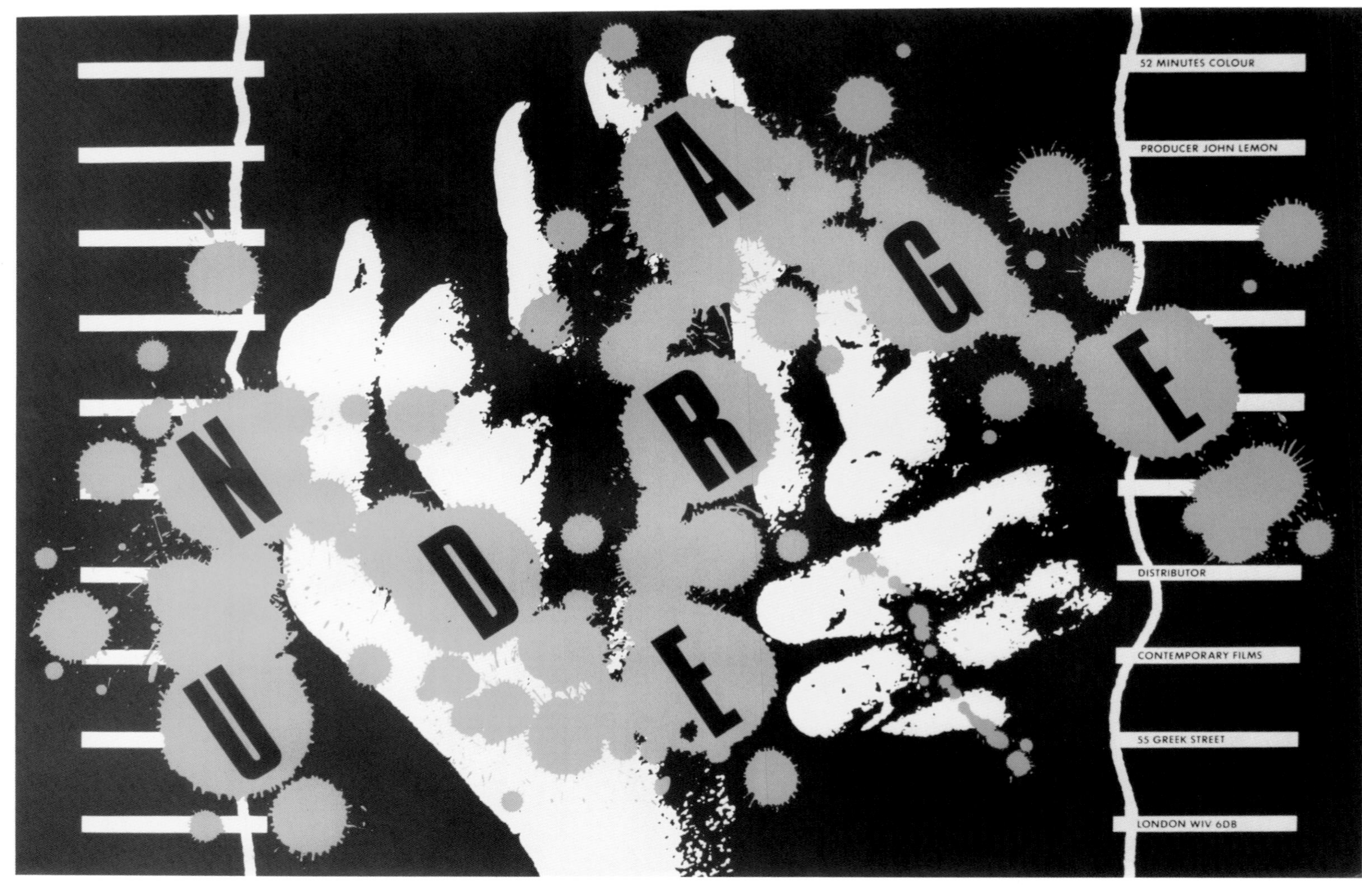

THIS PAGE: *Underage*. Poster. 750mm x 900m, 1983.

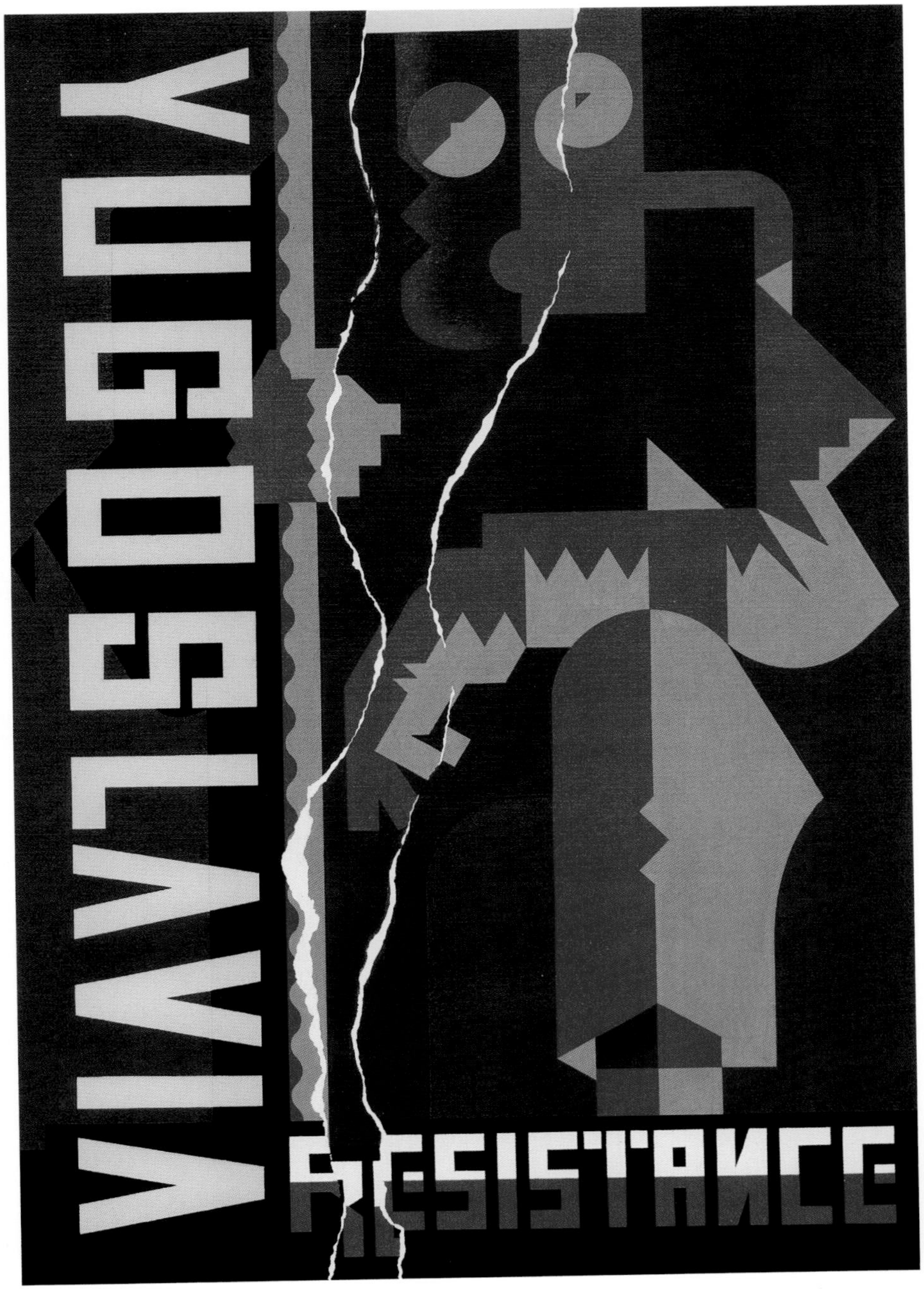

TOP: Yugoslavia, Resistance. Poster. 900mm x 600mm. 1983.

RIGHT: We'll Never See You Again. Resistance. Poster. 900mm x 600mm. 1983.

TOP: Artwork. Mango Crazy, Roger Chapman & The Short List. 1983.

BOTTOM: Front cover. Imperial Bedroom, Elvis Costello And The Attractions, F-Beat. 12in album. 1982.

CREDIT: Sal Forlenza 1942.

TOP: Artwork. You Really Got To Me, Mercy Ray. 1983.

BOTTOM: Front cover, The Art Of Roger Béchirian, Vol 1, F-Beat. 12in album. 1982.

TOP: Artwork. Billy Bragg tour. 1983.

BOTTOM: Artwork. Punkadelic, Inner City Unit. 1982.

THIS PAGE: Artwork. Ersatz,
The Imperial Pompadours. 1982.

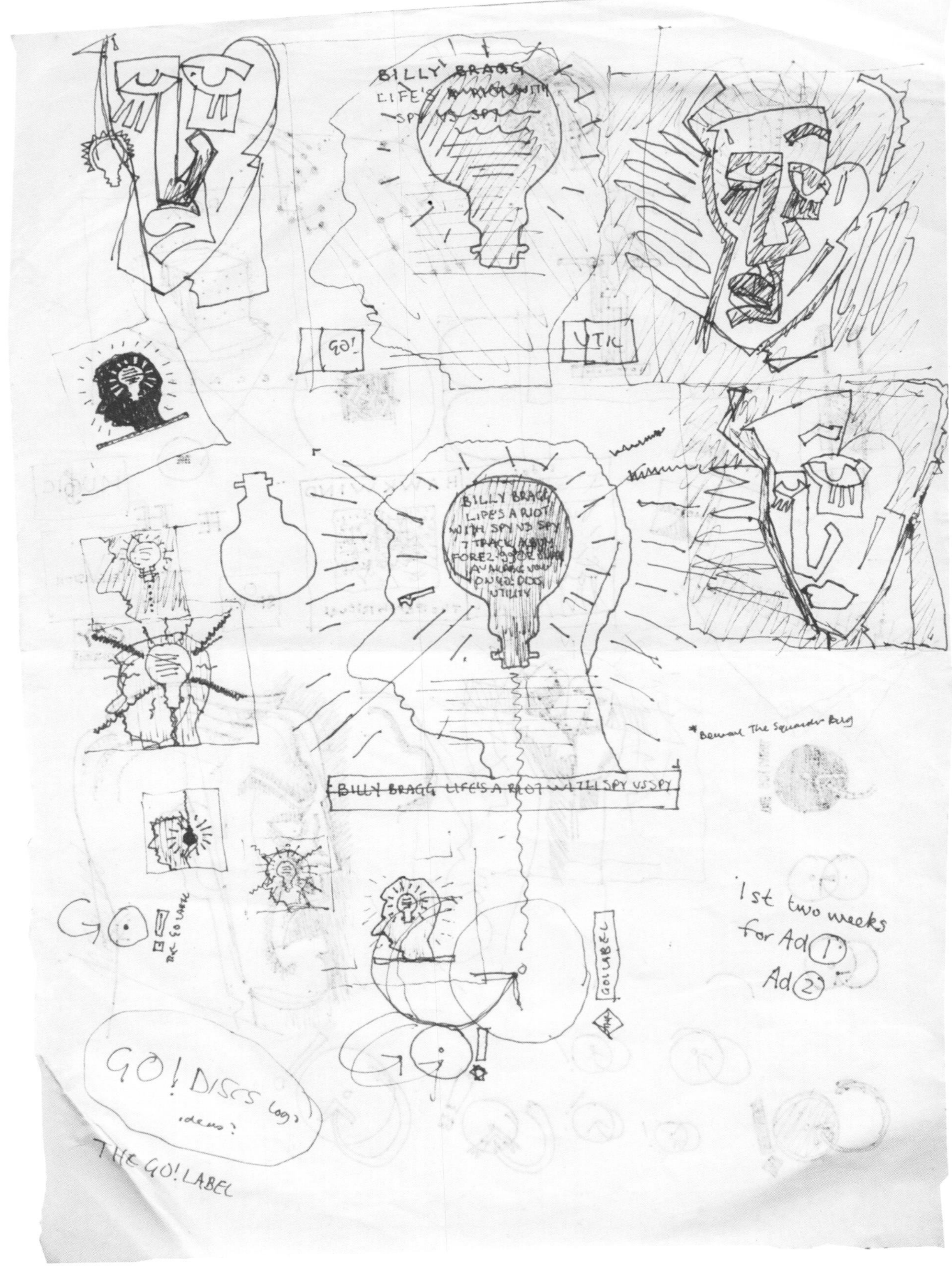

THIS PAGE: Sketches. Life's A Riot With Spy Vs Spy/Go! Discs. 1983.

THIS PAGE: Billy Bragg club residency.
Poster. 750mm x 500m. 1983.

THIS PAGE: Front and back cover. Life's A Riot With Spy Vs Spy, Billy Bragg, Utility. 12in album. 1983.

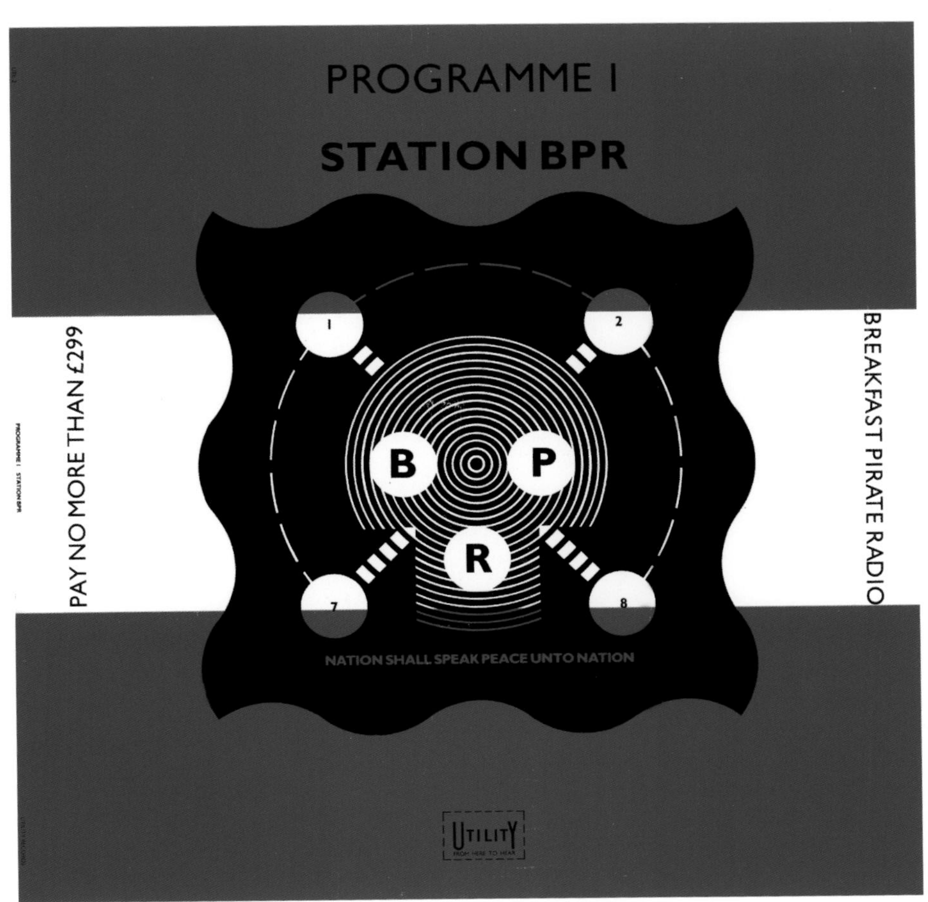

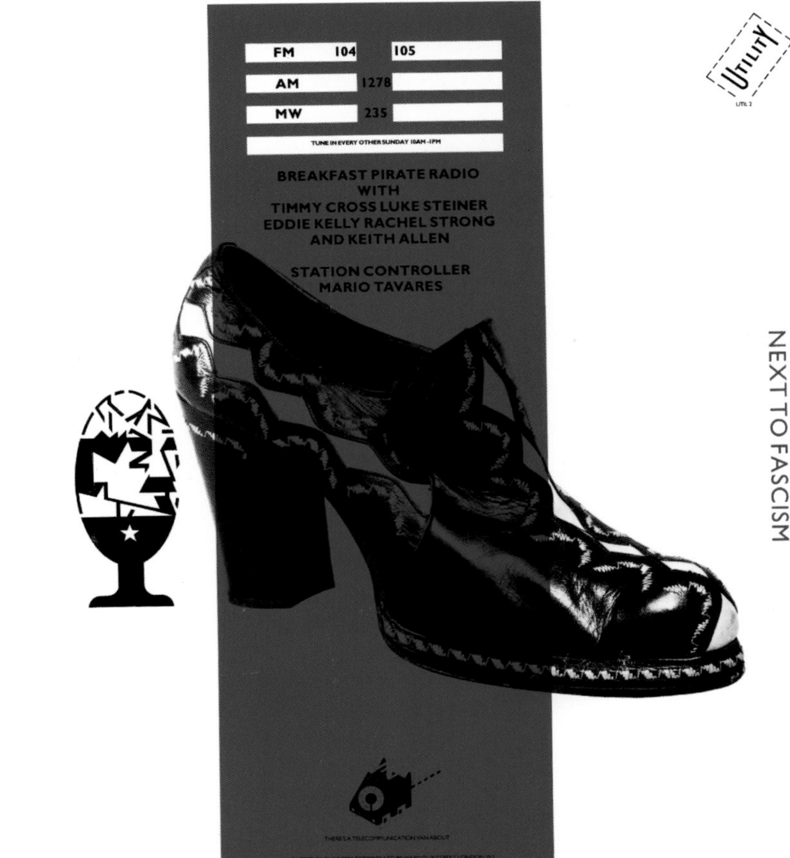

THIS PAGE: Proof. Front and back cover, Programme 1, Station BPR (Keith Allen). 12in album. 1983.

SIDE 1
LET THEM ALL TALK
EVERYDAY I WRITE THE BOOK
THE GREATEST THING
THE ELEMENT WITHIN HER
LOVE WENT MAD
SHIPBUILDING
THE WORLD AND HIS WIFE
SIDE 2
TKO (BOXING DAY)
CHARM SCHOOL
THE INVISIBLE MAN
MOUTH ALMIGHTY
KING OF THIEVES
PILLS AND SOAP
PRODUCED BY
CLIVE LANGER AND ALAN WINSTANLEY
ELVIS COSTELLO
Epiphone, Gretsch and Fender guitars,
'One-finger' Synclavier and Casiotone
STEVE NIEVE
Bosendorfer piano, Emulator, Fairlight CMI,
Vox organ, Hammond organ, Synclavier
BRUCE THOMAS
Electric Wal bass guitar
PETE THOMAS
Gretsch drums, Sabian cymbals
THE TKO HORNS
JIM PATERSON Trombone
JEFF BLYTHE Alto/Baritone sax/Clarinet
PAUL SPEARE Tenor sax/Flute
DAVE PLEWS Trumpet
STUART ROBSON Trumpet/Flugelhorn
on The World And His Wife
CARON WHEELER CLAUDIA FONTAINE
Backing Vocals Afrodiziak
CHET BAKER Trumpet solo on Shipbuilding
DAVID BEDFORD String arrangements
MORRIS PERT Percussion
Recorded at Air Studios, London
Assisted by GAVIN GREENAWAY and COLIN FAIRLEY
Mixed at Genetic Studios, Reading
Assisted by JIM RUSSELL
Pills And Soap is a Fairley/Costello original recording
Re-modelled by Clanger/Winstanley
CUTE
CUTE
CUTE

OPPOSITE AND THIS PAGE: Proof. Front and back cover, Punch The Clock, Elvis Costello And The Attractions, F-Beat. 12in album. 1983.

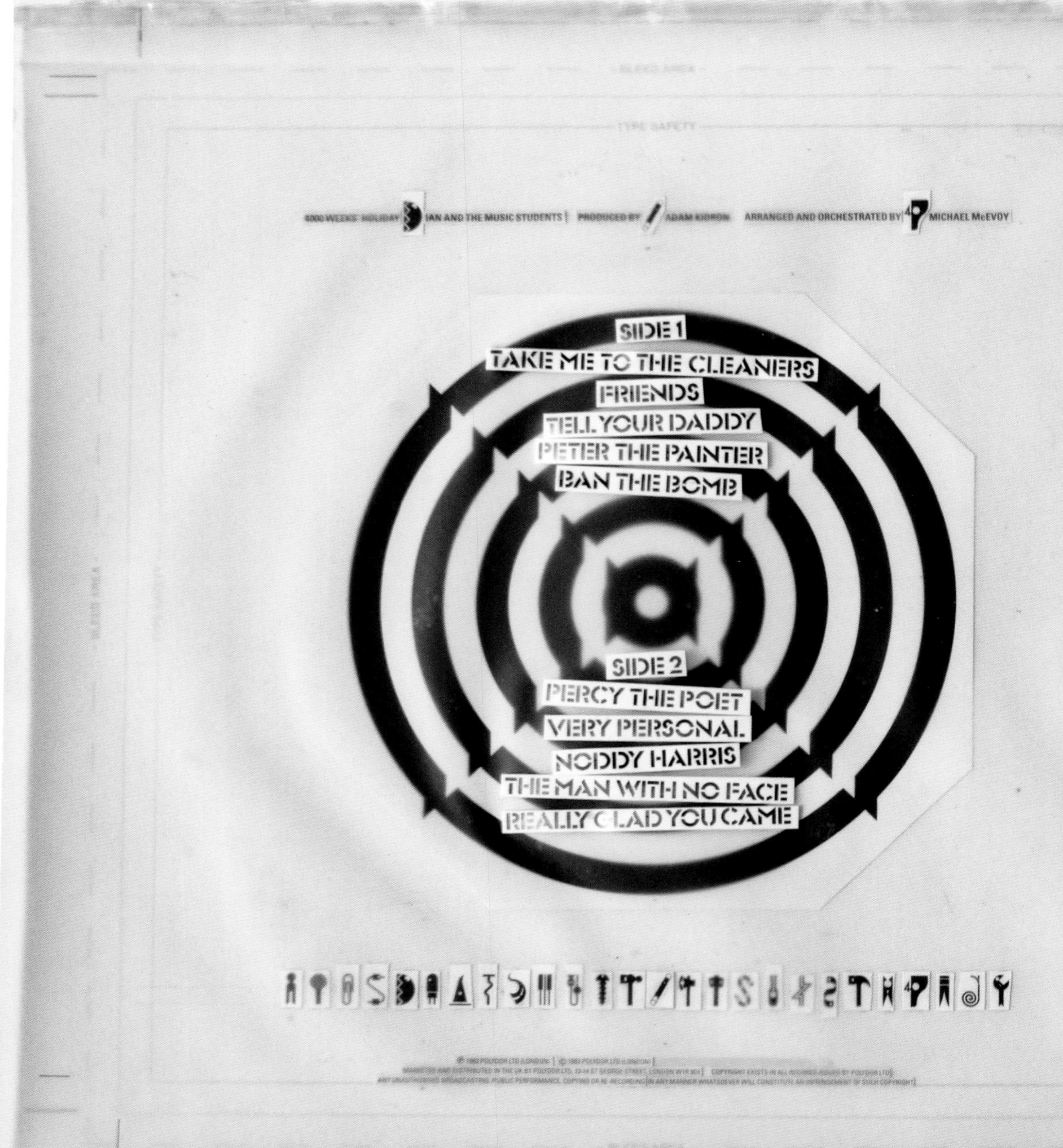
4000 WEEKS' HOLIDAY
IAN AND THE MUSIC STUDENTS
PRODUCED BY
ADAM KIDRON
ARRANGED AND ORCHESTRATED BY
MICHAEL McEVOY
SIDE 1
TAKE ME TO THE CLEANERS
FRIENDS
TELL YOUR DADDY
PETER THE PAINTER
BAN THE BOMB
SIDE 2
PERCY THE POET
VERY PERSONAL
NODDY HARRIS
THE MAN WITH NO FACE
REALLY GLAD YOU CAME

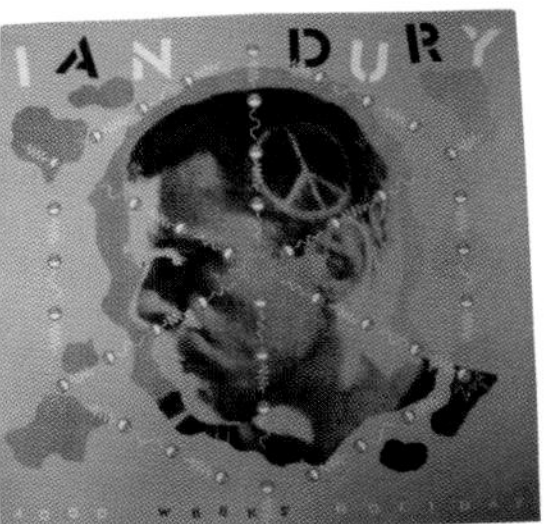

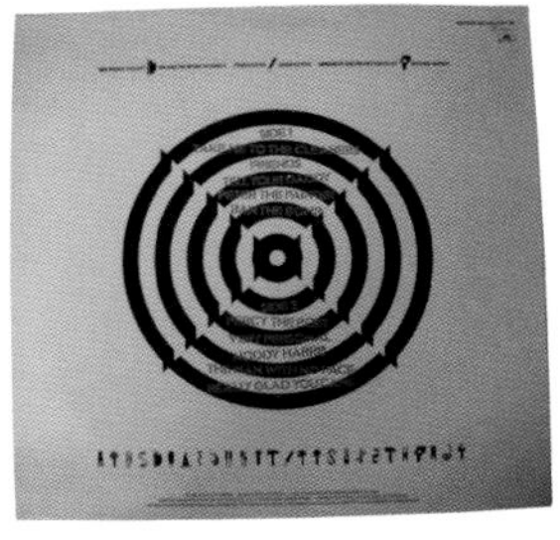

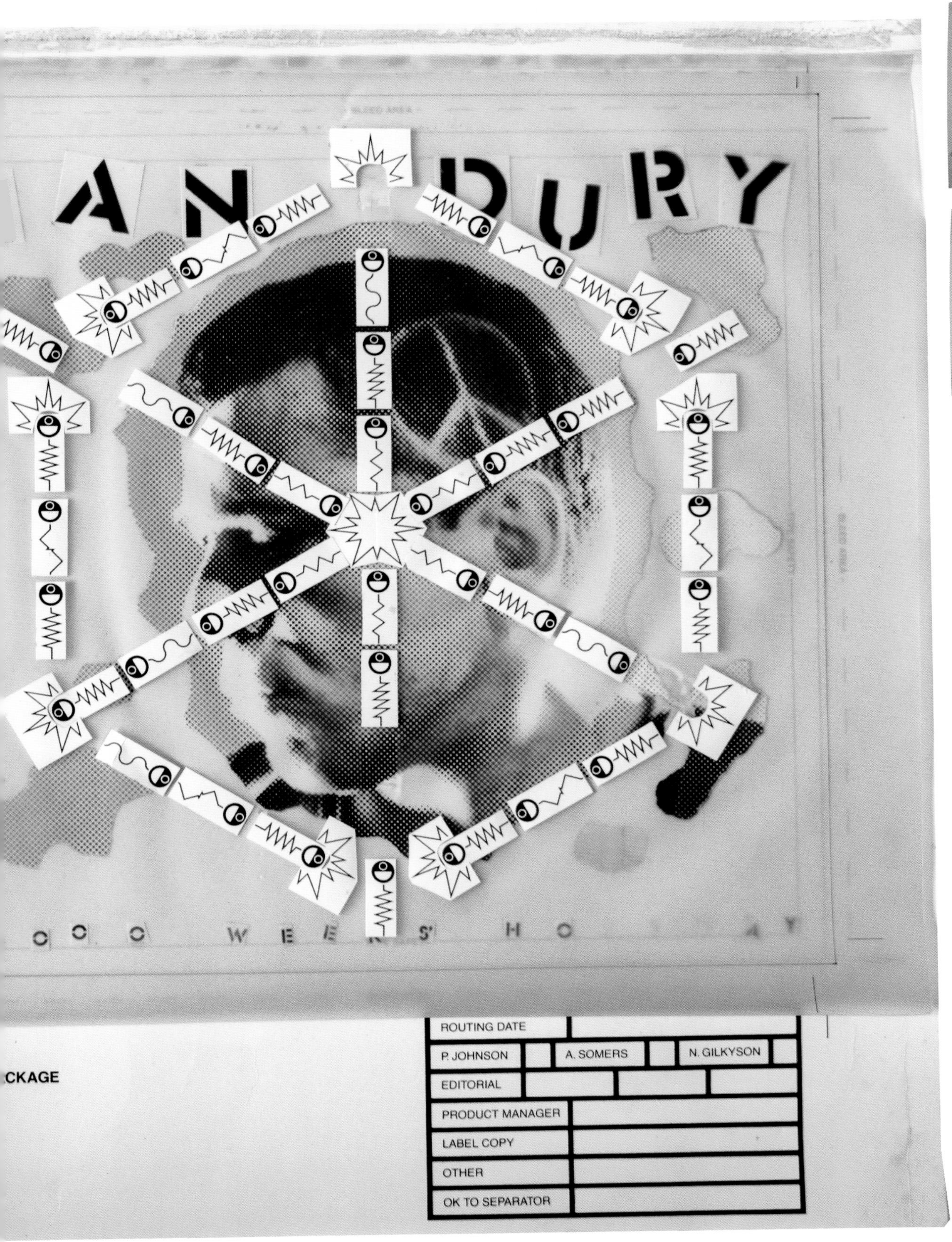

OPPOSITE AND THIS PAGE: Artwork. Front and back cover, 4000 Weeks Holiday, Ian Dury. 1983.

ABOVE: Front and back cover. 4000 Weeks Holiday, Ian Dury, Polydor. 12in promo album. 1984.

THIS PAGE: Sketches, including designs for Go! Discs logotype and Hawkwind album cover The Earth Ritual, Autumn 1983.

The M!ss!ng L!nks

In the decade or so since the publication of the second edition of this Barney Bubbles monograph, many more of his designs have emerged, such was the graphic artist's prodigious work rate over the 20 years leading to his untimely death in 1983.

The following collection provides a snapshot of the dizzying diversity of Bubbles' output. It also demonstrates his nimbleness in generating engaging graphic art that transcended disciplines and in some cases lifted his work out of the realm of print by shifting from 2D to 3D.

In this way this selection offers a series of previously missing links that further enhance Barney Bubbles' extraordinary oeuvre.

Paul Gorman
London 2022

Dr Colin's Elixir. Hand-drawn label. 1963.

Soon after the 2008 publication of the first edition of this monograph, Barney Bubbles' friend the artist Lorry Sartorio invited me to visit her at her apartment in north London. I hadn't previously been able to make contact with her since she had been living under the radar and had lost contact with those who had known her during his lifetime.

That afternoon Lorry showed me an array of Bubbles-related materials she had carefully kept in the quarter century following his death, including teenage love-letters (they met at Twickenham art school and remained on friendly terms for the rest of his life), invitations to parties, photography, postcards, drawings, student sketchbooks and watercolours. There was also this charming parody of a Victorian health elixir label which Bubbles – then Colin Fulcher – made when they were art students to cheer her up.

Lorry and I subsequently became matey and met up from time to time. I was very happy to reconnect her to members of Bubbles' circle.

Lorry died a few years back; she was an unforgettable bohemian figure with a pixielike presence, permanently garbed in black with matching boots enlivened by flouro pink accessories and a blonde crop. I treasure the letters and heavily decorated cards Lorry sent me over the years; as a devout animal-lover she always made sure to offer her fond regards to our dog Rita.

Strongbow Archer. Ashtray. 1967.

In 2011 I obtained a condition ashtray in the shape of, and bearing, the Strongbow archer logo created by Colin Fulcher when he was senior graphic designer at Terence Conran's central London studio.

STRONGBOW

Galactic Tarot. DPS advert in *IT*. 1971.

The Galactic Tarot set formed the basis for this double-page spread advertisement for Hawkwind in a December 1971 issue of the underground magazine *IT*.

Gone with the Wind kite. Double-page spreads from *Frendz*. 1972.

Obtaining a copy of the 14 July 1972 issue of underground magazine *Frendz* enabled me to understand the scope and ambition of Bubbles' design for a kite he incorporated into suitably psychedelic page layouts for a Hawkwind cover story.

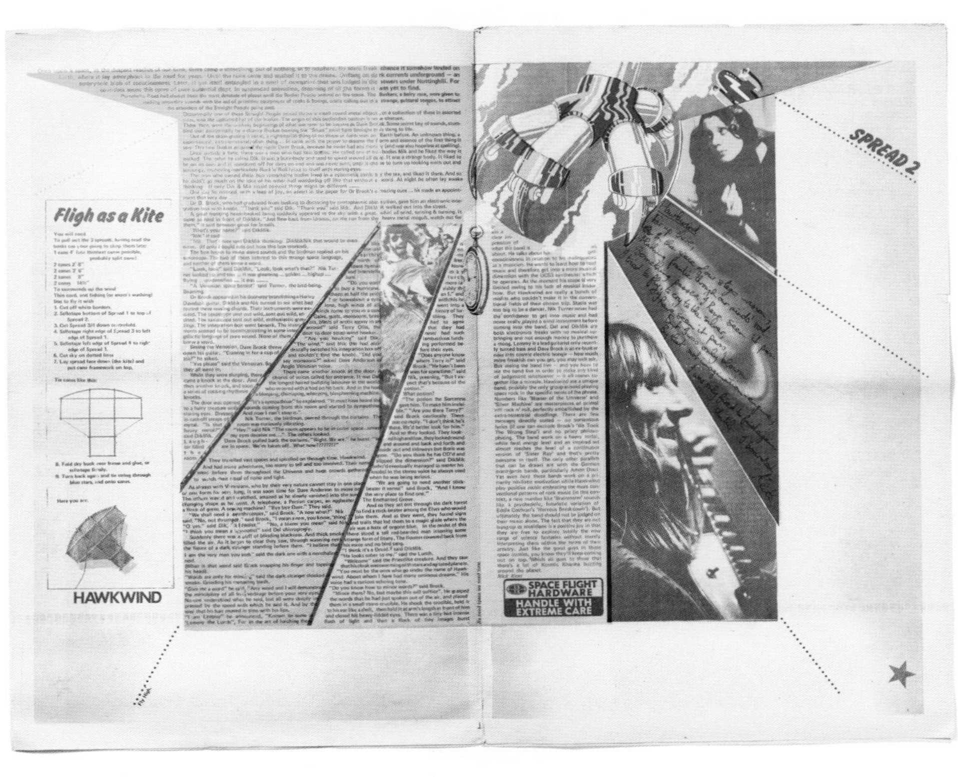
Fligh as a Kite
HAWKWIND
SPREAD 2
SPACE FLIGHT HARDWARE
HANDLE WITH EXTREME CARE

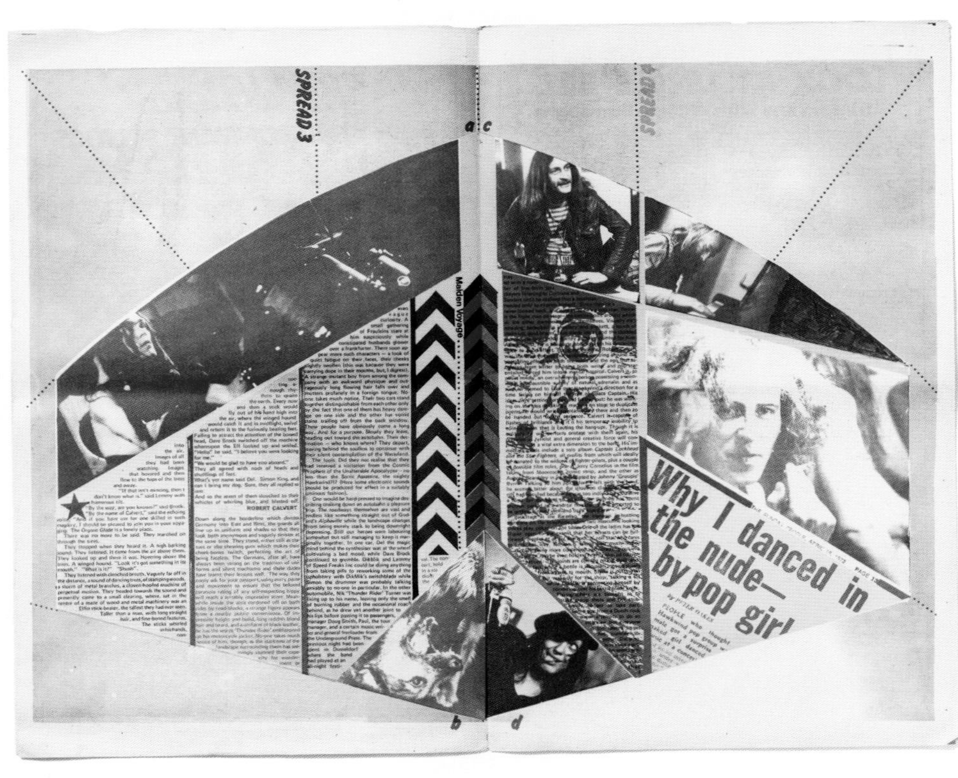
SPREAD 3
a c
Maiden Voyage
ROBERT CALVERT
Why I danced in the nude— by pop girl
b
d

Front cover. You'd Better Believe It/Paradox, Hawkwind, UA. 7in single. 1974.

This mask design was used for British music press ads for Hawkwind's 1973 tour the Ridiculous Roadshow and then repurposed by Barney Bubbles in gold and black for both sides of the sleeve of the single release of You'd Better Believe It/Paradox in Germany.

Love from Miss Stacia. A4 letterhead. 1974.

When Caz Facey and I were in the final stages of preparing the exhibition Process: The Working Practices Of Barney Bubbles – held at London gallery Chelsea Space from 27 September to 10 October 2010 – I received a letter from the artist Stacia Blake. As 'Miss Stacia', Blake's experimental dancing was a key element of the live experience of the 1972-5 line-up of Hawkwind which is generally considered to have made this phase of the collective's existence its most creatively fruitful.

Blake's charming note was accompanied by a couple of examples of the letterhead Barney Bubbles designed for Blake to answer the sacks of fan mail she received during this period. We were happy to be able to add the letterhead, which channelled such fin-de-siècle influences as Aubrey Beardsley, to one of the Process exhibition vitrines. I remember such fans as Mick Jones of The Clash/Big Audio Dynamite and bass player Jah Wobble were delighted to see that Blake was acknowledged on the opening night of the show.

Love from Miss Stacia 15 Great Western Road London W9 Telephone 01-289 2053

Hawkwind/Pink Fairies, Roundhouse. Poster. 1975.

This holds particular personal significance for me since I attended this concert at Camden's countercultural centre as a raw youth and recall the impact of this poster as much as the performances which took up most of the afternoon and evening of that freezing February Sunday.

Feasts. Recipe book. 1975.

On the death of the restaurateur and food entrepreneur Justin de Blank – who featured prominently in Barney Bubbles' career in the late 60s and early 70s – I wrote an obituary for a national newspaper. I was invited to the funeral by de Blank's widow Melanie, who kindly sent me this copy of *Feasts*, the recipe book Barney Bubbles designed for her husband's company. Sadly Melanie died aged 65 in March 2021.

Dear Lorry,
Well after such a long period of inactivity, things are happening thick and fast – events whistling past the old ears.
My studio is really nice and getting nicer all the time. I seem to be able to keep on top of things (just) and the work is getting better with each job. I work exclusively for Stiff and Chiswick records now and they keep me continually busy. The people here are very nice and I'm thoroughly happy to be around people again.
The squat has gradually become cleaner and tidier. I have a fridge, a cooker, washing machine, record player and an aquarium! Apart from the electricity and water, I pay no rent!! The best news is that Frances will share the two rooms and in exchange I can go down to use her country cottage. So when London gets too much I can split for Mother Earth. Too much eh?
The address for my studio is 32 Alexander Street London W2. Tel: 01 229 7146. Do come and share a pot of tea and meet all the new people.

A girl called Berenice is exhibiting next. Great work. Pleasant personality. Good looking. Ah, if only I were younger/older, taller/shorter etc/etc)
I hope you are happy and feeling stronger in yourself with each new day. A belated happy spring and birthday. It's downhill all the way now.... believe me.
Anyway, I'm off to the pub for a beer or three with Gerry. Do come and see all the fun and I promise you a really funny SURPRISE whenever you can make it.
Much love, Barny.

Stiff Records letter, handwritten on notepaper. 1977.

This letter to Lorry Sartorio communicates the excitement felt by Barney Bubbles on being encouraged to re-enter the fray as an active designer for music by his friend Jake Riviera, who persuaded him out of retirement with regular work for independent labels Stiff and Chiswick.

Generation X Marquee residency. Poster. 1977.

One of four posters commissioned by Jonh Ingham, erstwhile music journalist and manager of Generation X for a four-week residency by the Billy Idol-led punk rock group at Soho venue The Marquee. As detailed elsewhere in this book, Bubbles achieved the startling imagery by taking photographs of a series of juddering freeze frames from a video of the band in performance, and embellished the static lines so that they made connecting graphic criss-crosses.

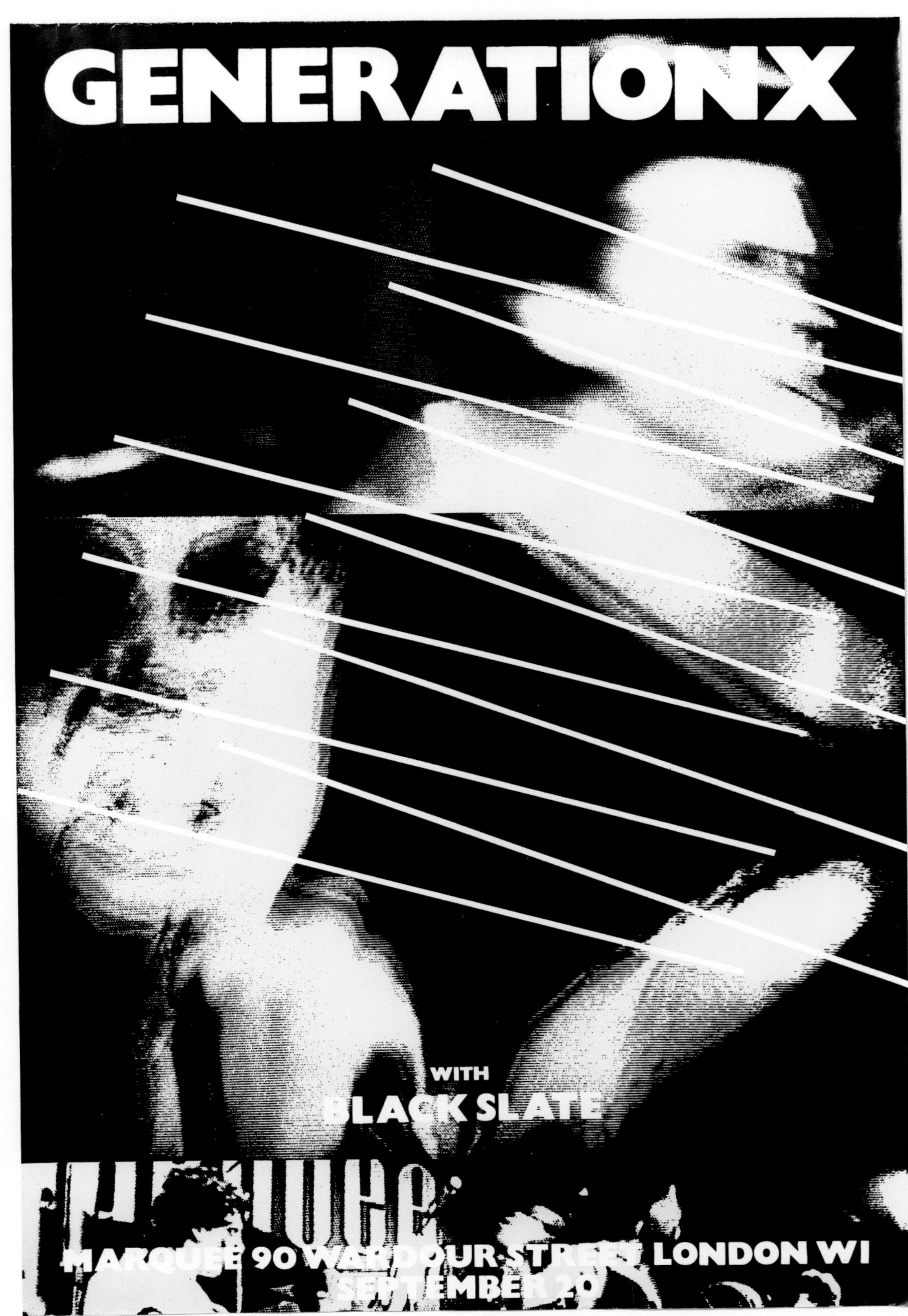
GENERATION X
WITH
BLACK SLATE
MARQUEE 90 WARDOUR STREET LONDON WI
SEPTEMBER 20

When You Kill Time You Murder Success. Clock. 1977.

Always one for a snappy slogan, Jake Riviera spotted this message on a sign in a Los Angeles dry cleaner's and Barney Bubbles applied it to clocks constructed from 12in vinyl records which were given away as Stiff promotional items.

Front cover. The Third Album, Big Star, Aura Records. 12in album. 1978.

In the spring of 2021 when that winter's lockdown easing began, I met up with Barney Bubbles' friend Cynthia Lole and she revealed to me that she hand-sewed a Tennessee flag over a single night so that it could be featured in a music video Barney Bubbles directed for The Third Album single track Kizza Me. As far as I know, the still which appeared on the album's front cover is the only remaining evidence that the clip was made, though I hold out hope that this, as well as many more pieces of the Barney Bubbles jigsaw, will emerge over time.

Radar logo. I Love The Sound Of Breaking Glass, Nick Lowe, Radar. 7in single. 1978.

Admission time: while it was referred to in the first two editions, and even appeared in tiny form on reproductions of record sleeves, I have not previously presented Barney Bubbles supreme logo for Radar, the record label he joined as art director in 1978. Here it is, in all its glory.

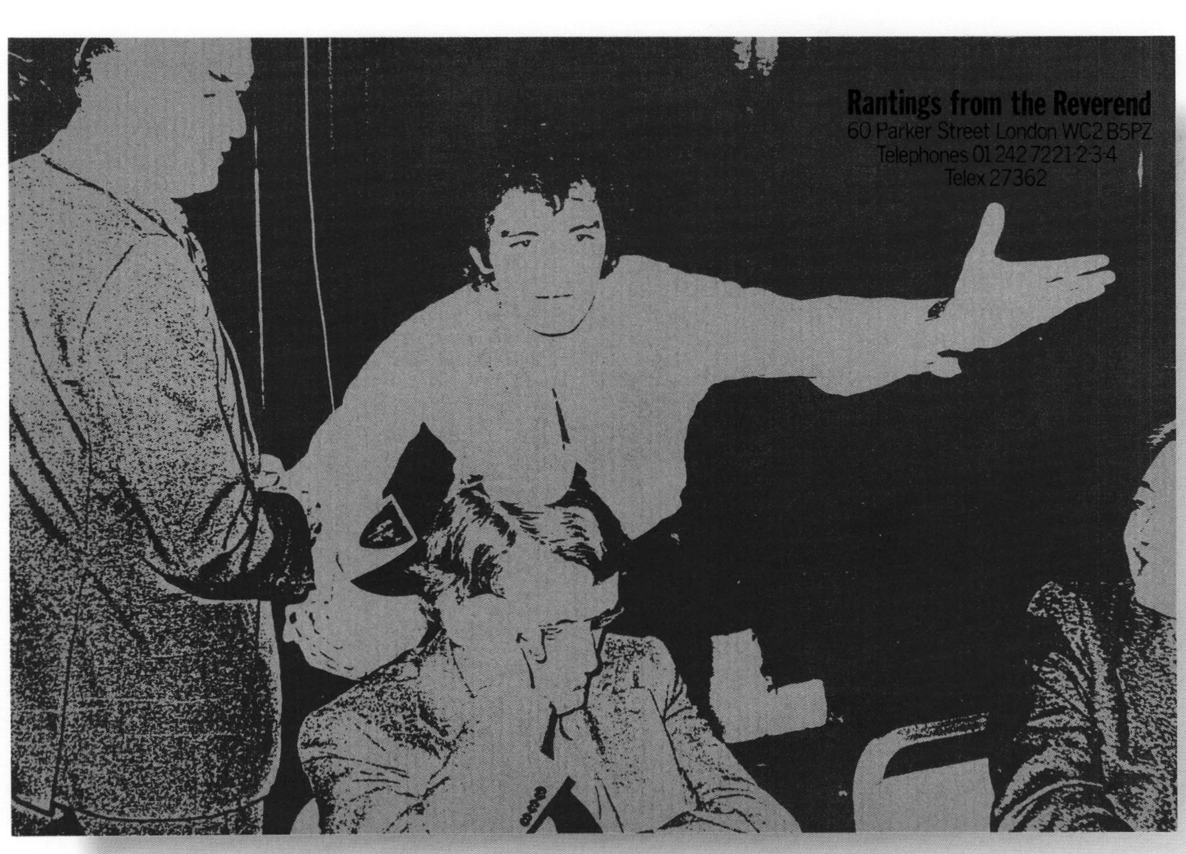

Rantings From The Reverend. Compliments slip. 1978.

Barney Bubbles invested as much energy in ephemera as he did in more official designs; this is one of a series of playful compliments slips and letterheads produced for Radar during his year-long tenure there, and utilises a photograph of the ebullient 'Reverend' Jake Riviera in full flight.

The M!ss!ng L!nk. Tattoo design. 1983.

While going through materials for the Process exhibition I came across this, the original artwork for the tattoo designed for drummer Rat Scabies. A humorous take on Rat's appearance, it bears poignancy as one of Bubbles' last designs. It also hammers home Peter Saville's point that the work of Barney Bubbles represents 'the missing link between pop and culture.'

Postscript

The public response to Barney Bubbles' death was swift and concentrated.

In the *NME*, journalist Roy Carr filed a heartfelt obituary and *The Face* paid tribute (pointing out Bubbles died on the day cruise missiles arrived in the UK from the US).

Soon Bubbles and his legacy were submerged under the new waves of design talent developing the visual identity of the on-the-rise CD format.

A book about Stiff Records published in the year of his demise mentioned the designer just once in 100 pages, and as the musicians with whom he was associated fell out of favour in the go-go 80s, so did Bubbles.

A relatively substantial appearance in Catherine McDermott's 1987 survey *Street Style: British Design In The 80s* was followed by occasional flickers of interest such as a 1989 piece on 'punk typography' in *Baseline* and a 1990 appreciation by designer Philip Brophy.

Bubbles' memory was kept alive by music fans, particularly the legions who followed Hawkwind as the band thrived through various incarnations.

And cult status was assured in 1992 when British design writer Rick Poynor used his editorship of graphics magazine *Eye* to commission a 16-page overview.

Two years later, Bubbles popped up in the designer Richard Hollis' survey *Graphic Design: A Concise History*.

'Barney Bubbles is much the most interesting British graphic designer, a key figure who can be put on the international level,' wrote Hollis. 'He had a direct line to creativity. Designers tend to manipulate image not create it. He was like a real artist.'

Around this time, Rebecca Brown and Mike Heath (who operate the design consultancy Rebecca & Mike) embarked on collecting information and material relating to Bubbles.

In the summer of 2001, they staged an exhibition dedicated to Bubbles at London's design shop Artomatic. Interest simmered with mentions in such volumes as Poynor's 2003 *No More Rules* and 2004's *Communicate: Independent Graphic Design Since The Sixties* (with David Crowley, Nico MacDonald and John O'Reilly).

Then, in January 2007, the dam broke. Designer John Coulthart posted a comprehensive illustrated career survey on his blog Feuilleton which provoked a torrent of comments and contributions from Bubbles' friends, fellow designers and admirers, including the author of this book.

It was at this stage that the first edition of this monograph crystallised, as *Reasons To Be Cheerful*. Within weeks of publication in November 2008, Barney Bubbles' name cropped up with increasing frequency, from the pages of the *New York Times* to Twitter to Shoreditch fashion blogs.

Two years later, in 2010, the second edition coincided with Process, an exhibition in London's Chelsea Space gallery organised by Caz Facey and myself that delineated Bubbles' working practices. This became one of the venue's most popular shows, attracting crowds of young designers and students beguiled by the analogue practices foreshadowing the eclecticism of the digital age.

Subsequently I organised for Bubbles' work to appear in the Victoria and Albert Museum's giant British Design show of 2012. The catalogue, designed by Jonathan Barnbrook's studio, paid tribute by featuring Bubbles' extraordinary 1977 Live Stiffs poster of a Chris Gabrin photo of Ian Dury among the handful selected to appear at the front with the likes of Cecil Beaton and David Bowie.

With French curator Sophie Demay I organised a giant Bubbles exhibition at the same year's international poster festival in Chaumont, and in recent years have consulted on the inclusion of Bubbles' works in a number of international shows, including Too Fast To Live at Michigan's Cranbrook Art Museum and New York's Museum of Art & Design.

The formalisation of the Barney Bubbles Estate, which benefits family members, has aided appreciation, and in 2017 a capsule collection with casualwear brand Fred Perry brought a range of Bubbles designs to a young and visually aware global audience.

Towards the end of 2020 an archive of Bubbles-related materials was purchased by Arts Council England as part of a government scheme, an indicator of the importance now attached to his work.

And so, it seems, the invisibility Bubbles craved in his insistence on anonymity and serial adoption of pseudonyms – Big Jobs Inc, Grove Lane, Sal Forlenza, Jacuzzi Stallion, Dag, Heeps Willard – is not to be.

But, as Nick Lowe said to Jake Riviera during a phone conversation in which they discussed whether Bubbles would approve of their involvement in this book: 'Barney was the closest we'll ever meet to genius; we've got no choice.'

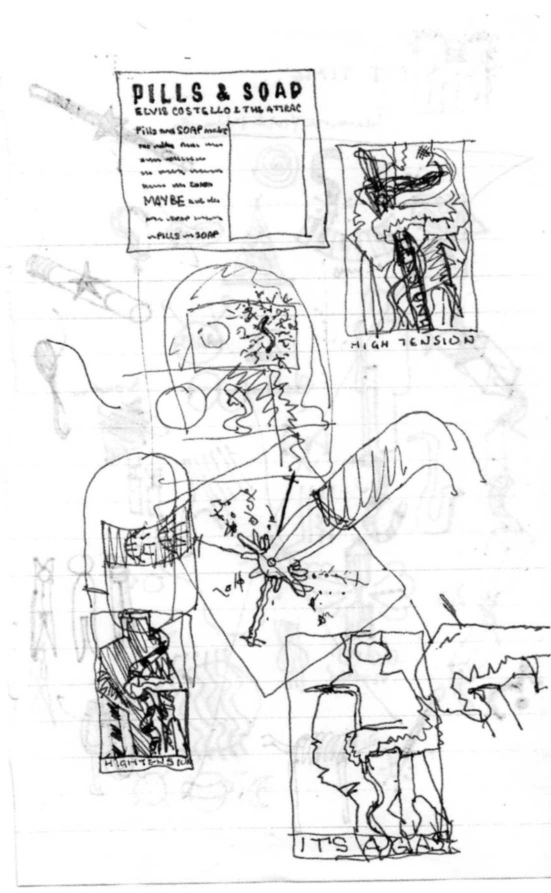

THIS PAGE: Sketches, including design for Pills & Soap by Elvis Costello And The Attractions. Spring 1983.

Picture credits

Ace Records 92, 119; Peter Barnes 142, 192; Will Birch 5, 194, 195; Justin de Blank 20, 21; Blockhead Ltd 93; Derek Boshier/Arts Council England 180, 181; Billy Bragg 211, 212; Marius Cain 142, 192, 219; Stafford Cliff 16, 19, 20, 23, 27, 36; John Coleman/Jeff Dexter 54, 55, 56, 57; Glen Colson 202; Jim Cook 217; Elvis Costello/Riviera Global 89, 90, 91, 105, 106, 107, 140, 147, 148, 149, 150, 151, 152, 153, 154, 155, 164, 165, 166, 167, 168, 169, 197, 206, 215; Alan Cowderoy 42, 43; Design Council, University Of Brighton Design Archives 26; Jeff Dexter 83; Baxter Dury/Ian Dury Estate 94, 95, 120–121, 132–133, 140, 144, 145, 146, 160, 161, 162, 163, 170; EMI 44, 45, 67, 68, 70, 71, 100, 171, 187; Carol Fawcett 118, 156, 157, 158, 199; Diana Fawcett 8, 14, 20, 24, 25, 116, 199; Chris Gabrin 89, 98, 108–109, 122, 126–127, 193; Chris Gabrin/Jake Riviera Collection 89, 105, 106, 107, 114, 125; Malcolm Garrett 10; Paul Gorman Archive 4, 5, 8, 11, 14, 17, 19, 22, 26, 28, 29, 30-1, 32, 34, 36, 203, 207, 216, 220, 221, 222, 223, 224, 225, 226, 227, 228, 229, 230, 231, 232, 233; Brian Griffin 96, 112, 124, 130–131, 147, 182–3, 203; Brian Griffin/Jake Riviera Collection 114; Bob Hall 138, 217; Peter Jenner 211, 212, 213; Brian & Jill Jewiss 108–9, 142; Pauline Kennedy 11, 86, 116, 207, 210, 216–17; Kingsland Lott Publishing 36; John (KosmicKourier) 37; Andrew Lauder 44, 45, 67, 68, 70, 71; Nick Lowe/Riviera Global 114, 115, 147, 158, 159, 196; Mercury/Universal Music Group 96, 97; Michael Moorcock 68, 75; Keith Morris Estate 104, 105; Keith Morris Estate/Jake Riviera Collection 89, 90; Music Sales 176–7; Mute Records 141; Richard Neville 23, 30, 31; Frances Newman 97; Humphrey Ocean 98; John Pidgeon 83; Tom Pogson 174–5; Riviera Global 58, 64, 65, 82, 99, 101, 115, 123, 140, 143, 146, 147, 148, 149, 150, 151, 152, 153, 154, 155, 158, 159, 164, 165, 166, 167, 168, 169, 172, 173, 184–5, 186, 187, 195, 196, 197, 198, 200, 206, 207, 214–5; Antoinette Sales 198, 201; Dave Robinson 44–45; Rat Scabies/Dave Vanian/The Damned 89, 102, 103, 110–11; Tom Sheehan 64; Phil Smee 67, 195; Doug Smith 20, 28, 29, 40, 46–7, 48, 49, 50, 51, 52, 53, 68, 70, 71, 72, 73, 74, 75, 76, 77, 78–79; Sony Music 194, 195; SPZ 83, 89, 98, 156, 157; Neil Spencer 113; Virginia Storey 19; Swan Song/Atlantic 171; B. Syme Frontispiece, 99, 128–9, 136, 190, 204, 205, 206, 208, 209, 213, 218; Genevieve Terry 138, 139; Uwe Tessnow/Line Records 194; Pete Thomas 5; Nik Turner 69, 74, 80, 81, 117, 171; Union Square 83, 141, 156, 171; UMG 37, 38, 42, 43, 58, 96–7, 138, 170, 171, 186; David Wills 14, 16, 17, 18, 23; Warner Music Group 59, 141; Mark Williams/Keith Morris Estate 104; Wise Publications/Music Room 178–9.

Selected reading

Ian Abrahams *Hawkwind: Sonic Assassins* (SAF Publishing 2004)

Phil Baines *Penguin By Design: A Cover Story 1935–2005* (Penguin/Allen Lane 2005)

Malcolm Barnard *Graphic Design As Communication* (Routledge 2005)

Will Birch *No Sleep Till Canvey Island* (Virgin 2003)

Derek Boshier *Lives: An Exhibition Of Artists Whose Work Is Based On Other People's Lives* (Arts Council 1979)

F. Carey, A. Griffiths *The Print In Germany 1880–1933* (The British Museum Press, 1984)

John Cooper Clarke Directory 1979 (Omnibus Press 1979)

David Crowley, Nico MacDonald, John O'Reilly, Rick Poynor *Communicate: Independent British Graphic Design Since The Sixties* (Laurence King Publishing 2003)

Carol Clerk *The Saga of 'Hawkwind'* (Music Sales Ltd 2004)

Roger Crimlis, Alwyn Turner *Cult Rock Posters* (Billboard 2006)

Stephen J. Eskilson *Graphic Design A New History* (Laurence King 2007)

Chris Foss *21st Century Foss* (Dragon's Dream 1978)

Helmut and Alison Gernsheim *A Concise History Of Photography* (Thames & Hudson 1971)

Paul Gorman *In Their Own Write: Adventures In The Music Press* (Sanctuary 2001)

Jonathan Green *Days In The Life: Voices From The English Underground* (William Heinnemann 1988)

Brian Griffin *Copyright* 1978 (Self-published 1978)

Brian Griffin, Richard Smith *Power: British Management In Focus* (Travelling Light 1981)

Paul Hill *Approaching Photography* (Focal Press 1982)

Richard Hollis *Graphic Design: A Concise History* (Thames & Hudson 2002 and 2021)

Lemmy Kilmister, Janiss Garza *White Line Fever* (Citadel 2004)

Emily King (ed) *Designed By Peter Saville* (Thames & Hudson 2003)

Eric Kohler *In The Groove: Vintage Record Graphics 1940–1960* (Chronicle 1999)

Sophie Lissitzky-Küppers *El Lissitzky: Life, Letters, Texts* (Thames & Hudson 1992)

Victor Margolin *The Struggle For Utopia: Rodchenko, Lissitzky, Moholy-Nagy, 1917–1946* (University Of Chicago Press 1998)

Ian 'Mac' McLagan *All The Rage* (Sidgwick & Jackson 1998)

Philip B. Meggs, Alston W. Purvis *Meggs' History Of Graphic Design 4th Edition* (Wiley 2005)

Michael Moorcock *King Of The City* (Scribner 2000)

Rick Poynor *No More Rules: Graphic Design And Postmodernism* (Laurence King Publishing 2003)

Alex Steinweiss, Jennifer McKnight-Trontz *For The Record: The Life And Work Of Alex Steinweiss* (Princeton Architectural Press 2000)

Dominic Strinati, Stephen Wagg *Come On Down? Popular Media Culture In Post-War Britain* (Routledge 1992)

Jon Wozencroft *The Graphic Language Of Neville Brody* (Thames & Hudson 1988)

Magazines and newspapers

Baseline 11 – Barney Bubbles Punk Typography (1989)

Eye 6 Vol 2 – The Secret Career Of Barney Bubbles, Julia Thrift (Spring 1992)

The Face 19 – Barney Bubbles, Dave Fudger (November 1981)

The Face 45 – Barney Bubbles 1942–1983 (January 1984)

Frendz 33 – Bowie Anti News (4 August 1972)

Friends – Hawkwind! (13 Sept 1970)

Independent – Osmund Caine obituary, David Buckman (7 December 2004)

Let It Rock – January 1975

Minerva Vol 41 – American Influence On British Higher Education: Science, Technology, And The Problem Of University Expansion, 1945–1963 (December 2003)

Mojo Classics The Greatest Album Covers – Barney Bubbles Master Of The Universe, Mark Paytress (April 2007)

New Musical Express – Barney Bubbles 1942–1983, Roy Carr (26 November 1983).

New Musical Express – *The NME Book Of Modern Music* (14 October 1978)

Nova – December 1968

Oz 12 – Fun & Games Tax Dodge Special (May 1968)

Oz 38 – Scoop! The Day The Earth Was Out To Lunch (November 1971)

Sleazenation 6, Vol 4 – Barney Bubbles, Rebecca and Mike (July 2001)

Spin 3 – Action Time Vision (2007)

Stuffing 3 – Philip Brophy *Melbourne, Post Punk Graphics The Displaced Present, Perfectly Placed* (1990)

Index